D1248218

First Ladies *and the* Fourth Estate

First Ladies

and the Fourth Estate

Press Framing of
Presidential
Wives

Lisa M. Burns

NORTHERN
ILLINOIS
UNIVERSITY
PRESS

DeKalb

© 2008 by Northern Illinois University Press

Published by the Northern Illinois University Press, DeKalb, Illinois   60115

Manufactured in the United States using postconsumer-recycled, acid-free paper.

All Rights Reserved

Design by Julia Fauci

Library of Congress Cataloging-in-Publication Data

Burns, Lisa M.

First ladies and the fourth estate : press framing of presidential wives / Lisa M. Burns.

   p.   cm.

Includes bibliographical references and index.

ISBN 978-0-87580-391-3 (clothbound : alk. paper)

1. Presidents' spouses—Press coverage—United States. 2. Presidents' spouses—
United States—Political activity. 3. Presidents' spouses—United States—History—
20th century. 4. Mass media—Political aspects—United States—History—
20th century. 5. Press and politics—United States—History—20th century. I. Title.

E176.2.B86 2008

973.09'9—dc22

2008018190

Contents

Preface

The year 1992 was the so-called Year of the Woman in U.S. politics. Women, in record numbers, were running for political office from school boards to the U.S. Senate. Journalists, pundits, and scholars credited this insurgence of women candidates to one specific event—the interrogation of Anita Hill by the Senate Judiciary Committee during the confirmation hearings of Supreme Court nominee Clarence Thomas. Hill's grilling at the hands of the all-white, all-male committee became a campaign issue for women candidates, representing everything from the continuing problem of sexual harassment in the workplace to the lack of women and minorities on Capitol Hill. One of the most heated races of 1992 was Lynn Yeakel's efforts to unseat incumbent Pennsylvania Senator Arlen Specter, who led the Senate Judiciary Committee's tough questioning of Hill.

In 1992 I was a reporter and news anchor at a National Public Radio affiliate station in Pittsburgh, Pennsylvania. The Yeakel-Specter race was one of the top stories of the year. I covered numerous campaign events for both candidates, but there is one instance that stands out in my mind. I was working on a feature story about an event attended by both Yeakel and Specter, and I was debating whether to open the story by describing Yeakel's bright red suit, which really made her stand out on a stage of dark-suited men. I asked one of my coworkers, also a woman reporter, why she thought we often talked about the appearance of women in stories, but we never focused on what men were wearing. Neither of us could come up with a good reason why we did this, although we agreed that most journalists were guilty of this gender bias in reporting. Stories about Yeakel often mentioned her "Dorothy Hamill wedge" hairstyle, yet none talked about Specter's thinning curly hair. And even TV reporters would comment on Yeakel's outfits (even though they could be seen in the video) but never described Specter's suits. After more introspection, I decided I would describe Yeakel's suit, as a way of setting the scene in my story, but I also noted that Specter wore red, in the form of a bright red tie that added a "pop of color" to his plain navy suit.

As I was studying press coverage of first ladies a decade later, I remembered my dilemma that day in the newsroom in 1992. I know I did not do anything remarkable that day, but I clearly remember being aware that I was bending, if not actually breaking, convention by describing Specter's outfit. In my mind it was a small, feminist gesture—an effort to "level the playing field," holding both candidates to the same standards. I could have left the references to appearance out of the story altogether. But Yeakel's red suit, which made her stand out in the sea of blue and grey suits on the stage, seemed to sum up her campaign. She was a woman seeking to break into a male-dominated field. She was a political outsider who had never run for office. And she stood in sharp contrast not only to her opponent but to most of the power brokers in Pennsylvania politics. Yeakel's campaign made it clear that she would bring a woman's perspective to issues such as health care, education, and employment opportunities. Her advertisements attacked Specter for his treatment of Anita Hill, and she often told audiences that she decided to run for the Senate because she was so angered by Specter's actions during the confirmation hearings. Yeakel's choice of bright outfits seemed to sum up the idea that she was different—she wanted to stand out. As a reporter I recognized that her red suit made a statement. It had multiple meanings that went beyond her appearance.

The resulting story was not particularly remarkable. It was just one of many that were filed during the campaign. But for me, it represents how my experiences as a reporter informed my analysis of press coverage of first ladies, which is the subject of this book. My professional background affords me insight into journalism practice, a perspective that I wanted to bring to my analysis of newspaper and magazine articles about presidents' wives. I am familiar with the conventions that shape newswriting, like framing. As a woman journalist I was often aware that there were gendered elements to my reporting. Yet I was not always as self-reflexive as I was with the Yeakel story. When I was working on deadline, I did not have as much time to think about my choices, let alone discuss them with a colleague. In many ways, reporting becomes a reflex. When time is limited, journalistic norms kick in. Those norms govern everything from story structure to wording. Journalists develop certain habits that show up in their stories. In coverage of women, gender framing is one of those habits. When covering campaigns, comparing and contrasting candidates is the norm. If there is a historical element involved in a story, it is common to assess the present in relation to the past. All of these habits are evident in stories about first ladies.

In my analysis of press coverage of first ladies, my focus is on the articles themselves. To use the language of critical scholars, my attention is on the texts and their messages, which are my objects of analysis, and the implications for both the subjects of the stories and the audiences who consumed the text. However, an admitted weakness of this research method is that it does not always consider how the texts are produced. For rhetorical critics, the focus on the message or text is a way of treading carefully around the problematic issue of intent. Because it is difficult to get at the intentions of a speaker, it is easier to focus on the message and its interpretation. For media critics, the production process can be difficult to analyze because there are so many aspects involved, from corporate and commercial concerns to the fact that numerous individuals may be responsible for creating a single text. In many studies of news coverage, including my own, journalistic conventions are pointed to as a blanket explanation for the production process. However, this explanation can give the false impression that journalists are automatons, who unthinkingly follow templates because they are trained to do so, or that journalists are lazy, falling back on convention because it makes their jobs easier.

As a former reporter, I recognize that the work of journalists, from news gathering to writing, is much more complicated and challenging. In this book my goal was to merge my training as a journalist with that as a scholar, allowing both standpoints to shape my analysis of first lady press coverage. Just as articles about first ladies provide a rich source of information about women's history, changing gender roles, and the evolution of the first lady position, I contend that these stories also offer us insight into the day-to-day practice of journalism. I also believe that covering the first lady involved more complexity than most editors and readers ever recognized, especially for women reporters who recognized the potential influence of this uniquely gendered political position.

When I decided to study politics and media at the University of Maryland at College Park, I never intended to focus on media coverage of first ladies. But three women inspired me to pursue this topic as my dissertation research: Dr. Maurine Beasley, Dr. Shawn Parry-Giles, and Ellen Axson Wilson. Maurine Beasley was one of the first professors I met at Maryland. I was intrigued by her work on Eleanor Roosevelt, particularly the way her studies of Roosevelt's relationship with the press shed light on the history of women journalists. Maurine supported me through a rough first semester, when I decided to make the switch from the Journalism to the Communication Ph.D. program. When I told her that I planned to study press coverage of first ladies in the twentieth century, she was extremely supportive. Her guidance, feedback, and encouragement have greatly shaped this project over the years, from its beginnings as a dissertation to the revised book manuscript. I am very grateful to have Maurine as a mentor.

In my second semester at Maryland, I took a class on presidential and first lady rhetoric from Shawn Parry-Giles. I never considered myself much of a history buff, but I found myself fascinated by the relationships between presidents and their wives. It was this course that sparked the idea for my dissertation, and Shawn agreed to be my advisor. She not only introduced me to the study of first ladies. She also aided my development as a rhetorical critic and writer. Her input was invaluable, and her support constant. Shawn was a skilled editor, and under her guidance I became a better writer. While the process was often frustrating, the lessons I learned helped me to grow as a scholar and a teacher.

Finally, if it had not been for Ellen Axson Wilson, I never would have considered studying first ladies. In the presidential and first lady rhetoric class, I decided to research the first Mrs. Woodrow Wilson, who has been overshadowed historically by Wilson's second wife, Edith Bolling Galt Wilson, and the charges of her "petticoat presidency." What I learned was that Ellen Wilson was a remarkable woman—an artist, an activist, and an advisor to her husband. I found it difficult to believe that her achievements had been virtually forgotten, and the journalist and scholar in me wanted to know why. In that question, the idea for this book was born.

There are many other people whom I must acknowledge for their support of this project. In addition to Shawn and Maurine, the other members of my dissertation committee at the University of Maryland, Dr. James Klumpp, Dr. Mari Boor Tonn, and Dr. Trevor Parry-Giles, all encouraged me to pursue publication. The members of my "dissertation support group" at Maryland—Dr. Amy Heyse, Dr. Leah Tuite, Dr. Laura Janusik, and Dr. Leslie Dinauer—have provided me with constant encouragement. They have been with me every step of the way. Meanwhile, my colleagues at Quinnipiac University have been very supportive. I would especially like to thank Dean David Donnelly and the Faculty Research Committee for granting me the time and funding needed to pursue publication; my faculty mentor, Dr. Nancy Worthington; my cat-sitter and confidante, Carol Marro; and my other faculty colleagues and students at Quinnipiac for their guidance and backing. I am also indebted to Dr. Edward Alwood. A fellow former journalist turned media historian, Ed has held my hand through my first venture into publishing, helping me with everything from writing query letters to translating contract language. In the process he has become both a mentor and a friend.

I consider myself very fortunate to be working with Northern Illinois University Press. Acquisitions editor Melody Herr, now with the University of Michigan Press, invited me to submit my manuscript to NIU Press for review. Her detailed instructions and feedback took much of the uncertainty out of the review process. I extend my appreciation to NIU Press Director Alex Schwartz and Managing Editor Susan Bean for taking on my project midstream. I also thank my copy editor, Pippa Letsky, for her thoroughness. Her attention to detail and pointed critique greatly improved the manuscript. My thanks to Designer Julia Fauci for her excellent cover design, to Marketing Manager Linda Manning for her help with promoting the book, and to the rest of the NIU Press staff for their skills. I also thank the three scholars who read my manuscript and recommended it for publication. Their comments were very insightful and supportive. The audiovisual archivists at the presidential libraries were very helpful in locating the first lady photographs included in the book.

Finally, I dedicate this work to my mother and best friend, Betty Roberta Williams, without whom none of this would be possible. She taught me to love learning, and she instilled in me the belief that I could accomplish anything I set my mind to, even if others did not share that viewpoint. Everything I am is a reflection of her love, her patience, her wisdom, and her belief in me.

First Ladies *and the* Fourth Estate

Press Images of First Ladies, 1900–2001

On May 16, 1789, a grandmotherly figure bade farewell to her beloved home and set out on a journey that would both change her life and influence the lives of many women to come. As she boarded her coach Martha Washington was not just leaving the serenity of her private life behind. She was traveling into uncharted territory for most females, making a journey into the public sphere and spotlight long reserved for men and only a handful of powerful women. In each town people lined the streets to wave to her, while reporters joined the procession and followed her all the way to New York. Washington seemed overwhelmed by all of the attention, but the press and the people apparently recognized the significance of her trip and the role she was to play in the burgeoning nation. A story in the *Pennsylvania and Daily Advertiser* described the reaction of the crowd: "every countenance bespoke the feelings of affectionate respect."[1]

The press and the American people have been fascinated by the first lady since the beginning of this nation's history, as we can see in the story of Washington's trip. But the institution itself is a complex combination of contradictions. The position of first lady is not outlined in the Constitution, yet it has been a part of the American presidency since inception. There are no set rules or guidelines, yet the first lady assumes important duties and faces high expectations. It lacks a clear job description, but being first lady is a matter of tradition probably more than any other U.S. institution. In over two hundred years a handful of women have shaped the first lady position through their personalities and their performance of her many roles. These women have been asked to live their private lives in the glare of the public spotlight, their every move subject to scrutiny.

Over the years first ladies have performed a variety of public and private roles from hostess, escort, and volunteer to advisor and policy maker. Because this is a gendered role, there are social norms and expectations associated with its performance.[2] The public nature of the position has given some latitude of performance, yet first ladies must also conform to gender standards reflecting the models of American woman-hood. And these standards often equate women's roles with the private sphere of home and family. Therefore, while the position has been shaped by the words and actions of each first lady, those in the role have never had total control over their performance because of historical, social, and political constraints.[3]

Standing between the first lady and the public is the ever-present press. Very few people ever have direct contact with the first lady, so the majority of the public's information comes from the media. The evolution of the position has undergone press scrutiny since the days of Martha Washington, but press coverage of first ladies expanded exponentially in the twentieth century as the number of media outlets grew and Americans' appetite for celebrity news flourished. Throughout the years journalists have played a significant role in shaping the position, reporting on everything from the first lady's fashion sense to her political activities.[4]

This study looks at press images of first ladies throughout the twentieth century and how press coverage has influenced and defined the first lady position over time. I have examined select newspaper and magazine articles covering the first ladies from 1900 to 2001 and traced how journalists have framed the first lady during different periods and the consequences of such framing. As a rhetorical critic, I was interested in analyzing these texts within their historical context, which required an understanding of the history of the first lady institution, gender ideologies, women's history, and journalism practices. As a feminist media critic and former journalist I was also sensitive to the news-writing process, particularly the journalistic practice of gendered news framing. What I discovered is that press coverage of presidents' wives is a rich source of information, not only about the history of the first lady institution but also about evolving gender roles, women's political participation, and media coverage of women in politics.

First Ladies and the Media—An Evolving Relationship

The relationship between first ladies and the media has been shaped by a number of factors over the years, including the dispositions of the individual women holding the position, the social norms governing women's publicity, the marketability of women's news, and institutional structures regulating journalists' access to first ladies. Starting with the coverage of Martha Washington, the relationship between nineteenth-century first ladies and the press varied widely, in part because there were no guidelines for either side to follow. Some first ladies attracted press coverage both positive and negative for their hostessing or their fashions, others actively sought publicity, and some avoided the press altogether. The emergence of publications targeting female readership in the mid-nineteenth century, including women's magazines and newspapers' women's pages, expanded press coverage of the institution. By 1900 articles about first ladies were regularly featured in the American press, which resulted in the need to institutionalize the relationship between first ladies and the media. Edith Roosevelt was the first to hire a social secretary, Belle Hagner, in 1902. Along with helping the first lady manage her many social commitments, Hagner's responsibilities included preparing press releases about the Roosevelts and talking to the press on Roosevelt's behalf, a practice that would eventually lead to the advent of press secretaries.[5]

The next major innovation in first lady press relations occurred during Eleanor Roosevelt's tenure when she began holding regular press conferences with women reporters. During her first White House press conference, Eleanor Roosevelt told the women assembled, "Your job is an important one and if you want to see me once a week I feel I should be willing to see you. . . . You are the interpreters to women of the country as to what goes on politically in the legislative national life and also what the social and personal life is at the White House." By limiting her press conferences to women journalists, Roosevelt gave them an opening for exclusive stories that sometimes led to front-page bylines —in a time when their work was often relegated to the women's pages. These reporters in turn often protected Roosevelt from tough questions and sometimes avoided printing potentially embarrassing answers. Roosevelt's relationship with reporters was strengthened by her own journalistic endeavors, which included writing a syndicated newspaper column, penning numerous magazine articles, and working as a radio commentator.[6]

Roosevelt's successors, however, were quick to abandon her approach to press relations. Instead they moved toward a more formal, managed relationship with reporters. Bess Truman, Mamie Eisenhower, and Jacqueline Kennedy limited their personal contacts with reporters and relied on their social secretaries to keep women journalists informed. Kennedy was the first to have a staff member assigned specifically to dealing with the media, and Lady Bird Johnson was the first to have her own press secretary, Liz Carpenter. Johnson was also considered the most open and accessible first lady since Eleanor Roosevelt. In the past forty years, press secretaries and their staffs have served as intermediaries between first ladies and journalists. As coverage of the first lady institution steadily increased throughout the twentieth century, so too have White House efforts to manage first ladies' relationships with the media.[7]

Media coverage of first ladies has evolved over the years and has played a significant role in shaping public expectations regarding the performance of the first lady position. By focusing on the social and ceremonial functions of the position, the early American press defined the first lady's duties and also set the boundaries containing her largely within the private sphere. Such coverage persisted throughout the twentieth century as journalists continued to scrutinize her performance and define her "proper" role. Some of the roles journalists have used to frame the first lady and to measure her performance include presidential escort, leader of social protocol, social advocate, policy maker, and political advisor. The first three frames—concerning the "traditional" roles of an upper-middle-class American woman acting in a supportive, nurturing capacity—dominated first lady coverage well into the twentieth century. The "nontraditional" frames of policy maker and political advisor appeared more frequently toward the end of the twentieth century, and often in critical news reports.[8]

Along with setting the standards of performance, media coverage has had other consequences for the first lady institution. One outgrowth of the media's fascination with first ladies is what some scholars refer to as the first lady's "cult of celebrity." Journalists have positioned the first lady as a media celebrity, as the embodiment of a cultural ideal of American womanhood. For the press, in some ways the first lady functions as a barometer of women's social and political status, reflecting shifting cultural views of American womanhood. Individual first ladies have both reflected the status of American women of their time and, because of the public nature of the first lady position, often expanded public understanding of women's "proper" place. Their celebrity status can be more a curse than a blessing, however. Journalists often expect first ladies both to embody traditional gender roles and reflect the changing times, simultaneously modern and traditional. First ladies are supposed to be comfortable socializing with kings and queens and movie stars, yet they must also be able to identify with "average" Americans. Their every move is critiqued, and they often find they can never please everyone.[9]

The focus of this study is the point where publicity, power, and gender intersect. The press is the primary way that the first ladies' ideas, images, and words move into the public arena. They become public women largely through the press, which details their public as well as private activities and circulates their images throughout the public sphere. Political figures, in particular, have long used the press as a vehicle for communicating with the American people, which some scholars have called "going public." Press coverage has always been a main avenue of "going public" for first ladies, making them some of the first female public figures, and in some cases the first female political celebrities, exhibiting political agency in their own right.[10]

But "going public" for women has always been a risky venture. Gender ideologies based on the notion of separate spheres have traditionally defined the public sphere as the domain of men. While being "a public man" was a highly valued ideal, the term "a public woman" was a euphemism for a prostitute, for example. Positive press coverage of American first ladies lessened the stigma of being a "public woman" and legitimized women's presence in the public sphere. First ladies have "arguably stood out for decades as the single most visible group of American women, apart from actresses and other performers who also rise or fall by dint of publicity." Yet, because press coverage often focused on first ladies as wives, mothers, and homemakers, the same stories that constructed these women as public figures simultaneously reinforced the idea that women's primary domain continued to be within the home.[11]

Press Framing

The practice of press framing has shaped stories about first ladies since Martha Washington's time, justifying their presence in the public sphere. Journalism is a specialized form of storytelling. Journalists construct narratives that include characters, plots, and settings, but they have a limited space available in which to tell their stories. So they rely on conventions such as framing that allow them to organize their stories into quick, concise packages in order to convey the maximum amount of information in the minimum number of words.

Frames have been defined as "organizing principles that are socially shared and persistent over time, that work symbolically to meaningfully structure the social world." Frames work by drawing upon prior knowledge of readers in order to explain and classify new information. Journalists thus use frames to make what is unfamiliar or new familiar to their audiences, and to make it newsworthy. The frames they select influence how they tell the story as well as how it is interpreted by its audience. For example, a popular frame is competition. A competitive frame structures a news story by presenting the characters as contenders engaged in battle, with the implication that there will be a winner (and a loser) when the battle is over. Such stories often describe the contenders by comparing one to another and frequently detail each contender's strategy for winning. The competition frame is frequently used in sports coverage and in political reporting, especially during campaigns. It shapes all elements of the story, fitting them into a tidy package that audiences can quickly comprehend, since people are familiar with the conventions. If the story deviates from the conventional form, audiences notice right away; if a story about a football game doesn't note who won, for example, readers will feel the story is incomplete. Thus, a frame provides a structure for a news story. Frames allow journalists to construct stories that not only ring true to their audiences but also are compelling and engaging narratives about the world in which we live.[12]

Journalists routinely use several frames to structure their stories about first ladies. Gender is most frequently used in coverage of women in politics. Reporters use gendered framing to "simplify, prioritize, and structure the narrative flow of events when covering men and women in public life." Gender is "a relevant peg for the story line whether covering candidates running for political office, voters at the ballot box, international leaders, or policy debates about welfare reform, abortion, and affirmative action." For women in politics it means their coverage always has a gendered element; they are always identified as female. And in the male-dominated world of politics, being female has often been a disadvantage.[13]

Journalists' notions of gender are drawn from competing ideologies that seek to define womanhood. When gender becomes part of a news story, it becomes "part of a culture described by a particular writer, class, power structure, or the like at a particular point in history." The result is a symbolic construction of gender in which various "ideals of American womanhood" emerge in the media. The notion that there is such a thing as the "ideal American woman" has persisted since the birth of this nation. However, gender ideals have evolved and shifted in response to historical, political, and social forces; and different conceptions of the "ideal American woman" have competed to define gender norms and roles. By using gender ideals to frame the first lady's activities, journalists reinforce the idea that the performance of the first lady's duties is always gendered.[14]

Tensions between ideologies that promote women's so-called traditional domestic roles and ideologies that promote the expansion of women's roles beyond the home into public and political life often result in double binds, especially for women in the public eye. A double bind "is a rhetorical construct that posits two and only two alternatives, one or both penalizing the person being offered them." The dichotomy is used to simplify complexities by categorizing them as either good or bad, right or wrong, public or private, political or personal. The historical basis for the double bind facing women is the dichotomy between public and private spheres: "Historically, the place for women is in the private sphere of the home—centered, metaphorically, not in the bedroom or the parlor, but in the nursery and the kitchen." When women venture out of their "proper sphere," they often find themselves "caught in situations in which they are damned if they do and damned if they don't." The first lady is automatically ensnared in a double bind by her position itself, which requires performance of private-sphere duties in the public sphere. Rosalynn Carter once said, "I had learned from more than a decade of political life that I was going to be criticized no matter what I did so I might as well be criticized for something I wanted to do." While journalists sometimes recognize the double binds facing the first lady, by continuing to use frames that draw on these dichotomies when discussing her position, they often reify the constraints, resulting in a no-win situation for the particular woman under scrutiny.[15]

An additional framing technique used by journalists in their coverage of the first lady institution is personification framing. Over the years the institution has been shaped by a combination of tradition, public expectations, and the individual performance and personality of each woman in the position. This is too much information to summarize in each news story, which results in a dilemma for journalists, who routinely rely on existing knowledge in order to contextualize new(s) information. Hence, they rely on ideological shortcuts, which allow them to sum up over one hundred years of institutional memory and the complexities of gender performance in one word, phrase, or name. The resulting personification frames allow journalists to present and evaluate information about each woman and about the first lady institution quickly, in a manner that fits their own narrative style.

These frames bring together the gender ideologies of the day, reporters' understanding of the historical performance of the position, and the experiences and activities of each individual woman. When used as a personification frame, a first lady or candidate's wife becomes the embodiment of gender ideologies and represents for journalists ideological definitions of American womanhood. This frame allows journalists to assess a woman's qualifications for the first lady role based on her performance of gender, which is then conflated with her ability to perform the first lady's duties. This framing can be both limiting and empowering, sometimes simultaneously. Either way, it is a powerful tool used by journalists to shape public understanding of the first lady position.

Press framing relies on organizing principles that are socially shared, and journalists often draw on history to provide context for their narratives. Reporters frequently reference shared memories of historic persons and events, "recycling of stories about certain key events. Journalists become involved in an ongoing process by which they create a repertoire of past events that is used as a standard for judging contemporary action." Journalists simultaneously draw from, reinforce, and contribute to U.S. collective memory, a "body of beliefs about the past that help a public or society understand both its past and its present, and, by implication, its future." Collective memory constructs symbolic bridges between the present and the past, using shared memories of the past to help people make sense of their present. Thus, collective memory, like news framing, both reflects and constitutes a society's values, beliefs, and attitudes.[16]

Historical persons or events are commonly used as news frames. One way that reporters use collective memory in coverage of a first lady is by referencing previous first ladies. They seek to define her performance by comparing her to prior presidents' wives who have achieved iconic status. Icons can be defined as "culturally resonant units that convey a familiar set of 'original' meanings and images." Icons "outlast single, short-lived versions of an event, character, or history: they are sites for repeated stagings of narratives, the sites on which the past, present, and future may be written." Icons also serve as sites of ideological contestation, embodying particular past performances that can be used to frame current debates.[17]

Iconic framing is an outgrowth of both personification framing and celebrity. Such historical memory is dependent on the frames that were used in years past to define performances of the first lady position. The problem is that often these first ladies, through the work of collective or media memory, are reduced to a single ideology or role. For example, Eleanor Roosevelt is presented as the icon of an activist first lady, while Jacqueline Kennedy is a fashion icon. While the memories of each woman are accurate, they represent just a small part of their overall performance. The complexities of their performance diminish as time passes. Iconic framing represents the limitations of media memory. These iconic first ladies are used by journalists to sum up the history of the first lady institution in just a few words or images. This practice reduces not only the individual women but the institution's historical legacy as well, frequently leaving readers with a very limited understanding of first lady history.[18]

While journalists use frames to construct their news narratives about first ladies, the wives themselves are not completely helpless when it comes to how they are presented in the press. Since journalists must draw on a variety of sources in constructing their narratives, framing often becomes a process of negotiation, especially when the subjects of news stories are aware of the importance of image-making. Presidents have always been concerned with constructing a favorable public image, but this concern has mutated into what has been called the "image-is-everything presidency" in which teams of consultants work to create a marketable image for the president. However, while presidents and their partisan rivals try to define the president's image, "an important intervening factor is the media—newspapers, magazines, and television," which play "an integral role in establishing the president's image." The same can be said of first ladies, who have more and more sought, with the aid of staffers and consultants, to construct their public image. The press "plays a critical role in transmitting both the image and substance of a First Lady." First ladies have the most influence over their images when they develop a coherent strategy for dealing with the media, which includes controlling their photographic and video images, as well as their public statements.[19]

First ladies have faced the added challenge of representing for the press their gender as well as their office, for their images are tied to both the first lady institution and American womanhood. For reporters first ladies "become 'sites' for the symbolic negotiation of female identity. Discourses by and about first ladies function culturally to shape our notions of femininity and so both foster and constrain women's agency." Despite the growing complexities of image negotiations, journalists play a significant part in image construction because the practice of framing allows them to explain, interpret, and even deconstruct the images presented by first ladies and presidents.[20]

Reporters also influence the celebrity status of first ladies through the various ways they present images of these women. A celebrity is "a person who is known for his well-knowness . . . the human pseudo-event" created by the media. The rise of a celebrity culture is considered a twentieth-century phenomenon. Scholars argue that celebrity is "a *modern* phenomenon, a phenomenon of mass-circulation newspapers, TV, radio, and film." The more media outlets available to circulate images of well-known persons, the more well-known they become.[21]

Celebrities are "overtly public individuals" who are given "greater presence and a wider scope of activity and agency" in the public sphere, largely through their access to and presence in the media. In the case of first ladies, celebrity status makes these women public figures in their own right and affords them the agency to act independently of their husbands. Furthermore, "Celebrity status also confers on the person a certain discursive power: within society, the celebrity is a voice above others, a voice that is channeled into the media systems as being legitimately significant." Press coverage of first ladies as celebrities positions them as a legitimate voice on cultural and political issues. However, celebrity can also be limiting because the individual is often lost in the image. A celebrity "*represents* something other than itself. The material reality of the celebrity sign—that is, the actual person who is at the core of the representation—disappears into a cultural formation of meaning." Such is the case with first ladies, who are often reduced by journalists to representations of American womanhood through the practice of personification framing. So, much like press framing, celebrity can be both empowering and constraining. Celebrity can also be lasting, or fleeting, depending chiefly on the media's memory.[22]

All of the concepts—framing, gender, collective memory, image-making, and celebrity—converge in press coverage of first ladies. Press practices like personification framing allow journalists to address complex topics, like gender or collective memory, in a single story. These theories provide a foundation for an analysis of newspaper and magazine coverage of first ladies throughout the twentieth century.

Print Media Coverage of First Ladies in the Twentieth Century

Television, radio, newsreels, and other media have contributed to the journalistic construction of the first lady institution, but this project examines articles about first ladies that were published in newspapers and women's magazines between 1900 and 2001, centering exclusively on campaign and inaugural years, when press attention to first ladies grows more intensive. Newspapers and magazines are important information sites because broadcast journalists tend to get their news from their print colleagues. Print journalism, thus, has considerable power when it comes to defining positions such as that of first lady and dictating the principle frames used by broadcast journalists.[23]

Analyzing print sources also provides a sense of continuity throughout the project. In terms of professional journalistic practice, the press, as we know it today, is very similar to its turn-of-the-century counterpart. Interviews, which became a journalistic staple in the late 1800s, gave journalists the power to question public figures as well as the power to decide what information was included in the resulting story. Such interviews were then packaged into narrative form to attract readers, including "leads" and the inverted pyramid style. Such interviews were then packaged into narrative form to attract readers, including lead sentences that grabbed readers' attention and the inverted pyramid style that presented the most important information first. Also, women's pages and successful mass market magazines began to target women and became staples of the print media in the late 1800s, boosting routine news media coverage of the first lady institution by the twentieth century.[24]

For this project I examined articles that appeared during presidential campaign and inaugural years, specifically the period ranging from the June of an election year, when the focus shifts away from the primaries to the national conventions and general election, through the June of the following year. I focused on stories that discuss the first lady position in general, including articles about former, current, and potential first ladies. I limited the study to campaign and inaugural years for several reasons. First, press coverage of first ladies has traditionally peaked during campaigns and their first six months in office. During campaigns, profiles on the candidates' wives evaluate their preparedness for the first lady position, often posing questions such as "What kind of first lady will she be?" Journalists also examine the relationship between these women and their husbands, assessing their level of influence, which is a key focus of this study. Reporters' interest in first ladies continues to be intense during their first few months in the White House and then has usually died down, after that time focusing mostly just on specific events or appearances. This was particularly true in the first half of the twentieth century.

In addition, almost all first ladies used their initial months to establish themselves and how they would approach the role. Thus, their activities during this time period were representative of their performance of the position throughout their tenure. Second, the period surrounding campaigns and inaugurations is when the past, present, and future come together, when Americans reconstitute themselves as a nation. Because my interest was in press framing of the first lady institution over time, as well as the individual first ladies, this time period was most germane because this is when reporters often focus on the history of the position and the various ways that previous first ladies have approached their roles. This focus includes articles examining the tenure of the outgoing first lady, touching on the highlights of her time in the White House. Finally, because of the breadth of the study, I needed a way to control the number of articles selected for analysis. Containing my study to campaign and inaugural years throughout the twentieth century still yielded thousands of articles. Some first ladies, such as Eleanor Roosevelt and Hillary Clinton, had almost daily press coverage, resulting in hundreds of articles about each woman from just one of the five publications included in this study.

This study centers on two major newspapers, the *New York Times* and the *Washington Post,* and three mass market women's magazines, *Ladies' Home Journal, Good Housekeeping,* and *McCall's.* Both the *New York Times* and the *Washington Post* are considered national newspapers. Their stories are often reprinted in papers nationwide, thus influencing audiences across the country. Because of their national status, both newspapers also employ reporters assigned to the White House press corps to cover campaigns full-time during election periods. *Ladies' Home Journal, Good Housekeeping,* and *McCall's* were selected because all three have consistently been among the most popular women's magazines published throughout the twentieth century. Women's magazines, because of their openly gendered content, serve as a counterpoint to mainstream newspapers, which have traditionally appealed to a broader audience despite the frequent relegation of first lady news to the women's pages.

My analysis of press images of first ladies is divided into the following chapters. Chapter One provides the study's historical context by examining the gendered press framing of the first lady institution prior to 1900. The gender ideologies of the nineteenth century, based on the concept of separate spheres, shaped journalists' framing of first ladies, which in turn aided the development of the first lady institution, with its series of duties, traditions, and expectations. In addition press coverage made many of these first ladies nationally visible public figures at a time when women's publicity was largely condemned. In some cases such publicity was used to criticize a first lady, but in general the women were positioned by the press as models of American womanhood. Combined, the gender ideologies of the nineteenth century, the duties of the first lady position, and the growing publicity surrounding first ladies provided the foundation for twentieth-century press framing of the first lady institution.

Chapter Two examines the news coverage of first ladies from 1900 to 1929. Beginning the analysis with the campaign of 1900 parallels the beginning of the modern era of American politics, an era that saw the emergence of the first lady as a public woman. The cultural debate regarding women's place in American society coupled with the growing popularity of women's magazines and women's pages heightened the publicity surrounding the first lady institution. In the press the nineteenth-century concept of true womanhood, which defined the home as woman's proper sphere, competed with the new woman's call for the expansion of women's roles into the public sphere. While turn-of-the-century first ladies personified the ideals of true womanhood, their successors represented a balance between the true woman and the new woman, embodying the modern era's version of the "superwoman." Such gendered framing was used by journalists to explain the growing duties of the first lady institution and to legitimate the emergence of first ladies as public women, which played a significant role in normalizing women's growing public presence and political activity.

The focus of Chapter Three is on how the depression, World War II, and the Cold War, especially in relation to women's roles, shaped the news narratives about the first lady institution from 1932 to 1961. The era was dominated by an ideology of domesticity that moved beyond the pages of women's publications and pervaded every aspect of private and public life. Women's roles as wives, mothers, and household consumers were imbued with political significance, offering them a sense of domestic empowerment, and recognizing that the "personal is political" long before second-wave feminism. However, by limiting women to traditional roles, women's political power was simultaneously contained to private-sphere concerns, which would be pointed to as the root of the "feminine mystique" by second-wave feminists. For the journalists (many of whom were women) covering the first lady, the first ladies of this era embodied the domestic ideal by personifying social feminism or Cold War domesticity. Thus, even Eleanor Roosevelt's precedent-breaking performance of the first lady position was framed primarily as an extension of her role as wife and homemaker. Yet such gendered framing and the rise of the first lady as public woman in the previous period had led to the emergence of specific first ladies as political celebrities. These first ladies served as models of women's civic engagement, an engagement that ranged from the volunteer and political activities of Eleanor Roosevelt to the Cold War consumerism of Mamie Eisenhower and Jacqueline Kennedy.

Chapter Four looks at coverage from 1964 to 1977, in which the first lady institution became a site of contestation over women's roles, reflecting the influence of the women's liberation movement on press framing. Just as domesticity had dominated the frames of the previous era, feminist ideals now permeated discussions of women's issues. In women's magazines the first ladies of this era, with the exception of Pat Nixon, embodied the contemporary (super)woman who successfully balanced home and family with a career and outside interests, thus supporting women's liberation without rejecting domesticity. In contrast Nixon represented the feminine mystique, which often resulted in critical coverage of her more "traditional" performance of the first lady position. The growing public and political activities of these first ladies were viewed through a feminist lens, particularly by women journalists, many of whom were sympathetic to the women's movement. This led to the emergence of first ladies as political activists in press framing. Because their status as public women and political celebrities was now linked with their political activism, there was more press scrutiny of first ladies during this period. In some articles journalists used iconic first ladies, who personified historical performances of the position, to gauge the activities of contemporary first ladies. Other stories reflected the ideological contestation over women's roles that characterized this era, pitting activist women against their more traditional counterparts, which often resulted in a no-win situation for everyone involved. While the activist first ladies were judged too influential, Nixon was criticized for not being influential enough. Such critiques of the performance of the first lady position began to evidence the double binds facing these women and pointed to a growing backlash against the second-wave of feminist activity.

Chapter Five examines the framing of the first lady institution from 1980 through 2001. By the end of the century Americans were still debating women's "proper" place, as "family values" became a major campaign issue. The backlash against second-wave feminism saw the return of the Cold War domestic ideal and its baby boomer counterpart, new traditionalism. When juxtaposed with the careerism of second-wave feminism, this set up a political catfight between candidates' wives. Media framing —which throughout the century had facilitated the emergence of first ladies as public women, gendered celebrities, and political activists—now worked primarily to establish boundaries to limit the gendered performance of the first lady position. Concerned with the "hidden power" of first ladies, journalists framed political wives who overstepped the boundaries of first lady and gender performance as political interlopers whose influence allegedly trespassed too far into the male political sphere. Drawing on iconic first ladies as boundary markers and on the double binds that developed in the previous era, gendered media framing worked to contain those wives who were perceived as political interlopers. Hillary Rodham Clinton, in particular, before she even moved into the White House aroused age-old fears of the sexualized public woman who refuses to be contained and who thus is a danger to her husband and her community.

At the beginning of the twenty-first century, gendered framing continues to influence the coverage of the first lady institution. The Conclusion looks at the themes that emerge from this analysis and reflects on the implications generated by this study of gendered framing for the first lady institution, for journalists, and for political women. In the end, this study demonstrates first ladies' unquestionable presence in the public sphere through press framing; such framing likewise reveals the visible boundaries that still persist for first ladies' involvement in the political sphere. This book examines how, throughout the twentieth century, the press provided first ladies with a forum in which to become public women, political celebrities, political activists, and political interlopers. However, before we turn our attention to the twentieth century, it is important to examine the history of first lady press coverage prior to 1900. The roots of such gendered media framing reach back to the earliest coverage of the first lady institution, back to Martha Washington's 1789 journey.

CHAPTER ONE

Representations of Womanhood in the American Press before 1900

By the time Martha Washington reached the final stage of her journey from Mount Vernon to New York City, it appears she had become accustomed to seeing her name in the newspapers. On May 27, 1789, in Elizabethtown, New Jersey, she boarded a forty-seven-foot presidential barge that carried her to Manhattan, and in a letter to her niece she noted, "the paper will tell you how I was complimented on my landing." Within weeks, however, anti-Federalist papers were criticizing rather than complimenting the president's wife. Soon after she arrived, Washington settled into a schedule of weekly social engagements, including receptions that she hosted on Friday evenings. Republican papers were quick to refer to the gatherings as "court-like levees" and "queenly drawing rooms." In a time when an accusation of royalist leanings was the ultimate insult, these comments were designed to incite the ire of Federalists.[1]

Newspaper criticism of Washington would eventually become a campaign issue. In 1792 Thomas Jefferson, through the republican newspaper the *National Gazette*, launched a campaign against the Washington administration by attacking Martha's levees. In private and in print Jefferson charged the president's wife directly with acting "too queenly."[2] Thus Martha Washington was no stranger to press coverage, and the stories about her would establish a continuing relationship between presidents' wives and the press.

As perhaps the most visible woman in America, the first lady has always been a popular topic of press accounts. For many journalists, the first lady position has served as a barometer to measure shifting ideals of American womanhood. The position is unique in that it calls upon women to perform the private-sphere roles of wife and mother in the public spotlight, making these women public figures. The position also affords its holders an avenue for public and political participation.

Journalists have consistently employed gender ideals in their framing of the institution. The news media constitute one social institution that helps shape gender norms and roles. Many feminist scholars note that the media are particularly influential in teaching American ideals of gender through its representation of sex-role stereotypes. Through their representations of gender in practices such as framing, journalists play an important role in shaping how Americans understand womanhood.[3]

At the same time, the ideals of American womanhood have never been static. The status and social expectations of women have fluctuated between traditions rooted in the past and progress made in the present; these contradictions are reflected in press coverage of all women, and particularly of first ladies. Because the first lady position straddles the public and private spheres, its mediated construction serves as a site of contestation over the ideals of American womanhood. As one scholar notes: "Historically, first ladies have functioned as 'symbols' of traditional white middle- to upper-class femininity in America, a condition that has both constrained and empowered them."[4]

Gender ideologies developed during the nineteenth century impacted the representations of American womanhood that appeared in newspapers and magazines, which in turn influenced the performance of the first lady institution. First ladies were nationally visible public figures at times when women's publicity was condemned. Sometimes their publicity was turned against them, making them the targets of harsh criticism; in other times their public role was justified as a requirement of their position. Regardless of the tone of discourse, first ladies were granted access to rhetorical spaces (in this case the pages of newspapers and magazines) that were closed to most women. The gender ideologies of the era were routinely employed by journalists to frame their stories about first ladies. What resulted is one of the many paradoxes of the first lady institution. Journalists used the first lady's status as a public figure to construct her as a model of American womanhood; such a focus, though, often promoted the home as woman's proper place, far away from the public spotlight.[5]

This chapter has three goals. The first is to outline the gender ideologies that influenced definitions of womanhood throughout the nineteenth century and into the twentieth. The second is to trace the development of the first lady institution, foreshadowing the roles and expectations of first ladies in the twentieth century. The last is to discuss press coverage of first ladies prior to 1900, with an emphasis on the gendered frames that continue to characterize coverage of the institution. These three goals then provide a foundation for the following analysis of news framing of the institution in the twentieth century. The following historical periods roughly coincide with shifts in gender ideologies, which impacted both the performance and the coverage of presidential wives.

The Era of Republican Motherhood and Parlor Politics, 1789–1833

Women played a significant role in the American Revolution and continued to shape the new nation, albeit from a position that has long been devalued. As Linda Kerber notes: "Like most women in preindustrial societies, eighteenth-century American women lived in what might be called a woman's domain. Their daily activities took place within a feminine, domestic circle." The notion of a woman's domain—a separate sphere that is private, physically located in the home, and constructed in opposition to the public domain of man—can be traced back to Aristotle and has been used over the years to define, describe, and critique women's place in society. The concept of separate spheres has informed the gender ideologies defining American womanhood since the revolutionary era, simultaneously constraining and empowering women. This paradox can be seen in the ideology of republican motherhood and the role of parlor politics in the fledgling republic.[6]

REPUBLICAN MOTHERHOOD AND PARLOR POLITICS

Women's participation in the American Revolution disrupted the barrier between the male political world and the female domestic realm. The ideology of republican motherhood "was an effort to bring the older version of the separation of spheres into rough conformity with the new politics that valued autonomy and individualism." Republican motherhood emphasized women's moral influence on men and ascribed importance to their maternal role and "recognized that women's choices and women's work did serve larger social and political purposes, and that recognition was enough to draw the traditional women's 'sphere' somewhat closer to men's 'world.'" But the ideology rejected the feminist stance that claimed for women a direct connection with political life and instead upheld the conventional separation of spheres. For example, republican motherhood promoted at least a basic education for females. However, girls were taught to read and write only to prepare them for their role as mothers of the next generation of citizens. While their access to education empowered women, the ideology imposed limits on that power by linking education to motherhood and containing women's knowledge within the private sphere, hence the paradox of republican motherhood.[7]

Because republican motherhood and the notion of separate spheres recognized the home as the woman's domain, American women, particularly political wives, would play a key role in building the new nation. According to Catherine Allgor's study of "parlor politics," America's founders "had not yet developed a clear delineation between a private sphere of home, emotion, and family and a public sphere of office, bureaucracy, and business." Because of this, "'work' happened in all arenas of life, especially in a town such as Washington. In a government with little mandated structure, the unofficial sphere proved as crucial as the official one." Social events served as both private events and political arenas, and since women assumed the role of hostess within the home, they were key players in the "parlor politics" of the new Republic. Allgor argues that, "in a republican culture that frowned upon official men engaging in such old-fashioned aristocratic politicking, women assumed more responsibility for creating the political machine and keeping its operations smooth." Thus, hostessing was both a political and a social role. Because hostessing was the province of women, they also bore the responsibility of balancing republican simplicity with the status symbols associated with aristocracy. Scholars have often overlooked this powerful position of post-revolutionary women because of its association with the feminine domestic realm.[8]

Early first ladies found themselves in positions infused with political significance, but the roles they played were often devalued or criticized. The ideology of republican motherhood and the importance of parlor politics in the new republic were influential in the development of the first lady institution and its resulting press coverage.

THE BIRTH OF THE FIRST LADY INSTITUTION

When Martha Washington joined her husband in New York, she knew she would be helping him in his latest venture, but there was no blueprint to follow in determining the extent of her responsibilities. While the duties of the president were detailed in the Constitution, there was no mention of the role of the president's wife. Washington's tenure and that of other early first ladies shaped the institution as "a public ceremonial office . . . responsible for social functions and hosting formal affairs of state."[9] The six presidential wives of this era—Martha Dandridge Custis Washington (1789–1797), Abigail Smith Adams (1797–1801), Dolley Payne Todd Madison (1809–1817), Elizabeth Kortright Monroe (1817–1825), Louisa Catherine Johnson Adams (1825–1829), and Rachel Donelson Robards Jackson (1828)—learned quickly that their private lives were now a matter of public record and that they were each expected to perform a variety of roles including hostess presidential helpmate, and public figure.[10]

The parlor politics of hostessing played an important role in the formative years of the United States. The female relatives of political leaders, like those of farmers and shopkeepers, "participated in the family business—in this case, however, the family business was politics." Social events served both private and political functions: "Men could maintain public virtue in the official sphere while working cooperatively and politically behind the scenes," while women "used a veil of respectability to work aggressively toward their political goals."[11] Of the early first ladies, Dolley Madison and Louisa Catherine Adams were particularly adept at social politicking. Madison, whose social events received universally high praise, was successful because of her ability to combine republican simplicity with federalist high style: "she created a public space for the executive that reassured both Federalists and Republicans, while impressing European visitors and officials with the sophistication of the new nation." But even Madison at times faced criticism, what Patricia Brady calls the "damned-if-you-do, damned-if-you-don't factor, the hypercritical attention lavished on every aspect of presidential entertainment—too lavish, too formal, too free." Washington social events were covered intensely by the partisan editors, who recognized their political importance.[12]

The behind-the-scenes activities of presidential wives were also of interest to the press. Early spouses often acted as confidantes and informal advisors to their husbands on political matters. Every woman of this era accepted the notion that her role as helpmate involved duties that impacted her husband's job performance, supporting scholars' claims that the presidency has always been a two-person career. Because the presidential workplace and residence were one and the same, wives had to be familiar with politics: "With a husband who 'worked at home,' she could not, as John Quincy Adams' wife, Louisa, liked to point out, escape knowing something about his job—who supported him and who opposed."[13] This knowledge was essential in social politicking and positioned the wives as partners in their husbands' political careers. Their political influence was often tempered by the republican motherhood notion that these women were serving as mere helpmates to their husbands rather than political actors in their own right, keeping their actions safely contained within the private realm. Such ideological limitations on their influence, however, did not prevent the occasional critique that wives wielded too much power. Regardless of how their performance was viewed, the helpmate and hostess roles made first ladies more visible publicly, especially when their activities were reported in the press.

Washington realized during her journey to New York, as she attracted crowds of well-wishers and newspapermen, that she had become a public figure. By treating them as newsworthy, the press and public promoted the status of these early presidential wives as public figures. Early first ladies were among the most visible women in the country, attracting press attention in a period when stories about women rarely appeared in partisan newspapers. However, because the press was not yet a mass media, first ladies' publicity was often limited to the elite readers of partisan publications.

These women recognized that, paradoxically, the publicity and political considerations of their public role placed severe constraints on their private lives and personal expression. Presidents' wives were scrutinized by both supporters and political rivals, as well as by the partisan press. In a letter to her niece, Washington complained, "I think I am more like a state prisoner than anything else, there is certain bounds [*sic*] set for me which I must not depart from—and as I can not doe [*sic*] as I like I am obstinate and stay at home a great deal." Abigail Adams noted, "I have been so used to freedom of sentiment that I know not how to place so many guards about me, as will be indispensable, to look at every word before I utter it, and to impose a silence upon myself, when I talk." Thus, despite being among the most recognizable women of their era, early first ladies' voices were often stifled by their status. The silence of these women gave considerable power to the partisan press to construct their images and interpret the "proper" role of the president's wife.[14]

PARTISAN PRESS FRAMING OF THE FIRST LADY INSTITUTION

The press of this era was characterized by its partisan nature. Editors believed their purpose was to win supporters for a particular political viewpoint; they published news from a political standpoint, defending the party's view and attacking opponents, while politicians sought out sympathetic editors to publicize their arguments.[15] Stories featuring women rarely appeared in partisan publications, which is not surprising given women's absence from politics and partisan papers' emphasis on political information.[16] One study of several major partisan era publications found that, when women did appear in news stories, they were usually portrayed as victims, "most likely of men from the opposing political party, but also of criminals and even the weather. Women were killed, raped, pillaged, made to work as prostitutes, beaten and terrified." The rare stories telling of women who asserted themselves in public were critical of their actions, often labeling them as "public women" or "Jezebels." According to Glenna Matthews, "public woman" was an "epithet for one who was seen as the dregs of society, vile, unclean," and to be a public woman "in any of the several senses of the term—was to risk the accusation of sexual impropriety."[17] The partisan press employed the notion of separate spheres. Partisan editors also often employed the rhetoric of republican motherhood in the process: "The periodicals became voices of authority in terms of disseminating a new conception of woman's role—one that kept her in the home but elevated the significance of what she did there." Republican motherhood recognized that women contributed to civic life by instilling democratic values in their children.[18]

Gender ideology converged with journalism ideology in the framing of first ladies, whose positions made their private lives of interest to the press. When women appeared in partisan papers, they were simply used for the editors' own political purposes, that is, promoting a particular political ideology by supporting allies and attacking opposition. First ladies were considered secondary and subservient rather than as political actors in their own right.[19] The press framing of first ladies between 1789 and 1833 exemplifies the debate over woman's place in the new republic. Early presidents' wives were generally represented in one of three ways: as a queen, as a republican mother, or as a Jezebel. Each of these press constructions reflects the politics and gender ideologies of the period. Even stories about first ladies' fashions were imbued with political significance during the partisan era. The coverage of these early presidential wives began to shape the institutional memory of the first lady position.

Partisan era editors did not have a template to follow for covering the first lady, and many treated her as a queen. Depending on the political perspective of the editor, this treatment provided a frame through which to praise or attack her. Federalist editor John Fenno institutionalized the practice of referring to Washington as "Lady Washington," a title he bestowed on all society females. But republican editors were quick to criticize the use of royal titles and pointed to "Lady Washington" as exemplifying the monarchical leanings of the Federalists. Abigail Adams was criticized for being a royalist to an even greater degree than Washington. She was often referred to as "Her Majesty" by republican editors. Dolley Madison was lovingly called the "Queen of Hearts," but her successor, Elizabeth Monroe, was accused of suffering from "queen fever."[20] Monroe's preference for all things French, including her clothing and the furniture in the newly redecorated White House, was criticized in the press as a sign of aristocratic airs. During her time in the White House, Louisa Catherine Adams was criticized by the Jacksonian press for living in "regal magnificence." Adams fought back, writing a detailed account of her life that appeared in the June 1827 issue of *Mrs. A. S. Colvin's Weekly Messenger.* This makes her the first president's wife to write openly for a publication.[21]

Partisan editors often employed the royalty frame when discussing social events. Early first ladies sought to establish a "republican court" that balanced royal dignity and republican simplicity. Washington's levees became a target of partisan press criticism for awkwardly imitating European court receptions. Madison was the first to develop a style that appeased both Federalists and Republicans. Many of her early drawing rooms were advertised and reported on in newspapers. Madison's "republican court" was national news. "*Intelligencer* stories about her wit, fashions, and parties were read across the young nation, by men and women alike."[22] Even anti-Madison publications at times carried flattering accounts of her popular receptions. The press's royal framing of Madison's events helped make republicanism, "with its particularly ideological and abstract ideals of manners, into a working reality" for Americans.[23]

Even the fashion choices of first ladies carried political significance during the partisan era. The partisan press set the first ladies up as trend-setters, like European royalty, and editors often connected their popularity to their husbands' political fortunes. Madison's turbans became a national fashion craze, thanks in part to their descriptions in press accounts. She was also the first president's wife to grace a magazine cover, now offering Americans a visual representation of the popular first lady.[24] Monroe's French gowns were often described in detail by partisan editors, many of whom criticized her regal tastes. In contrast, federalist papers praised Washington's decision to wear American-made garments and touted her as a model of republican values for supporting her country rather than coveting the latest European fashions.[25] Coverage of first ladies as trendsetters established them as recognizable public figures.

The first ladies of this era not only circulated in the public sphere via press coverage, they also engaged in volunteerism, one of the few public activities deemed appropriate for women. Partisan editors often used the values associated with republican motherhood to frame first ladies' volunteerism, a topic that received limited coverage during this period. Stories about Washington frequently mentioned how she helped care for her husband's troops during the Revolutionary War and noted her continuing support of veterans' causes as a symbol of her patriotism. Madison was the first to have her volunteerism covered extensively by the press.[26] She served as the "First Directress" of the newly founded Washington Female Orphan Asylum, donating a cow and twenty dollars to the cause as well as making clothes for the orphans. The *National Intelligencer* regularly advertised the organization's meetings and fund-raisers. The press covered the opening of the asylum and continued to report on its progress in raising money.[27] Volunteerism was sanctioned by the press as an acceptable public-sphere activity for women because it reflected the domesticity and patriotism of the republican motherhood ideal. Volunteering was a way for women to extend their maternal caretaking skills beyond the home. This type of press coverage would continue as first ladies adopted various volunteer and social advocacy projects, and the publicity surrounding such activities would also expand women's presence in the public spotlight.

However, because women's publicity was generally frowned upon, first ladies' status as public women was sometimes used against them. Campaign coverage during the partisan era was often extremely negative, and several presidential wives found themselves at the center of political scandals in which they were cast as Jezebels. During her husband's presidential campaigns the anti-Madison press circulated "lewd rumors of a scandalously graphic nature," claiming that Dolley Madison was Thomas Jefferson's mistress. Editors charged that the Madisons were childless because James was impotent and Dolley was oversexed. Other stories implied that Madison "had relations" with Democrats who could deliver electoral votes. During the campaign of 1828, the Adamses were accused by Jacksonian editors of having had premarital relations.[28]

These charges were minor compared to the attacks leveled by the pro-Adams press against Rachel Jackson. During the campaign of 1824 word began to spread that Jackson was still married to her abusive first husband when she married Andrew in 1791.[29] Many were aware of the situation, but it did not become a major campaign issue until 1828. By then, Anthony reveals, Jackson was called a "bigamist," "an American Jezebel," "a convicted adulteress," and "a profligate woman" in pamphlets and the press.[30] Jackson went on to win the election, but Rachel suffered a heart attack just before Christmas. "Rumor held that the slanders of the campaign had brought on Rachel's death, shocking and shaming the Washington community, who had been joking for months about the country woman smoking her pipe in the White House drawing room."[31]

The partisan press established a template for covering the first lady that continues to frame coverage of the institution. "The groundwork for the media's depiction of women was laid in the 1790s, almost sixty years before the women's movement began, and the media since that time have often conveyed the same thinking on women's place that appeared in these publications 200 years ago."[32] However, the social upheaval of the following era would also impact how journalists framed the first lady position. The Jacksonian era is credited with ushering in a new democratic ideology that championed the common man while at the same time further diminishing the political activity of American women.[33]

Meanwhile conflicting notions of American womanhood were in competition to define women's roles. While the true womanhood ideology intensified the concept of separate spheres, the fledgling woman's rights movement advocated expansion of women's participation in the political sphere. These very different ideals of womanhood impacted both the performance and the press framing of the first lady institution.

The Emergence of True Womanhood and Woman's Rights, 1833–1865

The notion of separate spheres continued to inform gender ideology. Republican motherhood remained salient particularly during the Civil War, but during this era the emerging "cult of true womanhood" dominated discussions of women's roles, particularly in publications targeting female readers. The sweeping social and political changes of this period drew many women into the public sphere, however, and eventually led to the development of the woman's rights movement whose early leaders promoted a gender ideology that directly challenged the separation of spheres.

DEFINING WOMEN'S PROPER PLACE

The ideology identified by Barbara Welter as the "cult of true womanhood" first appeared in the 1820s. With cardinal virtues of piety, purity, domesticity, and submissiveness, true womanhood was based on a strict separation of the public and private spheres. Many feminist scholars have viewed true womanhood as an ideology that "controlled women and narrowed their options." True womanhood's strict separation of spheres meant that republican motherhood lost its political importance during the antebellum era. True womanhood constrained women's rhetorical activities and agency: "femininity and rhetorical action were seen as mutually exclusive. No 'true woman' could be a public persuader." Women who did speak or act in public risked their reputations, unless they could prove how their actions were sanctioned by true womanhood.[34]

While true womanhood worked to confine women to the home, it also afforded women a certain level of authority within their sphere of influence. Women were viewed as the moral superiors of men, and they were entrusted with the spiritual health of their families, an idea that would eventually justify their public involvement in moral reform and benevolent organizations. When Alexis de Tocqueville visited the United States in the 1830s, for example, he observed that "although the women . . . are confined within the narrow circle of domestic life, and their situation is in some respects one of extreme dependence, I have nowhere seen women occupying a loftier position."[35] In the mid-1800s true womanhood had a favorable impact because "for the first time in American history, both home and woman's special nature were seen as uniquely valuable." Domesticity was viewed as an alternative to patriarchy and was legitimized as a social force, both inside and outside the home.[36]

Volunteerism expanded during this era, engaging more women from various social classes in public-sphere activity. In the antebellum era thousands of charitable associations were formed, and more controversial reform efforts such as abolition were supported largely by women. These benevolent organizations gave women experience in leadership, organizing, fund-raising, and financial management and also offered a network of female acquaintances. The organizations also neutralized the negative connotations associated with women acting outside of the private sphere.[37]

The moral reform movement was one of the first to be initiated and controlled by women. Many female abolitionists drew on the religious elements of true womanhood to justify their public-sphere activities. During the Civil War the U.S. Sanitary Commission (staffed primarily by women) provided food and medical services for the soldiers. Meanwhile Southern women created similar organizations dedicated to the war effort. The number of voluntary associations exploded following the Civil War, as many women sought activities that took them out of the home.[38]

Women's experiences in the abolitionist movement, particularly with the obstacles they faced as public women, led to the formation of the woman's rights movement. At the first Woman's Rights Convention, held on July 19, 1848, Elizabeth Cady Stanton read the "Declaration of Sentiments," which called for a number of reforms, including marriage law, property rights, and suffrage for women. Early leaders—including Stanton, Susan B. Anthony, Lucretia Mott, and Angelina Grimke—promoted a natural rights philosophy that viewed women and men as equals, a viewpoint contradicting that of true womanhood. After the Civil War, when the Fourteenth Amendment added the word "male" to the Constitution in relation to citizenship and voting rights, movement leaders focused their energies on the suffrage issue. An active woman's movement challenged not only laws but also the gender ideologies that dictated women's roles in society. These competing ideals of public versus private womanhood can be seen in the individual performances of the first lady position during this era.[39]

THE ANTEBELLUM FIRST LADY INSTITUTION

Most of the presidential wives of this era were less active and less influential than either their predecessors or their successors. "The roles and responsibilities during this time were not expanded, and the institution was much less visible than it was during the earlier period." Ten different presidents served between 1833 and 1865. Two of them were widowers: Andrew Jackson (1829–1837) and his successor, Martin Van Buren (1837–1841). James Buchanan (1857–1861) was a bachelor. Five presidential wives claimed poor health and delegated their first lady duties to stand-ins: Anna Tuthill Symmes Harrison (1841), Letitia Christian Tyler (1841–1842), Margaret Mackall Smith Taylor (1849–1850), Abigail Powers Fillmore (1850–1853), and Jane Means Appleton Pierce (1853–1857). Each of the remaining first ladies of this era—Julia Gardiner Tyler (1844–1845), Sarah Childress Polk (1845–1849), and Mary Todd Lincoln (1861–1865)— accepted her role and the inevitable publicity that went along with being first lady. This period was influential in the development of the institution, despite the limited expansion of her roles. Antebellum first ladies "helped to establish a 'traditional' approach to the office, that of a publicly passive and seemingly nonpolitical first lady," a performance duly reflecting the true womanhood ideology.[40]

Tyler, Polk, and Lincoln, the more publicly active antebellum first ladies, continued to play the well-established roles of hostess and helpmate. All three, like their predecessors, were recognized for their hostessing and sought to use social events to garner support for their husbands. The youthful Tyler was well aware of the importance of both image-making and parlor politics; in her brief time in the White House, she used hostessing to bolster the popularity of both her husband and herself. The Polks entertained regularly, often holding two public receptions a week. Lincoln believed that keeping a regular schedule of entertaining, even as the Civil War loomed, was important in maintaining a sense of stability and presidential authority. Her plan backfired, however, and her hostessing became a frequent subject of press attacks. Along with their social politicking these women also served as behind-the-scenes advisors. They all showed an interest in politics, and Polk was acknowledged as the most knowledgeable and influential. She acted as both political partner and advisor to her husband.[41]

Whereas most of the wives of the antebellum era were rarely mentioned in the press, Tyler, Polk, and Lincoln were exceptions. Tyler actively sought publicity and had her own unofficial press agent. Polk received universally good press, praised both for her intelligence and for exemplifying "the elegance, charm, and dignity that marked the pinnacle of true womanhood." In contrast Lincoln was the target of some of the most virulent negative press coverage of any first lady in history. She seemed to attract attention for all the wrong things. Even the ideologies of republican motherhood and true womanhood were not enough to frame Lincoln's activities in a positive light.[42]

True womanhood may have limited press coverage of most antebellum first ladies, but it prized two roles that would become important in the press framing of future first ladies: that of wife and that of homemaker. Margaret Taylor, Abigail Fillmore, and Jane Pierce, along with Sarah Polk, "contributed to their husbands' administrations in varying degrees as loyal wives, homemakers, hostesses, cultural arbiters, intercessors, helpmates, and advisors."[43] Because true womanhood demanded that women avoid publicity, the roles played by most of these first ladies received little attention from the press. In later years, however, the roles of wife and homemaker would receive considerably more press coverage.

FRAMING THE ANTEBELLUM FIRST LADY

Unlike partisan papers, which rarely mentioned women unless it was in connection with politics, the antebellum period saw the rise of the penny press with its stories of average men—and average women, who became both writers and subjects of newspaper content. Several women broke into the field of journalism at this time. The majority worked for the newly developed society and women's pages, as well as for growing numbers of women's magazines. These publications were developed specifically to satisfy the advertisers wishing to court female consumers. Some sixty magazines aimed at women were founded between 1830 and 1850. Many of these publications featured female editors and writers.[44] Society news and articles about fashion and beauty became press staples, as a result, in an effort to attract women readers. Despite the general expansion of women's news, however, first lady coverage during this era in fact diminished, with a few exceptions, due to the women who held the position. The press continued to treat first ladies like royalty, covering their social and political activities. Whether focusing on the first ladies' fashion or the scandals surrounding them, journalists drew upon gender ideologies to frame their coverage while simultaneously using first ladies to gauge often competing ideals of American womanhood.

Despite the democratic spirit of the Jacksonian era and the penny press, many journalists continued to frame first ladies as American royalty; and first ladies such as Julia Tyler and Mary Lincoln even courted this coverage. The royalty frame was especially prevalent in stories about the ladies' appearance and fashion. Tyler made history by hiring a press agent, *New York Herald* writer F. W. Thomas, to promote her activities, a move that evidences her understanding of the importance of image management and self-promotion. Thomas wrote glowing stories about Tyler's youth and beauty, calling her the "Lovely Lady Presidentress" and "the most accomplished woman of her age." These stories representing Tyler as American royalty reached a national audience because of the *Herald*'s huge circulation. Lincoln was also interested in promoting a regal image, which she believed would legitimize the White House in the eyes of visiting dignitaries. Shortly after Lincoln entered the White House, *Leslie's Weekly* praised her regal tastes: "No European court or capital can compare with the President's circle and the society of Washington this winter in the freshness and beauty of its women." The magazine also complimented the new first lady fashions for "displaying the exquisitely moulded shoulders and arms of our fair 'Republican Queen,' . . . absolutely dazzling." Both Tyler and Lincoln were praised by the press for their beauty and style, which positioned the first lady as a trendsetter for American women and reinforced the notion that physical attractiveness is a defining quality of womanhood.[45]

While royal comparisons persisted, particularly in the society columns of the penny press, there was a shift from the frame of queen to that of lady, a Victorian ideal tied to true womanhood. The lady represented all that "was chaste, unworldly, and moral in American culture," and true womanhood, praising piety, purity, domesticity, and subservience, "promulgated the lady as the ideal type of American woman." Press coverage of Sarah Polk reflected the discourse of true womanhood, which is interesting, given scholars' claims that she was her husband's most trusted advisor and one of the most politically astute women to become first lady. Polk was a strict Calvinist and was praised by the religious press for banning drinking and dancing during her time in the White House. Polk received universally positive press coverage: "Capital social arbiters who sized up her 'feminine charms' could hardly fault her, and the more intellectually inclined, who wanted a thinking woman in the White House, apparently approved of her too." An editorial in a New York paper noted the "legitimate influence of a pious wife . . . his guardian angel." Thus, despite her political activities, Polk's piety made her an accepted model of the true woman.[46]

The focus on society news in the penny press intensified interest in White House social activities as well. John Tyler caused quite a stir in the press when he became the first president to wed while in office, marrying twenty-four-year-old New York socialite Julia Gardiner in June 1844. Like her predecessors from the partisan era, Tyler used social events (covered by all of the major papers) to garner support for her husband's policies. She hosted several social events that helped her husband lobby successfully for the annexation of Texas, as well as a grand final ball that reclaimed her husband's social status after he was turned out of his own party. Abigail Fillmore also garnered press coverage when she invited public figures to the White House during her tenure, including singer Jenny Lind and authors William Thackery, Charles Dickens, and Washington Irving. Coverage of such events established the White House as the center of Washington society and cast the first lady as a society doyenne.[47]

Along with the additional attention to the first ladies' roles as hostesses and social arbiters, the press included more coverage of their volunteerism also. The values of republican motherhood continued to legitimate their philanthropic activities. Lincoln was praised by some newspapers as a patriot for her volunteerism during the war. The *Washington Star* characterized her as a motherly figure in a story about her visits to Union hospitals, where she delivered flowers, food, and sympathy to wounded and dying soldiers. Some papers also noted her personal donations to the U.S. Sanitary Commission, which raised money for soldiers, and her fund-raising efforts on behalf of the Contraband Relief Association, which provided aid to freed slaves flooding the nation's capital.[48]

It is ironic that the values of republican motherhood were used also to criticize Lincoln's performance of the first lady position. Initially she was praised for her hostessing skills, but then she faced harsh criticism from female journalists who denounced her expensive clothing and extravagant entertaining as unpatriotic and selfish. Columnist Mary Clemmer

Ames claimed that, while American women were making bandages for wounded soldiers, the president's wife spent her time traveling between Washington and New York, making extravagant purchases. Eleanor Donnelly published a poem, "The Lady-President's Ball," which told of a fictitious soldier dying in the street as a party raged in the White House. When Lincoln cancelled weekly band concerts, however, she was criticized again, placing her in a no-win situation. One of the most crushing rumors printed was that she abused her children. The stories that accused her of being a frivolous woman and a bad mother were just as critical of her performance of the first lady role as those that claimed she was a traitor and Southern sympathizer because some of her male relatives were fighting for the Confederacy.[49]

As the lineage of the first lady institution extended, journalists started to construct the collective memory of the institution through stories that focused on the history of the institution and the links between past and present. Reporters often compared Julia Tyler to Dolley Madison, in part because of her close relationship with the former first lady. Tyler herself sought to publicize the relationship, insisting to her press agent at one point, "Can't you get into the New York papers that Mrs. President Tyler is coming to town accompanied by Mrs. Ex-President Madison?" Tyler recognized that linking herself publicly with her popular predecessor could only boost her own popularity. Like Madison, Tyler continued to garner press coverage that tied her to the first lady institution until her death, and she often commented on her successors when interviewed. Sarah Polk remained popular with the press following her White House tenure. Reporters often visited her Tennessee home to seek her opinions on political matters and her successors. To this day journalists continue to refer to Mary Lincoln as an example of everything a first lady should not be. Such media coverage impacts the collective memory of the institution and influences future reporting on it. By contrasting "proper" and "improper" performances and by positioning certain first ladies as historical role models to be either emulated or rejected, journalists shape expectations of the first lady performance.[50]

The Civil War brought about great social change in the United States, particularly for women. Women expanded their social roles and challenged the boundaries of private and public spheres. Meanwhile, journalists would take an even more active role in defining the first lady institution within a context of contestation over women's roles in American culture.

True Womanhood, New Womanhood, and Social Reform, 1865–1900

Although the ideology of true womanhood dominated the pages of newspapers and the growing number of women's magazines at mid-century, American women's daily experiences were taking them increasingly out of their homes and into the public spaces. The Civil War "encouraged many women to give their first speech, organize their first club, or take their initial trip out of home territory."[51] Whether shopping at a department store, going to the theater, or working at a settlement house, women were becoming more visible in public life.

FROM TRUE WOMAN TO REFORMER

True womanhood continued to shape discussions of women's roles in the late nineteenth century, yet the true woman of the Gilded Age was very different from her antebellum sister, particularly as portrayed in the press.[52] True womanhood was championed by the mass market women's magazines and women's pages that proliferated following the Civil War, in part because the ideology promoted the rapidly expanding consumer culture. Women's domestic roles made them responsible for the household shopping, drawing them into the marketplace, part of the public sphere previously closed to white middle- and upper-class women. Women's publications, aimed primarily at white women, "promoted for women readers traditional 'women's values' and full participation in the consumer society. Contradictions naturally followed." For example, while advocating domesticity and women's place in the private sphere, women's magazines in the 1880s and 1890s simultaneously encouraged women's participation in the public sphere of commerce.[53] As true womanhood became tied to consumer culture, the boundaries of the domestic sphere became much more elastic. Such ideological repositioning allowed true womanhood to remain a viable ideology in the debate over women's roles.

The redefined true womanhood was still viewed as restrictive, however, by woman's rights leaders such as Anthony and Stanton working on behalf of suffrage and other women's issues. The energies of suffragists were focused on two fronts: lobbying for a constitutional amendment and stumping for state propositions granting women the vote. Egalitarianism, which promoted gender equality, continued to be the dominant ideology of the movement. Suffrage leaders routinely experienced discrimination and ridicule, especially when they spoke in public. Women's rhetorical action was still viewed as improper, a violation of the separate spheres: "When a woman spoke, she enacted her equality, that is, she herself was proof that she was as able as her male counterparts to function in the public sphere." Suffrage activity was still viewed as suspect by both men and women because it was such a far departure from true womanhood.[54]

Neither the ideology of true womanhood nor the woman's movement could fully account for the roles women found themselves playing in a rapidly changing society. Thus a new ideology was needed. Industrialization, urbanization, and immigration from 1865 through the turn of the century dramatically altered the social, cultural, and political landscape of the United States, and American women were greatly impacted by these developments. The "new woman" ideology that emerged during these years claimed the middle ground between true womanhood and suffrage. Combining true womanhood's moral authority and concern for family with the public activism of suffrage leaders, the new woman was interested in social reform and personal improvement. The new woman ethos was "concerned with substantive matters such as reform rather than empty party-giving. It meant having opinions and an identity of one's own." Women of the era were now allowed to be college educated, and many who had taken that path believed that the ideology of the new woman reflected their experiences.[55]

New womanhood was promoted by the growing number of women attracted to reform activities such as the temperance and settlement house movements. The Women's Christian Temperance Union (WCTU) under Frances Willard's leadership became the largest women's organization in the nation, lobbying for a broad welfare program. By appealing to women's moral authority and domestic concerns, the WCTU attracted women from various walks of life and convinced them to support various reform efforts, including suffrage.[56] In a similar way, the settlement house movement channeled women's domestic talents into social reform efforts. By the end of the century, progressive movements were drawing countless women into the public sphere. Meanwhile the growing number of women's clubs and literary societies (many of which were more politically active than their titles suggest) meant that, by the end of the century, an overwhelming majority of women from all walks of life were involved in women's club activities. This participation in women's clubs and reform movements was often justified as a logical extension of true womanhood's moral influence. In order to bridge the separate spheres, female reformers created a "public female sphere" in which they established their own networks, managed their own organizations, and commanded an actual physical space as well as a figurative spot in the male-dominated public sphere. This space, in the late nineteenth century, allowed women to reconcile conflicting gender prescriptions and be publicly active true women.[57]

TRANSITIONAL SPOUSES AND THE EVOLUTION OF THE FIRST LADY INSTITUTION

The first ladies of this period were a mix of true and new women. In general they were sociable, well educated, and intellectually gifted. Yet many scholars express disappointment with these women's performance of the first lady position, referring to the "unfulfilled possibilities" of this era and the "limited promise of the 'new woman.'" Although these first ladies were generally more active and influential than their immediate predecessors, they "fell short of their potential; they did not make lasting impressions on the first ladyship or on the status of women in U.S. society."[58]

News coverage of the first lady tells a different story, however. With the exception of Eliza Johnson (who proclaimed herself "an invalid"), the women of this era expanded the duties of the first lady, providing the foundation for the development of the modern institution. By the end of the nineteenth century, first ladies were more than just hostesses, help-mates, and volunteers; they were also White House managers and preser-vationists, campaigners, and social advocates. Meanwhile their roles as supportive wives and mothers were also garnering more attention. They routinely dealt directly with the press and appeared in public more often than their predecessors. The seven women who occupied the White House at the end of the nineteenth century—Eliza McCardle Johnson (1865–1869), Julia Dent Grant (1869–1877), Lucy Ware Webb Hayes (1877–1881), Lucretia Rudolph Garfield (1881), Frances Clara Folsom Cleveland (1886–1889, 1893–1897), Caroline Lavinia Scott Harrison (1889–1892), and Ida Saxton McKinley (1897–1901)—often found themselves at the center of the social debate over women's roles.

Each first lady of this era contributed to the increasing public visibility of the position, and each in a different way. Grant strongly believed that the first lady was a public position, and she took an active role in creating and promoting herself and the first lady institution. She was the first always to recognize reporters, and she issued the first press release. She attended several ceremonial functions, including the opening of the 1876 Philadelphia Exposition marking the U.S. centennial, because she recognized the publicity opportunities of such events.[59] Hayes traveled across the country with her husband, giving the thousands that turned out a chance to see the president's wife firsthand. For others Hayes's image was readily available in the press. She became "the most familiar woman's face in America. Advertisers used her picture, without her approval, to promote household products, and popular magazines carried photographs of her."[60] Hayes's popularity would be mirrored in the tenure of Cleveland, whose image was also appropriated to sell numerous products. Cleveland was frequently chased by photographers, who, like today's paparazzi, went to extreme lengths to capture a picture of the popular young first lady. She also issued a press release in response to reports saying she was an abused wife.[61] The volunteer activities of both Hayes and Cleveland received due press attention, which created the public expectation that the first lady should support a charitable cause. Garfield appeared frequently in public, often accompanying her husband on tours of government facilities, including a naval shipyard.[62]

First ladies also became more visible through participation in their husband's campaigns. Garfield was the first candidate's wife to appear on a campaign poster. McKinley was the first to have her image appear on campaign buttons; she was also the subject of the first campaign biography of a candidate's wife. Harrison and McKinley were active in their husbands' front porch campaigns, entertaining guests and posing for the media. Harrison, almost daily, reviewed campaign parades that featured marchers numbering upward of seventy-five thousand. Despite her poor health McKinley often "emerged from the house to pose for photographs with various delegations who came to pay their respects to her husband."[63] Stories about candidates' wives became common features of newspapers and magazines. These articles usually focused on their roles as wives, mothers, and homemakers, outlining their qualifications for the position of the first lady. Such stories would become staple campaign coverage in the twentieth century.

Ironically, the swelling publicity of the first lady institution was accompanied by an intensified focus on the first lady's domesticity and femininity. The press used gender ideologies to justify the first lady's public activities, and several first ladies of this era were constructed as personifications of a particular ideal of American womanhood. The language of true womanhood, the spirit of the new woman, the patriotism of the republican mother were all used to frame the public and private activities of first ladies at the end of the nineteenth century.

NEW JOURNALISM AND THE NEW WOMAN: FRAMING FIRST LADIES

The conflicting ideologies of womanhood shaped representations of women in the press during this era. Both true womanhood and the emerging new woman found a voice in newspapers and women's magazines. Coverage of the first lady institution intensified substantially during the era of new journalism, because of factors such as the expansion of women's pages, the proliferation of women's magazines, and the marketability of women's news, as well as the first lady's own heightened visibility.

The expansion of women's publications following the Civil War led to a rise in both the number of female journalists and the coverage of women. By the end of the nineteenth century, more women worked for the press than ever before. Indeed some of the most prominent journalists of this era were women. Several of the society reporters and female columnists who had made their start before the Civil War were now among the highest-paid journalists at their respective publications, and women journalists formed their own professional organizations.[64] By the 1890s women's magazines were proven commodities, already reaching millions of readers. The growing importance of women's consumerism led newspapers to focus more on their female readers, and to create evening and Sunday editions targeting women, to accommodate the large number of advertisements aimed at female consumers. These editions were mainly filled with advertisements for department stores hoping to attract women as customers. The newspapers also expanded the society and women's pages in order to carry more articles about fashion, beauty, and health, subjects all linked to advertising. These articles promoted domesticity and the true woman ideology in an effort to cultivate women as consumers.[65]

In stories about the first ladies, the press continued to use the frames that had been prevalent in earlier coverage. The focus on women as consumers encouraged stories about the first lady's appearance and fashion, sometimes using her to promote various products. The private lives of presidential couples were of growing interest to reporters, recalling in some cases the partisan era's focus on scandal. The first lady's political activities (such as volunteerism) also received more attention during this era, as journalists began making more connections between gender ideals and the public performance of the first lady position.

First ladies had long been viewed as style setters, and the more frequent use of illustrations and photographs in newspapers and magazines, coupled with advertisers' desires to promote women's consumerism, heightened the attention paid to first lady fashion and appearance. When Julia Grant issued the first press release, she declared she was not interested in being a "fashion dictator," but this did not keep her fashions from being discussed in the press.[66] Lucy Hayes also did not wish to be a trendsetter, yet her prim and proper style was the focus of much of the early media coverage of her. The *New York Herald* described Hayes as "singularly youthful" and a "most attractive and lovable woman."[67] Mary Clemmer Ames covered the Hayes inauguration in her column, praising the first lady's prim appearance. Ames compared her eyes to those of "the Madonna" and wondered how fashion magazines such as *Vanity Fair* would represent the new first lady, asking would they "friz that hair? powder that face? . . . bare those shoulders? shorten those sleeves? hide John Wesley's discipline out of sight, as it poses and minces before the 'first lady of the land?'"[68] Ames's description positioned Hayes as a model of true womanhood, simultaneously constructing her as a public figure. Popular magazines frequently featured photographs of Hayes, often posing with her children; advertisers also used her image without her permission to promote their products. Frances Cleveland faced a similar problem. Weeklies such as *Leslie's Illustrated* and *Harper's* could not get enough of the young first lady; advertisers unscrupulously reproduced her likeness to sell just about every product imaginable, including soaps, perfumes, liver pills, ashtrays, even women's underwear. Women imitated her hairstyle and her fashions. People lined up by the thousands at White

House receptions and public appearances just to catch a glimpse of her. Both Hayes and Cleveland were treated by the press as models of consumption, foreshadowing the celebrity coverage that would emerge during the mid-twentieth century.[69]

Several first ladies were held up as models of true womanhood in articles praising their piety and purity. The *Philadelphia Times* lauded Hayes as a "true woman" for her pious dress and the lack of pretension at her White House events. Ames considered her a model of true womanhood in her columns, noting her religious devotion. Ida McKinley was also positioned by the press as a true woman. Following her husband's election, popular magazines published numerous posed photographs of the new first lady and articles praising her womanliness and virtue.[70] An article in *Harper's Bazaar* noted, "Mrs. McKinley's faithful presence beside her husband at state functions, her frail form clad in the rich, ceremonious dress proper to the occasion, describes a gentle martyrdom, the indescribable pathos of which is written in the expression of her sweet pale face." The article further described McKinley as "a revelation of the glory of the woman at home" and a "First Lady who exalts mere womanliness."[71] McKinley's press construction reflected the true woman ideal at the end of the nineteenth century. The publicity given to these "true women"— so perceived by the press—helped carve a space for women in the public sphere that would be explored further by the first ladies of the early twentieth century.

Domesticity, another key theme of true womanhood, also framed the coverage of first ladies. In the campaign of 1880, newspapers promoted the Garfields as the ideal nineteenth-century couple. Republican party literature bragged that Lucretia Garfield had "the domestic tastes and talents which fitted her equally to preside over the home of a poor college president and that of a famous statesman." When Garfield decided to redecorate the White House to reflect the history of the mansion, she promoted her plans in the press. Similarly, Caroline Harrison was referred to by her contemporaries as the "best housekeeper the White House has ever known." The press touted her domesticity, which included her plans for a major White House renovation. When Harrison decided to renovate the White House, she, like Garfield a decade before her, used the press to lobby congressional support for the renovation. Such stories presenting first ladies as White House homemaker would start a trend stretching well into the twentieth century.[72]

True womanhood's emphasis on domesticity and the private sphere, coupled with the fact that the White House serves as both a private residence and a public place, in some ways legitimated public stories about the private lives of presidents and their families. Coverage of life inside the White House intensified the spotlight on both presidents and their wives. Articles about the Clevelands were representative of this type of news framing. When bachelor president Grover married twenty-two-year-old Frances in June 1886, the newspapers followed the couple's every move. The press was barred from the White House wedding, but the story made the front page around the nation. Eager reporters followed the couple on their honeymoon, hiding in trees in order to get pictures of the newlyweds. A few years later Cleveland staunchly defended her husband during a campaign scandal. In 1888 rumor spread that Grover beat his young wife. In response, Watson reports, Cleveland issued the second press release in first lady history, calling the reports "wicked and heartless lies" and said she wished women "no greater blessing than their homes and lives be as happy and their husbands may be as kind, attentive, considerate, and affectionate as mine." By highlighting the relationships of presidential couples, newspapers promoted first ladies as traditional wives while simultaneously recognizing them as public figures in their own right.[73]

Despite the dominance of the true woman ideal, the involvement of many middle-class women in social movements heightened journalists' interest in the private and public activities of first ladies. The image-making activities of the women of this era also prompted the press to pay more attention to the first lady's roles as advisor and presidential surrogate. Hayes, the first college graduate to become first lady, was recognized for her political intelligence. She was reported to be one of her husband's respected advisors. According to an article in the *National Union*, "Mrs. Hayes is said to be a student of politics and to talk intelligently upon their [*sic*] changing phases."[74] Hayes was one of the earliest first ladies to travel regularly, sometimes serving as a surrogate for her husband, and expanding the press coverage of the position. When the Hayeses traveled through the South in an effort to reunify the country, the *Richmond Dispatch* reported, "Mrs. Hayes has won the admiration of people wherever she has been in the recent tours of the President." Garfield was also her husband's trusted advisor. One journalist noted Garfield was "in all senses the 'helpmeet' of her husband, his companion in all sorts of studies and reading, his confidante and advisor in all things." Ames, in her column, observed that Garfield had "a strength of unswerving absolute rectitude her husband has not and never will have."[75]

The frame of the new woman was most often employed to describe the volunteerism of first ladies during this era. Hayes was linked to the temperance movement. Although she refused to publicly support the WCTU, the organization used Hayes's likeness to promote their cause by commissioning a portrait of the first lady with a symbol of the temperance movement in the background. Ames averted criticism of the portrait by arguing in her column that the portrait be considered "a tribute to Mrs. Hayes—to the grace and graciousness of her womanhood."[76] Cleveland represented the new woman ideal. A Wells College graduate, she balanced her home life with a concern for social reform efforts. The press of the era noted that, rather than championing a specific cause, Cleveland supported several, including the WCTU's "Hope and Help" campaign, the Washington Home for Friendless Colored Girls, the Colored Christmas Club, and the Cincinnati Orchestra Association. Despite her domestic public persona, Caroline Harrison was deeply interested in politics and was an ardent advocate of many women's issues. She was the first president's wife to associate herself publicly with struggling women's organizations such as the Daughters of the American Revolution, and her support garnered needed publicity for such groups.[77]

As the lineage of the first lady institution extended, journalists had more history to draw from when constructing narratives about the position. Simultaneously the image-making activities of some first ladies encouraged coverage that highlighted the history of the institution. Grant often avoided journalists' criticism by orchestrating press events that ensured a positive portrayal of the first lady. For example, when the former first lady Julia Tyler visited the White House in 1871, reporters were present as she gave a portrait of herself to Grant to be hung in the White House to mark the start of the first ladies portrait collection. A reception was later held in Tyler's honor, and reporters remarked on the two Julias standing side by side in the receiving line. Events such as this encouraged the press to construct the institutional memory of the first lady position. The number of articles comparing candidates' wives during campaigns also increased in this era. In the campaign of 1876, for example, the serious Hayes was contrasted with the fun-loving Grant; reporters speculated on how the difference in their personalities would impact the role of the first lady.[78]

By 1900 journalists had a century of experience in covering the first lady institution, and many of the trends of previous years coalesced by the end of the century. While several themes carried over from earlier eras, new journalism heightened the publicity surrounding the position, accentuating the various roles played by first ladies. The popularity of women's pages and magazines created a market for women's news, and first ladies helped fill these pages. At the same time the competing ideals of the true woman and the new woman were used by journalists to frame—and scrutinize—the private and public activities of first ladies. To an even greater extent than in previous years, journalists positioned first ladies as representatives of various interpretations of the ideals of American womanhood.

Conclusion

Since the birth of this nation, the notion of separate public and private spheres has dominated discussions of gender roles in the United States. American women have subsequently adopted, promoted, questioned, and rejected the gender ideologies seeking to define their lives. Yet the notion of an ideal American woman persists, thanks in part to women's publications that use this ideal, no matter how unrealistic, to frame their articles about women. First ladies, in particular, are subject to this framing because of their visibility and the gendered aspects of their position. This discussion of competing gender ideologies, the development of the first lady position, and press framing of the institution lays the groundwork for the following analysis of the press images of first ladies in the twentieth century. There are four key points that inform the following analysis.

First, the metaphor of separate spheres plays a significant role in shaping gender roles. The one element common to all the gender ideologies reviewed above is the reference to separate public and private spheres, defined by gender, race, class, and physical location. Republican motherhood and true womanhood used the separation of spheres to distinguish between the respective duties of women and men and to highlight women's realm of influence. These ideologies both empowered and inhibited women, by allocating them power but dictating that they wield this power only within the confines of the home or of philanthropic extensions of the domestic sphere. The natural rights philosophy promoted by early woman's rights leaders did not reject outright the notion of separate spheres but, instead, demanded women's access to the public sphere. These women knew firsthand the limitations on women's public activity because they were themselves constrained by social norms and laws aimed at keeping women out of the public sphere. The new woman and the revised true woman of the late nineteenth century sought a more indirect route into the public sphere by stretching the boundaries of the private sphere into public spaces and creating a "female public sphere." The concept of separate spheres continues to influence gender ideology and American life: "For all our vaunted modernity, for all that men's 'spheres' and women's 'spheres' now overlap, vast areas of our experience and consciousness do not overlap. The boundaries may be fuzzier, but our private spaces and our public spaces are still in many important senses gendered."[79]

Second, gender ideologies are not static, and they are not absolute. Ideology "is dynamic and a *force,* always resilient, always keeping itself in some consonance and unity, but not always the *same* consonance and unity." Gender ideologies such as that of true womanhood have adjusted to social and cultural changes in order to remain viable, and they continue to alter in order to accommodate the cultural shifts of the twentieth century. Women's lived experiences and the ideals of American womanhood were often at odds. If gender ideologies are placed on a continuum, most women would fall somewhere in between "feminist" and "traditional" values, "often holding some part of each set of values simultaneously." This was often true of most first ladies.[80]

Third, by the end of the nineteenth century, the foundation for the first lady institution had been established, which shaped both the collective memory of the first lady position and future expectations of presidents' wives. First ladies were expected to perform a variety of duties, many of which straddled the private and public spheres. The media memory of their performance defined both proper and improper performances of the first lady position. Meanwhile, first ladies were required to perform their duties in the public spotlight amid much public and press scrutiny, and no first lady has ever received unanimous acclaim for her performance.[81] News articles support this statement. As the public visibility of first ladies expanded, so did the press coverage of the institution. Meanwhile, the publicity of the position via the press heightened the visibility of the institution.

Fourth, and finally, press framing of the first lady conflates the performance of the first lady's duties with performances of gender. While the royalty frames of the early republic gave way to descriptions of ladylike true women, press frames have always included a gendered element. These frames have reflected social, political, and historical conditions while reifying the prominent gender ideologies of the various eras. This trend intensified at the end of the nineteenth century as the publicity surrounding first ladies grew and continued to do so throughout the next century.

CHAPTER TWO

The First Lady as Public Woman,
1900–1929

"Who will be the First Lady of the Land the next four years?" According to a *Harper's Bazaar* article of August 1900, this was "the paramount woman question of the pending Presidential campaign." The story, comparing the candidates' wives, stated, "The election of Mrs. McKinley or Mrs. Bryan means elevating to a place of eminent dignity and importance a typical American woman, of contrasting schools of culture."[1] These contrasts were evidenced for the press in each woman's performance of gender.

The *Harper's Bazaar* story positioned each woman as a personification of a gender ideology; Ida McKinley exemplified the true woman ideal, and Mary Bryan personified the new woman of the era. The reelection of McKinley, the author believed, "would provide the American people a First Lady who exalts mere womanliness above anything that women dare to do." The writer praised her performance of the first lady role, claiming "she has done her utmost" despite being an "invalid for many years past," and concluded that McKinley was "an inspiration to all women who for one reason or another are hindered from playing a brilliant individual role in life." Bryan, in contrast, was introduced as "a woman of action—a successful woman" who "has been admitted to the bar—a full-fledged lawyer." The story noted she was a club woman interested in social reform. However, Bryan's individual accomplishments never outranked her roles as wife and mother. Bryan's "mind is a storehouse of information on all subjects that pertain to her husband's duties and ambitions." It was a "well-known fact that she does assist her husband in his work," even writing some of his famous speeches. "Yet," the author continued, "with all the rest, Mrs. Bryan is versed in the domestic arts and sciences—a good housekeeper and a good mother." She was praised as "the rare instance of the logically impossible woman who accomplishes a man's success at no expense of her own." She was the epitome of the new woman. The article concluded that, despite their differences, each woman personified a type of American womanhood that should be emulated: "Mrs. Bryan's influence as wife of the President of the United States would compel women to know and to think about the questions of the day. She would be a needed stimulant to the woman who aims at nothing at all. Mrs. McKinley—a vivid antithesis—is always a needed gentle sedative to the typical woman of today who aims to do too much."[2]

The McKinley-Bryan dichotomy is an excellent example of the gendered journalistic framing of the first lady institution. It illustrates how these women personified for the press the gender ideologies competing to define womanhood at the turn of the century. This magazine story points to the various roles first ladies were expected to play and evaluates each woman's ability to do so. Finally, it also evidences the growing publicity surrounding the first lady position, especially during campaigns.

Press coverage of first ladies established these women as highly visible public figures and role models for American women by circulating their images and stories about their activities and interests in the public sphere. In turn the first ladies of the modern era were performing more duties that garnered press attention and thus contributed to the rise in press coverage. This group of women forged new roles for the first lady institution, laying the foundation for the notion of the modern first lady as an active presidential partner.[3] Eight women served as first lady between 1900 and 1929. Two of them, Ida Saxton McKinley (1897–1901) and Florence Kling Harding (1921–1923), had their time in the White House cut short by the deaths of their husbands. Their successors, Edith Kermit Carow Roosevelt (1901–1909) and Grace Goodhue Coolidge (1923–1929), went on to occupy the position longer than the other first ladies of this era. Ellen Axson Wilson (1913–1914) died just seventeen months into her tenure, leaving the White House without a first lady until her widower, Woodrow, married Edith Bolling Galt (1915–1921). The remaining first ladies of the modern era, Helen Herron Taft (1909–1913) and Lou Henry Hoover (1929–1933), held the position for only one term. The personalities of the women holding the position, the many duties of the modern first lady, and the public expectations regarding the performance of those roles were all reflected in the journalistic framing of the first lady institution.

During the modern era, press framing reflected the changing status of women in American society. While turn-of-the-century first ladies such as McKinley and Roosevelt embodied true womanhood, their successors personified both true womanhood and the new woman, despite the conflict in gender prescriptions. Such framing empowered women by recognizing the multiplicity of private and public roles they play and by considering their activities as newsworthy.

Journalists also used gender framing to judge how these women performed the first lady duties at this time. Stories focused on the first lady's various roles as helpmate, hostess, campaigner, and volunteer. At first true womanhood dominated discussions of role performance, but as the era progressed the new woman ideal became more common in media articles. In 1901 Edith Roosevelt avoided campaigning and chose not to involve herself in volunteer work, and the ideology of true womanhood explained her limited performance of her position. But as early as 1908, wives were taking a more active and more public role in their husbands' campaigns, and every first lady of this era except Roosevelt and McKinley worked publicly on behalf of a social cause, mirroring the new woman ideology. By the end of the modern era, press coverage indicated that first ladies were expected to perform various private- and public-sphere roles in ways that reflected both traditional and newer gender ideologies, despite the inherent conflicts.

The expanded publicity surrounding the first lady, coupled with journalists' framing of her as the personification of American womanhood, fashioned her as an important public woman. Editors needed stories to fill the women's pages and magazines, and because of the visibility and various duties associated with her position, the first lady made good copy. During the modern era, journalists routinely began to treat the first lady as a newsworthy public figure, regardless of the individual disposition of the woman who held the position. Unlike their nineteenth-century counterparts, first ladies could no longer avoid the spotlight or their institutional duties, which subsequently challenged traditional notions regarding women's avoidance of publicity. Journalists often managed this contradiction by continuing to frame first ladies as true women or republican mothers, characterizing their increasing political activity as extensions of their wifely role or domestic concerns. Just as expediency arguments garnered support for woman's suffrage, reporters' reliance on traditional gender ideologies as framing devices helped first ladies become public women with less controversy surrounding their publicity. Thus, the gendered framing of modern era first ladies resulted in the emergence of the first lady as a public woman—recognized by the press as a positive role model for American women.

Competing Gender Ideologies—The "New" Modern Woman

The modern era was a period of great social change, and particularly for American women. During this time more women were actively participating in public-sphere activities. The Nineteenth Amendment granted women the vote in 1920, which boosted women's formal political participation in governance. Meanwhile the progressive and women's club movements reached their zenith during the early years of the twentieth century, providing a politically charged space for middle-class women. Growing numbers of women entered colleges and the workplace, and they joined organizations that reflected their educational and occupational interests. All of this activity was reported in women's magazines and in the women's pages of major newspapers, which boasted millions of female readers. Despite this budding acceptability of public activity, there remained a lack of consensus regarding the ideals of American womanhood. In fact, this rise in women's political participation stimulated public debate over the conflicting gender ideologies of true womanhood, the new woman, feminism, and republican motherhood.[4]

The nineteenth-century notion of true womanhood—valuing piety, purity, submissiveness, and domesticity—dominated the political and popular culture discourse surrounding women's behavior well into the twentieth century. "Social-structural changes further heightened the ironic tensions that developed between the dictates of the Cult of True Womanhood and the realities of the bourgeois matron's life," however. Such changes prompted women to seek ways to justify "new roles for women outside the family."[5] One way to do this was to use the language of true womanhood to defend women's expanding roles. Many female reformers were quick to claim that their outside interests were actually an extension of their domestic duties. Such "municipal housekeeping" and "domestic reform" was a hallmark of both progressivism and social feminism. The use of domestic metaphors and maternal rhetoric appealed to journalists, who continued to promote true womanhood, particularly in publications aimed at women. Both women's magazines and the women's pages in newspapers used the frame of true womanhood to justify women's public activities, even long after they had acknowledged the growing phenomenon of the new woman.[6]

The new woman represented new social, political, and economic opportunities for women. The image of the new woman varied greatly between 1900 and 1929, however. She started out as a serious-minded college or working woman interested in social reform and devolved into the flirty flapper, whose only interest was in having fun. In the early twentieth century the "new woman" stood for self-development, as contrasted to subservience to the family. One avenue of self-development was a college education; by 1920 women made up nearly half of the expanding college population. Many of these college-educated women became involved in reform efforts such as the settlement house movement, turning social work into a profession.[7]

But most middle-class women continued to enter the public sphere through participation in women's clubs and voluntary associations. Roughly one million women were affiliated with women's clubs in 1914. The reform spirit of progressivism prompted such groups to take a more overtly political stance, although most continued to cloak their new woman practices in the rhetoric of true womanhood. These female reformers specialized in lobbying and pressure-group politics and were highly successful in gaining support for reform legislation throughout this era. However, by the end of the 1920s, most reform-minded women would not have considered themselves new women, primarily because "the flapper was the dominant image of the new woman," and especially in the media.[8] The changes in new woman ideology were reflected in journalists' use of the new woman as a framing device. As the new woman evolved from serious reformer to sexualized flapper, journalists routinely returned to promoting the frame of true womanhood. Reporters often pointed to the "new" new woman as proof that the values of the true woman should continue to define American womanhood, creating a backlash not unlike the one Susan Faludi argues occurred in the 1980s against second-wave feminism.[9]

The term "feminism" also came into common usage during the modern era as a way to characterize the expanding political activities of American women. Carrie Chapman Catt, president of the National American Woman Suffrage Association, defined feminism in 1915 as "world-wide revolt against all the artificial barriers which laws and customs interpose between women and human freedom."[10] Feminism often was associated with suffrage, but the term was also used by women involved in the temperance, labor reform, and the settlement house movements. Meanwhile, by the 1910s, the suffrage movement was garnering nationwide support, in part because some of its leaders rejected the natural rights argument supported by early suffrage leaders in favor of an expediency argument. This approach "claimed the vote for women not as an end in itself but as a means to rid the society of vice and corruption and to make it a good place for families, women, and children."[11] Feminism and suffrage, like the new woman ideology, started to reflect the rhetoric of true womanhood. By 1929, according to a magazine article by journalist and suffragist Ida Clyde Clarke, the "modern feminist" combined the best elements of true womanhood, the new woman, and the suffragist, resulting in a "well rounded, perfectly balanced, thoroughly informed and highly intelligent person . . . who manages her home, holds her job, and so on, in the normal way."[12] The feminist frame, in just a few short years, had evolved from a way to describe women's collective political activities to a more individualistic frame that conflated feminism with other existing gender ideologies such as that of the new woman.

The persistence of maternal rhetoric explains why even an eighteenth-century ideology such as republican motherhood continued its currency as a news-framing device in the modern era. Republican motherhood allowed the American woman to claim a significant political role, even though it was often tied to her domestic role. As "citizen-mothers," modern era women felt empowered to care for those in need just as they would care for their own husbands and children. First ladies often extended the ideology of republican motherhood beyond the home by characterizing social politicking and volunteerism also as women's duties as citizens.[13] Presidents Wilson, Harding, and Coolidge reflected the values of republican motherhood in their public statements regarding suffrage. In Wilson's statement urging Congress to support suffrage, for example, he offered "good reasons why women could be viewed as good citizens while working both inside and outside of their homes during the war." Harding's inaugural address envisioned republican mothers rocking the "cradle of American childhood" and providing the "education so essential to best citizenship," while Coolidge praised women for "encouraging education" and "supporting the cause of justice and honor among the nations."[14] Republican motherhood was similarly used, albeit limitedly, by modern era journalists to frame the volunteer and political activities of first ladies. Like the presidents, journalists invoked republican motherhood in their discussions of women's patriotism and wartime contributions and their newfound status as citizens in the years immediately following suffrage.

Despite their mounting public presence, most women continued to avoid publicity of their reform activities. With the exception of the leaders of various women's movements, who gave voice to their causes, the majority of women continued to work "behind the scenes" within a distinctly female though also public sphere. While women benefited from the experience of controlling their own organizations, they were not truly integrated into the male political sphere. Thus, their political influence often was indirect. Female reformers were very successful at lobbying on the individual level, for example, but rarely enjoyed (or sought) direct access to legislative bodies. Instead, male lawmakers spoke for them within the official political sphere.[15] Avoiding publicity, especially public speech, allowed politically active women to present themselves as true women, who justified their actions as extensions of their domestic roles. In doing so, however, they diminished their political agency and often surrendered their voices to the men, including journalists, who would speak on their behalf, as fathers and husbands had been doing for years.

The ideological shifts in the definitions of the modern American woman can be traced by looking at the ways journalists (many of whom were women) employed these overlapping gender ideologies and dealt with the paradoxes of public womanhood throughout this period. Because of the gendered nature of the first lady position, its expanding duties, and increased publicity, coverage of the institution became a place where journalists could report on these changing gender ideals and offer their own definitions of the ideal American woman, which allowed for the performance of the first lady as public woman.

Framing the First Lady in the Modern Era

Gendered framing devices employed by journalists shape their narratives about the first lady institution. By conflating performances of the first lady position with gender performance, journalists further feminize an already gendered institution. The journalists' framing can result in constraints on the performance of the position when they hold first ladies to institutional as well as gender ideals. First ladies not only have to measure up to historical standards set by their predecessors, but they must conform to social expectations regarding the performance of gender as well. Such framing also recognizes the complexities of the first lady position and gender performance. Traditional ideologies such as true womanhood often are employed to justify the expansion of women's interests to the public sphere. By considering the private and public activities of first ladies as newsworthy, journalists give voice to women's experiences. Such publicity normalizes women's place both in the press and in the public sphere. Coverage of the first lady institution then acts as a site of contestation over the private, public, and political roles of American women. The following examples illustrate the various ways gender framing shaped stories about the first lady institution in the modern era.

FROM TRUE WOMAN TO NEW WOMAN – PERSONIFICATION FRAMING IN THE MODERN ERA

The press, the public, and scholars have long considered the first lady a symbol of American womanhood. The *Washington Post* argued in 1928 that the first lady position was "the highest dignity which can come to an American woman," and a *New York Times* article the following year stated, "Just as every American boy may hope to become President, so every American girl may hope to become a President's wife." According to a *New York Times* article in 1904, "The President's wife, the first lady of the land, is always an object of paramount importance, not only to the women of the country, but to the men as well."[16] When framed as a model of American womanhood, any individual first lady stands in for a particular gender ideology, and her performance of gender is upheld by the press as an example for American women to follow. This form of personification framing is commonly used in profiles of candidates' wives as a way to gauge their qualifications for and potential performance of the first lady position.

As the true woman ideology dominated the nineteenth century, it is not surprising that Edith Roosevelt, true to her Victorian upbringing, personified true womanhood for the press. One of the hallmarks of true womanhood was an avoidance of publicity. The same *New York Times* article of 1904, comparing Roosevelt to the wife of her husband's opponent Alton B. Parker, described both as model true women who remained within the boundaries of the domestic sphere, uncomfortable with any attempt to lure them into the public sphere. Roosevelt was praised for avoiding the "fierce limelight of publicity." The article claimed that she "always shrunk from being conspicuous in any way, and in fact would prefer to live the quietest and most domestic of lives." Mrs. Parker (whose first name does not even appear) was described as a subservient woman who avoided "any publicity, and whose life is so bound up in her husband's and in her own household that the affairs of the outside world . . . affect her not at all." These comments about how the women avoided publicity further anchored them in the private sphere, the proper place of the true woman, and also represented the characteristics of piety and purity.[17]

Both women were described as domestic, a prominent characteristic of true womanhood. Roosevelt, in particular, served as a model of domesticity for the press primarily because both she and her husband embraced the true woman ideology. According to the same *New York Times* profile, "Whichever way the election goes, however, the women of America will have a good representative in the wife of the head of the nation. Homemakers in the best sense of the word are Mrs. Roosevelt and Mrs. Parker," remarks that further position both women as role models by claiming "their success in the lines in which they have undertaken were something worth copying in these days when so much is said about the frivolity of women, their carelessness to their duties, and their lack of interest in anything serious."[18] This comment mirrored the views of Roosevelt's husband, who decried the attention paid to leisure pursuits and women's subsequent avoidance of motherhood (evidenced in the declining birth rates at the turn of the century).[19] In his famous speech "The Strenuous Life," Roosevelt stated, "when women fear motherhood, they tremble on the brink of doom; and it is well they should vanish from the earth, where they are fit subjects for the scorn of all men and women who are themselves strong and brave and high-minded." For Roosevelt, the ideal American woman was "the housewife, the helpmeet of the homemaker, the wise and fearless mother of many healthy children."[20] By constructing the candidates' wives as personifications of domesticity, the *New York Times* writer not only praised the women but also offered a critique of any woman who did not subscribe to domestic commitments.

Several first ladies of this era found themselves at the center of the debate over changing gender roles. During this period true womanhood was being challenged by the ideologies of the new woman and feminism. One way the press reconciled these competing ideologies was by emphasizing their more traditional aspects while still lauding the individual accomplishments of these women. A *Good Housekeeping* article from March 1913 discussed how Woodrow Wilson's first wife, new first lady Ellen Wilson, balanced her work and her home life. The article opened with a discussion of Wilson's career as an artist, noting that her paintings "have been shown this winter in art exhibits in New York, Chicago, Indianapolis, and Philadelphia." The author, Mabel Porter Daggett, tempered her discussion of Wilson's artistic pursuits, however, by focusing on Wilson's skills as a homemaker and concluded, "Woodrow Wilson's wife has a talent for painting. She has a genius for home-making." By framing Wilson as both a working artist (performing a public-sphere activity) and a homemaker (a private-sphere role), Daggett positioned Wilson as the embodiment of both the career-minded new woman and the domestic true woman.[21]

Similarly, Lou Hoover embodied the qualities of both the new and the true woman, according to the headline of the 1928 *Washington Post* article cited earlier: "Mrs. Hoover Seen as Cosmopolitan, Social Worker, Devoted Mother and Real Companion to Husband." This article concluded that "Mrs. Hoover will go to the White House with the ideal equipment of a point of view of the woman of the world, trained in official entertaining, combined with a healthy, sane grasp of world needs and things which are not strictly social and withal the dreams of the idealist and the social service worker." In a *New York Times Magazine* profile, Hoover was praised for her performance of roles associated with both the true and the new woman: "She is not only a homemaker of the first rank and a sympathetic and understanding friend of children, but also a scientist, a linguist, an amateur architect, an accomplished sportswoman, and an able organizer."[22] Hoover represented the growing number of college-educated women who balanced a number of roles that once were considered diametrically opposed. By using Hoover and Wilson to personify this blend of true and new womanhood, journalists were able to negotiate the complexities of gender performance while offering a preview of the women's tenures as first lady. Such framing allowed journalists to position these women as both modern (the new woman) and traditional (the true woman); it also reinforced an expectation that these women somehow had to do it all.

In the press, first ladies Edith Wilson and Florence Harding each personified republican motherhood, although in different ways. While Wilson confined her actions to the private sphere, Harding's activity took her into the public sphere. During times of war, the ideal of republican motherhood (reconciling politics and domesticity) was often used to justify women's political participation. Such was the case with Edith Wilson, Wilson's second wife, during World War I. The *Ladies' Home Journal* of July 1918 asked, "What Is Mrs. Wilson Doing?" in relation to the war effort. The article claimed that the women of the Wilson White House were deeply committed to the war effort: "Nor are these women at work in the war because they are members of the immediate family of the President, but because they are, like all other women of America, deeply patriotic." Furthermore, the writer stated, "So loyal are the present residents of the White House to the traditions of American home life, so far removed are they from all that is out of harmony with democratic simplicity, that their work in the war is almost unknown to Washington itself." The story detailed the various support efforts in which the women were engaged (such as knitting warm clothing for the soldiers) and praised the fact that there was no "blowing of newspaper trumpets" in relation to their work. The article concluded that the work of Mrs. Wilson "is a testimony not only of her own patriotic self-sacrifice, but of the spirit of American womanhood in this crisis of our nation's history."[23] These words echo the ideals of republican motherhood, which posit that women's domestic skills can have political worth; these same sentiments appeared in President Wilson's appeal in 1918 that women should be granted suffrage as a reward for their wartime service.[24] According to the *Ladies' Home Journal* article, Wilson claimed a significant political role, though she played it in the home. For the press, she came to embody feminine heroism.[25]

In contrast, Harding personified the ways in which republican motherhood extended into the public sphere. For journalists, Harding embodied her husband's vision of women's political participation. In his inaugural speech, within a discussion of economic conditions, President Harding stated, "We want an America of homes, illuminated with hope and happiness, where mothers, freed from the long hours of toil beyond their own doors, may preside as befits the hearthstone of American citizenship."[26] Harding actively participated in women's organizations, often writing letters of support to be read at their meetings when she could not attend in person, and recognized that such acts would receive press coverage. Yet her conception of political participation, like her husband's, encouraged women to extend their roles as homemakers and mothers to the public sphere. An example is offered in a *New York Times* story about the Southern Tariff Convention of Women. Harding's letter is quoted as saying, "Full citizenship with all its responsibilities has come to American women. It represents their opportunity to serve their homes and their country if they wisely exercise it." Harding argued that the tariff issue was "of the utmost interest to women, for they are the makers of household budgets, the managers of homes[,] . . . and on them falls large responsibility for those measures of thrift, economy, and careful expenditure which greatly concern the welfare of our country's and the world's affairs." While Harding's comments embodied the patriotism of republican motherhood, they also echoed the progressive and social feminism concept of "municipal housekeeping," which struck a middle ground between the activism of the new woman and the domesticity of true womanhood. By allowing her voice to circulate in the public sphere, reaching both the female audience addressed in her letter and the promiscuous audience of newspaper readers, Harding also contributed to the growing acceptance of the public woman.[27]

In all of the articles mentioned, these women personified gender ideologies, reflecting the shifting definitions of American womanhood in the modern era. Roosevelt embodied true womanhood to the same extent that Hoover was represented as possessing all of the qualities of the new woman. Yet Hoover also was framed as a true woman, simultaneously representing tradition and change in women's roles. In Harding's case, coverage captured a particular historical moment when woman's suffrage and subsequent political participation was widely celebrated and embraced. Harding also embodied republican motherhood, implying that women's new civic roles were simply an extension of their domestic duties. In wartime Edith Wilson, as a good republican mother, personified how women's domestic skills could be used for patriotic ends. For the most part, journalists emphasized what were viewed as the more traditional roles of women, namely those of wife, mother, and hostess, despite giving more attention to women's expanding roles. The new woman may have been praised for her individual accomplishments (such as Ellen Wilson's artistic endeavors), but these accomplishments paled in comparison to her homemaking skills or devotion to her spouse. Reporters were able to satisfy the expectations of people who wanted first ladies to be equally traditional and modern by having these women personify both traditional true women and the more modern publicly active new women.

By the end of the modern era, first ladies were expected to balance the domesticity of true womanhood and the republican mother with the social activism of the new woman and the political visibility of feminists, despite the contradictions inherent in these different ideologies. Yet even when these women embodied the more traditional gender ideologies, press coverage ensured that their performance of gender roles took place on a very public stage. This helped position even the most private first ladies as public women.

FROM HOSTESS TO ADVOCATE: FRAMING THE PERFORMANCE OF THE FIRST LADY POSITION

Journalists' use of gender ideologies as framing devices impacted the ways in which the duties of the first lady position were covered. The articles from the modern era show a shift toward a more public woman in the framing of the first lady institution. Such framing mirrored the changes in women's roles and the expansion of the first lady's duties.

At the turn of the century, the frame of wife and mother had dominated first lady coverage. Most of the stories about Edith Roosevelt revolved around her family. When they first occupied the White House, there were six Roosevelt children, ranging in age from three to seventeen. A profile of "Mrs. Roosevelt and Her Children" in the August 1902 *Ladies' Home Journal* praised Roosevelt's devotion to her family, noting that despite the demands of the first lady position she "finds time still for the companionship with husband and children, which is, after all, the chief end of her life." The article writer, Jacob A. Riis, proclaimed that Roosevelt's ideas "on home-making and child-training, which, if sometimes called old-fashioned, one may be permitted fervently to hope, for the sake of our country, will never quite go out of fashion." Despite acknowledging the public duties of first ladies, stories about Roosevelt located her primarily in the private sphere, the place where true women exerted moral influence and found happiness in being good wives, mothers, and homemakers. Roosevelt's influence on her family was noted in a *New York Times* story from the 1904 campaign, which framed her as a supportive spouse in the true woman tradition: "She found time amid the guidance and care of her little children and the directing of her household to always be with her husband when he needed her, to listen to his plans and again and again to aid him by her quiet counsel and good common sense." According to these reporters the ideals of true womanhood clearly influenced Roosevelt's performance of the first lady position. However, it is interesting to note that, even though stories lauded Roosevelt as a model wife and mother, the fact that her ideas were called "old-fashioned" in a 1902 article shows that social views on women's roles were already in flux.[28]

Presidential wives in the modern era were framed by the press more frequently as partners who played important roles in their husbands' private and political lives. The partner frame drew on the concept of a "companionate marriage" promoted by social scientists, social workers, and journalists as the "new marital ideal." Several first ladies were commended for the companionship they shared with their husbands. According to the *Ladies' Home Journal*, the Roosevelts would spend their evenings discussing "the high ideals they hold in common—in essentials always agreed, however they may differ, on points of less concern. For hers is no passive reflection of his robust intellect. She thinks as he acts, for herself, with full freedom and calm judgment—in this, as in all else, the helpmeet he needs."[29] The Coolidges and Tafts were described in a similar manner. The *Ladies' Home Journal* said of Grace and Calvin Coolidge, "Quite obviously both of these busy people manage to keep up a lot of interests and habits in common . . . now and again some phrase or a short conversation proves what a pleasant comradeship exists between the strong, still man and his animated, graceful wife." The *New York Times* claimed that Taft actively worked to keep abreast of her husband's interests: "To any subject in which Mr. Taft is interested or of which he is making a study she also gives her attention. . . . It has intensified the sense of comradeship existing between them."[30] Edith Wilson was credited by the press with helping her husband shoulder the burdens of World War I. According to the *Ladies' Home Journal*, "One can hardly speak of, much less attempt to measure, the results of her constant, never-failing companionship and sympathy." The Hardings' partnership combined their private and political lives. The *New York Times* claimed, "The two Hardings have blended their qualities and personalities perfectly through long experience in working together. Theirs has been a partnership of their work. . . . Together, they entered politics, Mrs. Harding in the background, devoted, confident, and forward looking, while her husband furnished the generous, amiable qualities that made him popular."[31] By positioning these couples as examples of the companionate marriage model, reporters recognized the president's wife as a partner who played an important role in her husband's career, even if that role was relegated to the domestic sphere.

Hostessing is another duty of first ladies, related to their role as presidential partner, and modern era journalists recognized both the social and the political significance of this institutional obligation. Hostessing in Washington, D.C., has always been both personal and political, governed by etiquette and political protocol, with "social events serving as both private events and political arenas, often at the same time." Yet hostessing is also highly gendered, long considered the province of women despite its influence on the public and the political lives of men. Washington society differed from the social scenes in other major U.S. cities, "because of the nature of American government and politics, Washington is a town where everyone is given a fighting chance; in Washington, everyone is essentially nice to everyone else—even to total strangers who wander in. Those strangers could, if nothing else, be voters."[32] Thus, hostessing demanded a delicate balance of democratic and aristocratic elements, requiring knowledge of etiquette, social customs, White House traditions, Washington and diplomatic protocol, and the political sentiments of both the administration and its guests, with the hostess always running the risk of being criticized for offending someone.

First ladies were expected by the press to be experts on etiquette. In 1909 an article in *Ladies' Home Journal* proclaimed that incoming first lady Helen Taft "enters the White House better equipped than most of the women who have presided there. . . . In addition to a familiarity with the usages of polite society, she enjoys a knowledge of precedence," which the author credited to the hostessing experience Taft had garnered during her husband's tenure as governor general of the Philippines. According to the article, Taft's qualifications included "an acquaintance with ceremonious etiquette which will make her an invaluable helpmate to her husband." In similar fashion, a *Washington Post* profile claimed that Hoover's experience of years of hostessing prepared her for the first lady position: "Official entertaining will be no novelty to Mrs. Hoover, who is a true cosmopolitan and through her eight years as Cabinet hostess in this capital knows the etiquette of Washington from A to Z."[33] Within the hostess frame, knowledge of "ceremonious etiquette" and experience with "official entertaining" are presented as qualifications for the first lady role.

Modern era journalists also recognized that a first lady's success or failure as a hostess could impact her husband's presidency, since the numerous social functions she must preside over can impact the president's political agenda and public image. Riis's 1902 *Ladies' Home Journal* article about Roosevelt alluded to the first lady's importance as hostess, saying that her style "assured the success of the administration from a point of view often of more account than is commonly supposed."[34] The *New York Times* argued that Taft recognized the political importance of the first lady's hostessing duties: "she considers a public office a public trust, socially as well as politically, and that the personal side of her husband's administration will be conducted on a plane of the highest and broadest democracy, yet with the dignity benefiting the home of the Chief Executive of the greatest republic on earth." This statement reflects the balance of democratic simplicity with the dignity associated with aristocracy. The *New York Times Magazine* credited Herbert Hoover's political success, in part, to his wife's hostessing abilities, claiming that "Mr. Hoover could not have gone as far as he did without the calm, assured and diplomatic backing of his wife. She made their home serene and hospitable, never stuffy or ostentatious."[35] In this case an aristocratic approach to hostessing is rejected in favor of a more democratic approach. The conflicting expectations surrounding the hostessing role highlight the complexities of this particular first lady duty. Some of today's scholars have dismissed hostessing as a merely ceremonial role.[36] But journalists covering the first lady have long recognized the political significance of hostessing, especially given the interconnectedness of society and politics in Washington, D.C.

Articles about the first lady institution during the modern era reflected not only the expanding duties of presidents' wives but also the changing views on women's roles. By this time journalists had developed a whole set of frames to shape their coverage of the first lady institution, and these reflected the changing expectations for women and public life. First ladies were expected to perform multiple duties, while continuing to embody often contesting ideologies, primarily those of true womanhood and the new woman. The domesticity of the true woman was the dominant frame in the coverage of McKinley, Roosevelt, and Taft. Their successors were framed more often as new women, both socially and politically active. Yet the true woman frame persisted, and often in the same articles. These ideologies, contradictory in many ways, reflected both the growing duties of the first lady and the tensions arising as modern era women both expanded their public roles and continued as the primary caretakers of their homes and families.

The First Lady Emerges as Public Woman

Stories about the modern era first lady reveal her emergence as a public woman, constructed by the press as a positive role model for American women. In her book *The Rise of Public Woman,* Glenna Matthews argues that women achieved "a new kind of public power" in the modern era: "they began to win electoral office, they saw the enactment of major public policy for which they had struggled, and they enjoyed an increasing public presence." However, she notes that "women's power and women's access to public influence still fell far short of that exercised by men."[37]

The first ladies' public presence expanded in part through the heightened press coverage provided by women's pages and women's magazines. The gendered framing used to describe their activities evidenced the new "public power" and influence they wielded. As first ladies became more visible and vocal in the public sphere (largely via the press), they became public women, demonstrating for the press the more roles women were playing in the political sphere. Yet by framing these women as both "true" and "new" women, journalists were able to justify the first ladies' expanded roles while still positioning them as models of the more traditional conceptions of American womanhood. The emergence of the first lady as public woman in press coverage paralleled the rise of the rhetorical presidency and the rhetorical first lady, as presidents and their wives began "going public" more frequently, targeting their messages to larger public audiences and developing new strategies for controlling their public image.[38] Articles show that the first ladies of this era "went public" in various ways, all of them significant in normalizing women's presence and political participation in the public sphere.

Journalists' access to the first ladies was a key factor in this process. By the turn of the century, first ladies were routinely the subject of news coverage. Modern era first ladies developed strategies for dealing with the press, practices that by the end of this period had become institutionalized, leading to the development of the "office of first lady." A major step in establishing this office occurred when Roosevelt hired a secretary, whose primary job was to handle press inquiries. Roosevelt's strategy was to satisfy the curiosity of the press and the public while maintaining her family's privacy, and she accomplished this mainly through the regular release of photographs of her family and press releases detailing their activities. This approach allowed Roosevelt to avoid direct contact with reporters while maintaining a sense of control over the publicity surrounding herself and her family. By participating in the image-making process, Roosevelt promoted constructions of herself as a dedicated wife, mother, and true (private) woman while simultaneously garnering the publicity making her a public figure. Thanks to Roosevelt, the first lady's social secretary became a permanent feature of the White House staff.[39]

Other first ladies "went public" by granting interviews. McKinley, Taft, Ellen Wilson, Harding, and Hoover all talked with reporters and were sometimes quoted directly, which was rare in articles prior to this period. These first ladies became public women by allowing their voices to circulate in the public sphere. By speaking to the press, they also played a more active role in constructing their public image. In some cases these women boldly engaged in the prominent social debates of their era, such as the question of woman's suffrage. Prior to this period no first lady had taken a public stance on suffrage. Yet during the modern era, both Taft and Ellen Wilson voiced their opinions on the issue. Taft assumed the anti-suffrage stance in a 1908 *New York Times* article, saying, "I am not a sympathizer with the woman suffragists." She explained that her opposition was based on the fear that suffrage and political participation would force women "to neglect other duties that they cannot possibly shift to others," such as child rearing. Her statements echoed her husband's position and reflected the anti-suffrage argument that suffrage placed an additional and unnecessary burden on women, whose focus should be home and family, not politics.[40] Taft further stated, "We are not ready for women to vote, as not enough of them take an interest in political affairs, and until the majority of women want the vote they will scarcely be given the right."[41] This was an interesting comment coming from a woman who was herself very interested in politics and actively involved in her husband's campaign and career.

In contrast Ellen Wilson was framed as a limited supporter of the suffrage cause. In a 1913 *Good Housekeeping* interview, Wilson credited her daughter Jessie, a settlement house worker, with influencing her views on the subject. "The arguments of my Jessie incline me to believe in the suffrage for the working woman." This reflected Wilson's progressivism and interest in social reform, without committing her fully to the suffrage cause. The vagueness of the statement, meanwhile, allowed her to comment on the issue without having "embarrassed the president who had not yet come out for suffrage on the national level."[42] Despite Taft's and Wilson's differing views, and the relatively conservative tone of their comments, the very act of speaking out on a controversial issue was a milestone in the first ladies' emergence as public women. By articulating a political position in public (considered taboo only a few years earlier), these women helped break down the barriers to women's publicity and political involvement. This new level of political and rhetorical activity for first ladies was further explored by Harding, whose written statements to women's political groups were often published, and Hoover, who gave public speeches and was the first president's wife to deliver a radio address.

The first ladies of this period also became more vocal, and visible, on the campaign trail, further normalizing women's place in political life. The most publicly active campaigner of the modern era was Harding, and reporters noted her influence on her husband's political career. During the 1920 campaign the *Washington Post* described her as a "heap of ambitions, dreams, and political aspirations, not for herself but for her husband." Harding routinely talked to the press and promoted her role in the campaign. She told *Washington Post* reporters, "I have taken part in all of Senator Harding's campaigns and no matter how many engagements I may have, I never miss an opportunity to be present when he makes a speech. . . . The campaign at Chicago during the convention was very arduous, but I have enjoyed every moment of it." Harding made it clear that she would be participating in her husband's "front porch" campaign, stating, "it is there we shall remain this summer and receive the delegates during the coming campaign."[43] Harding's contributions to the campaign were acknowledged by the *Washington Post*, which duly stated in an inaugural article that "hers had been an active part in bringing about this great triumph in her husband's life." This article was titled "Mrs. Harding Shares Tasks of President," and the lead read, "Just as through the presidential campaign, Mrs. Harding stood like a soldier beside her husband. During the great moments when he was delivering his inaugural address, she watched and weighted his every word. Yesterday, as always, Mrs. Harding shared his thoughts and aspirations."[44] Harding, the first president's wife ever to cast a ballot for her husband, was praised for her interest in politics. A *New York Times* profile called her "a woman of independent ideas" and proclaimed, "She likes politics. She likes to participate in activities until recently regarded as men's spheres. She heartily believes in woman suffrage."[45] Through her words and her actions, Harding shaped her image as a politically active public woman, while the positive press coverage of her rhetorical activities further legitimized women's presence in the political sphere.

Harding's successors were not as vocal, but they still played visible public roles in their husband's campaigns. Coolidge was one of the first candidates' wives to appear alone at political rallies, a considerable step forward for public womanhood. She gave no formal speeches but instead spent time interacting with audience members. The *New York Times* noted that, at a rally held by a Republican women's club, Coolidge "shook hands with all present" but "made no remarks."[46] Lou Hoover accompanied her husband on his "speech making tours" but, according to the *Washington Post*, "made no speeches" of her own and took "no active part in the campaign." This article surmised that "there is no doubt but that her smiling personality has been a vote-getter just the same."[47] Although Coolidge and Hoover took a more passive approach to campaigning, their presence on the campaign trail, either alone or standing alongside their husbands, signaled the growing political importance of candidates' wives. The fact that women's campaign involvement increased after 1920 can be attributed in part to the passage of the Nineteenth Amendment and the need to attract female voters.[48] However, society's changing views on women's roles also opened the door for politically inclined wives to assume a more public role without fear of recrimination from the press and public.

The political activities of modern first ladies were not confined to the campaign trail; some of them extended their political interests to the public sphere through volunteerism and social advocacy. Modern era first ladies regularly acted as honorary chairs of various volunteer organizations, drawing on their status as public figures. A *Ladies' Home Journal* article about Edith Wilson's wartime volunteer efforts commented, "Mrs. Wilson is not, of course, unaware of the prestige that attaches to her name and position. She has accordingly lent the use of her name, and has accepted honorary appointments when convinced that by doing so she could further the advancement of commendable causes, even though she might be unable to undertake active direction of the work itself."[49] First ladies such as Wilson had become respected public figures, to the extent that their name alone could assist an organization. Groups such as the Girl Scouts of America recognized that the first lady's involvement promoted their organization. Both Harding and Hoover were honorary leaders of the Girl Scouts and were often associated with the organization in news articles. Harding acted as a ceremonial figurehead, while Hoover was actively involved with the group. She had served as the national president of the organization and had led her own troop before becoming first lady; she continued to work closely with the national office after entering the White House. Hoover promoted the organization as a model of the volunteerism her husband encouraged in response to the Great Depression.[50] The press credited her with having "sold the Girl Scout movement to social and official Washington," much of which then became actively involved with the organization. First ladies' involvement with voluntary organizations reflected the national trend of women's civic involvement during the progressive era.[51]

While most first ladies of this time confined themselves to charitable work, Ellen Wilson's social advocacy extended into the policy-making arena and serves as another example of the first lady's emergence as public woman. During the modern era, "some women leaders began to engage in a new—for women—kind of intense politicking of the two parties and of male officeholders."[52] Wilson engaged in such politicking in her efforts to improve the housing of those living in the squalid alleys of the capital city. Housing reform was a key component of progressivism. Women's efforts often centered on improving the quality of life in American cities by improving poor living conditions. And after 1910, "women increasingly turned to the government, especially at the federal level, to implement their reforms."[53] It is not surprising that social advocates enlisted the help of a first lady who shared their interest in progressive reform. A May 16, 1913, article titled "Mrs. Wilson Slumming" noted that Wilson was touring the alleys, "seeking first-hand information for the movement to improve the living conditions of the poor in Washington." The article concluded that Wilson was "deeply impressed with the necessity of legislation to do away with the alleys."[54] While the article recognized the political aspects of her alley tours, the title's play on the word "slumming" reflects a sarcastic tone that can be read as a subtle critique of Wilson's involvement in slum clearance.

The press continued to follow Wilson's work on behalf of housing reform. An article noted a week later that Wilson had donated "$100 toward cleaning up the slums of the capital," and that this was part of a larger fund-raising effort, with the money going to "further eliminating unsanitary dwellings in the slums, and the substitution of clean and wholesome houses that can be cheaply rented." The article also mentioned Wilson's donation of a White House automobile for tours of the alleys.[55] Legislation related to slum clearance was introduced on May 24, 1913, and the *New York Times* noted that the project was "indorsed [*sic*] by Mrs. Woodrow Wilson, who has made a personal inspection of the alleys and courts." The legislation was dubbed "Mrs. Wilson's bill," the first ever to be named for a first lady, and was passed by both the House and the Senate shortly before her death in 1914, marking the first time that a president's wife was publicly acknowledged for her active involvement in policy making. (The legislation never went into effect, however, due to a lack of funding.)[56]

Wilson's political activities, from fund-raising to lobbying, were representative of the forms of political action engaged in by female reformers during the years prior to woman's suffrage. Although her political influence was indirect, reminiscent of the "parlor politics" of early first ladies, the press coverage of Wilson's involvement added an element of necessary publicity to garner widespread public support for such causes. Given the progressive political climate of the time and the active involvement of women in social reform efforts, Wilson's social advocacy and policy making were, for the most part, positively framed. Such coverage of the institution expanded the acceptable roles and the political agency of first ladies.

Despite the emergence of positive representations of public womanhood during the modern era, Matthews contends that women faced more constraints than opportunities. She paints a bleak picture of public womanhood, noting that "the middle-class white woman of the 1920s confronted unpleasant realities should she contemplate becoming publicly active. There was no cultural expectation that a woman should be able to 'have it all.' If she chose serious engagement with politics, for example, she was unlikely to combine this with a husband, let alone raising children."[57] Yet this is exactly what modern era first ladies were able to do. Not only did these women become more publicly active; they were applauded by the press for doing so. Modern era first ladies, as a group, were more vocal, more politically active, and more publicly visible than the majority of their predecessors. Even the most reticent first ladies such as Roosevelt and Coolidge played a role in constructing their public image and presenting themselves as public figures.

I contend that the gendered press framing of their public activities meant that first ladies could avoid the pitfalls of public womanhood described by Matthews. First ladies in the modern era were indeed expected to "have it all," or at least to be able to balance their private role as wives with the public duties of the first lady position. By framing first ladies as true women or republican mothers, journalists lessened the criticism usually associated with publicity surrounding women, whose growing presence in the public sphere was justified primarily as an expansion of their wifely duties, just as their increased political participation during this period, including suffrage, was largely defended as an extension of women's domestic concerns. The heightened publicity surrounding first ladies was also a product of rising public interest in and press coverage of the presidents and their families. Combined with a social climate that recognized women's changing roles, such factors facilitated the emergence of first ladies as public women.

Conclusion

Coverage of the first lady institution during the modern era can be viewed as the basis for contemporary reporting on the first lady. First ladies personified various gender roles for journalists, and coverage of the first lady institution served as a site of contestation where the prevailing gender ideologies competed to define women's roles. The true woman dominated coverage at the turn of the century, and the ideal never was replaced by the new woman or by feminism. Instead, the modern era press often used the competing ideologies to frame different aspects of a woman's life, a practice that reflected the complexities of gender performance as first ladies "went public." The representations of first ladies also reflected the expanding expectations and publicity associated with the position in the twentieth century and the idea that first ladies must somehow be simultaneously modern and traditional, a concept that would lead to double binds in later years as the press amplified their critique of first ladies' performance of their institutional duties.

Publicity surrounding the first lady institution expanded during this era, thanks in part to the popularity of women's magazines and women's pages in newspapers. The positioning of first ladies as public figures in the political sphere neutralized the stigma associated with women's public-sphere activity. This was accomplished primarily through the press practice of gendered framing. In framing first ladies as true women or republican mothers, journalists made the mounting political activity of these women appear less controversial by linking their actions to women's traditional roles. The first ladies handled press scrutiny in different ways. Some issued press releases as a way to avoid reporters, while others granted interviews. As the era progressed, first ladies made more frequent public appearances independent of their husbands, meeting the public, posing for photographs, and sometimes making speeches. They also became more vocal in their support of social and political causes. But because the first ladies of this era played a limited role in the construction of their public image, the press had considerable control in defining and interpreting their actions. The resulting constructions often tempered their individual agency by emphasizing their domestic roles. While women such as Ellen Wilson and Florence Harding served as models of women's enhanced political efficacy, the press continued to remind readers that they were also true women. Such gendered framing in some ways undermined their standing as independent public figures, yet it also made their presence in the public and political sphere less controversial because their actions were not seen as an overt attempt to challenge or change traditional gender roles.

Press coverage of the first lady institution in the modern era was influential in promoting positive representations of public women by positioning first ladies as visible public figures and role models for American women. Stories and images of first ladies were disseminated to a wide audience through newspapers and magazines, establishing these women as prominent public figures acting in the political sphere. However, because these articles appeared primarily in publications targeting female readers, first ladies' publicity remained gendered and their actions remained confined largely to a female political sphere. Such gendering justified their status as public women while also limiting their sphere of influence. Although none of these first ladies achieved the celebrity of some of their successors, each woman was recognized by the press as playing an important role both in her husband's life and in American culture. Their various ways of "going public" created a climate in which first ladies could be more publicly and politically active without fear of serious recrimination. The flexibility of gender ideologies allowed journalists to present first ladies as both traditional and modern, both private and public women. Hence, the modern era first ladies did not face the same double binds that would prove problematic for their successors, but they did encounter mounting expectations. A reporter for the *New York Times Magazine* noted in 1929, for example, that first ladies were often held to a "superwomanly ideal," a term that is often associated with the women's liberation movement of the 1970s.[58] In recent years the "superwoman" expectation has been used to describe the struggles facing the "modern" woman at the end of the twentieth century.[59] That the writer's comment would not seem out of place in an article published today is further evidence that coverage from the modern era continues to serve as the foundation for journalistic constructions of the first lady institution.

Eleanor Roosevelt at Works Progress Administration Negro nursery school in Des Moines, Iowa, June 1936. (The Franklin D. Roosevelt Presidential Library)

Eleanor Roosevelt appearing on CBS radio, 1946. (The Franklin D. Roosevelt Presidential Library)

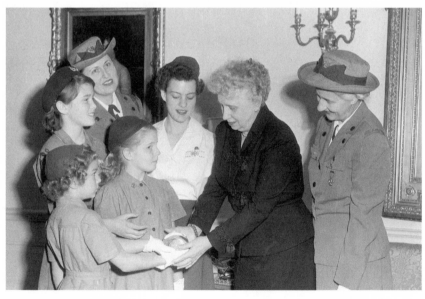

Bess Truman with delegation of Girl Scouts, December 1952. (The Harry S Truman Presidential Library)

Bess Truman with Mamie Eisenhower, visiting the White House in December 1952. (The Harry S Truman Presidential Library)

Jacqueline Kennedy displays a silver pitcher donated to the White House, December 1961. (Abbie Rowe, The John F. Kennedy Presidential Library and Museum, Boston)

Jacqueline Kennedy with her family at Hyannisport, August 1963. (Cecil Stoughton, The John F. Kennedy Presidential Library and Museum, Boston)

Lady Bird Johnson's 1964 Whistlestop tour, October 1964. (The Lyndon Baines Johnson Presidential Library)

Lady Bird Johnson planting a cherry tree, April 1965. (The Lyndon Baines Johnson Presidential Library)

Big Bird from "Sesame Street" visits Pat Nixon at the White House, December 1970. (The Richard M. Nixon Presidential Library)

Betty Ford holds impromptu press conference outside the White House, August 1974. (The Gerald R. Ford Presidential Library)

Betty Ford holds first press conference as first lady, September 1975. (The Gerald R. Ford Presidential Library)

Rosalynn Carter chairing a meeting, President's Commission on Mental Health, April 1977. (The Jimmy Carter Presidential Library)

Rosalynn Carter and Betty Ford at an ERA rally, November 1977. (The Jimmy Carter Presidential Library)

Rosalynn Carter in the Oval Office with her husband, April 1978. (The Jimmy Carter Presidential Library)

The Reagans in the Oval Office, November 1981. (The Ronald Reagan Presidential Library)

Nancy Reagan at a "Just Say No" rally at the White House, May 1986. (The Ronald Reagan Presidential Library)

Barbara and Laura Bush visit Bryan's House for Children with AIDS, Dallas, TX, October 1991. (The George Bush Presidential Library)

Hillary Clinton appears with C. Everett Coop at a public forum, Fall 1993, to promote President Clinton's Health Security Act. (The William J. Clinton Presidential Library)

Hillary Clinton speaking at a health care rally, March 1994. (The William J. Clinton Presidential Library)

CHAPTER THREE

The First Lady as Political Celebrity, 1932–1961

In a 1932 *New York Times Magazine* article profiling the "Candidates for the Post of First Lady," reporter Alice Rogers Hagar articulated the difficult duties of the first lady: "The President's wife must be a silent partner. The unwritten law is that the First Lady gives no interviews, makes no public utterances. She appears at State functions, where her presence is expected, and she must have a smile for every guest, though guests number legions. She must do her utmost to shield the President from importunities, even when his secretaries are equally on guard. She must be prepared, when he is tired, to cover up his lapses with a friendliness so sincere that they are forgotten. She must never show weariness or distress." Given the demands of the position, Hagar argued that it was the job of journalists to "discover what manner of American women are 'candidates' for this most difficult post . . . and to try to understand the character, background, training, and talents of the two, one of whom will spend at least four years as the exemplar of American living."[1]

The two women in question were Lou Henry Hoover and Anna Eleanor Roosevelt. According to Hagar, both "remarkable women" were equally prepared for the post: "There is no question of comparing them— each is a personality distinct. Yet contrasts are few and far to seek, for, broadly speaking, their lives run parallel. In greatness of heart, in quality of mind, in education, in spiritual independence, in vivid approach to living and in depth of experience they are sisters." Hagar's profile revealed that both Hoover and Roosevelt were committed to "outside interests of philanthropic or an educational nature." Hoover was said to have "aided her husband in his career," while the Roosevelts' "fine, frank comradeship" was commended. Devotion to their children was discussed, but each woman was also applauded for her individual accomplishments. In particular Roosevelt was said to have "fingers in more pies at one moment than most mortals in a lifetime," demonstrated by a list of her professional and organizational affiliations. Following her assessment of each woman, Hagar concluded, "The Great American Home would seem to be in excellent hands for the next four years when we can present two such 'candidates' for the First Ladyship as these American gentlewomen, Mrs. Hoover and Mrs. Roosevelt."[2] While recognizing the superwomanly qualities needed to perform the first lady position, Hagar ultimately reinforced the domesticity of the institution in her closing statement. This article reflected the growing expectations faced by first ladies, and the complexities involved in performing the first lady position in accordance with gender norms of the era.

The first ladies of the early twentieth century had laid the foundation for the modern first lady by institutionalizing many of the duties that had been performed by their nineteenth-century predecessors. They also evidenced the rise of the first lady as public woman, a rise tied to increased publicity of the first lady institution. However, as one author claims, "Before 1933, none of the First Ladies had exploited fully the possibilities inherent within the celebrity status of the institution." For the next thirty years only four women served as first lady: (Anna) Eleanor Roosevelt (1933–1945), (Elizabeth) Bess Wallace Truman (1945–1953), Mamie Geneva Doud Eisenhower (1953–1961), and Jacqueline Lee Bouvier Kennedy (1961–1963). It was during the tenure of Eleanor Roosevelt that the first lady "blossomed as a national celebrity in ways that permanently altered the expectations for presidential wives who followed her."[3]

This can be credited largely to the regular press coverage Roosevelt garnered through her many activities. Articles about Roosevelt were not only a constant feature of women's pages and magazines but also appeared at times on the front pages of the *New York Times* and *Washington Post*. Such positioning signaled that stories about the first lady were considered of interest to both male and female readers, extending her newsworthiness beyond a solely female audience. Although Roosevelt's successors did not emulate her approach to publicity, they each had to deal with the public image, personality, and celebrity issues related to the first lady institution. The heightened publicity granted agency to these women by recognizing their individuality and legitimizing the roles they played in their husbands' careers, but their individuality was sometimes limited by expectations of the institutional role and by the gender ideologies visible in press frames.

The frames used in stories about the first lady between 1932 and 1961 reflected the cultural changes of this period, particularly in relation to women's roles. Women were more frequently recognized as citizens making important contributions to American political culture, whether through rationing during wartime or endorsing Cold War consumerism. Women's contributions were tied primarily to the roles of wife and homemaker, however, reflecting an ideology of domesticity that permeated both personal and political areas. Many feminist scholars have pointed to the postwar era as a period of "domestic containment," which trapped (primarily middle-class white) women in their suburban homes, where they sublimated personal ambition and independence to the needs of their families. The domination of the so-called feminine mystique during this era, which has been traced to the period between the world wars, became an ideological catalyst that led to the emergence of the women's liberation movement in the 1960s.[4]

The notion of "domestic containment," while valid in many respects, ignores the positive facets of this era's domestic ideology, primarily the sense of domestic empowerment, which granted women control over the private domain and authority within the home. Homemaking was often treated as a profession, an integral part of a two-person career, and the homemaker's consumer responsibilities were now imbued with political significance. Such constructions of homemaking and consumerism, even if contained within the private sphere, legitimate women's roles, and they contribute to the second-wave feminist idea that "the personal is political." Thus, although this "in-between" period may have lacked the organized feminist activity that characterized the so-called first and second waves of feminism, gender roles continued to be in flux. While frustration with the domestic containment of this period unleashed a new tide of feminist activity in the 1960s, the domestic empowerment of homemakers, which began to recognize the personal as political, fostered the female consciousness necessary for social action in the coming years.

Press coverage of the first lady institution in this era reveals both the expansion and the limitation of women's roles that proved significant in the history of feminism and contribute to our understanding of women's place in American culture. The journalistic practice of personification framing promoted domesticity. With such ideological shortcuts, Roosevelt became a stand-in for both social feminism and republican motherhood, while her successors embodied various aspects of Cold War domesticity. Such gendered framing also impacted journalists' coverage of the first lady's duties. Most framing reflected the concept of the two-person career, acknowledging the wife's role in her husband's career, as hostess, advisor, or protector. This type of framing now recognized the political importance of the first lady, evidencing the domestic empowerment of the homemaker role. But such stories also reinforced traditional gender roles by framing the first lady's duties as an extension of her role as wife and homemaker.

Gendered framing was also tied to a growing focus on the first lady as celebrity. First ladies had begun to seek and to attract more press attention, legitimating their status as public women without fear of reproach.

The first ladies of this era with the exception of Truman gained celebrity status as personalities independent of their husbands. Roosevelt, Eisenhower, and Kennedy all garnered celebrity status to the extent that the public and press felt comfortable referring to them as Eleanor, Mamie, and Jackie. In articles focusing on the first ladies' celebrity, their husbands were rarely, if ever, mentioned; these women were recognized as public figures in their own right. However, they were at times reduced to their fashions and other superficial representations of their personalities because reporters often focused only on their physical appearances and consumer behavior. Their celebrity was thus both empowering and constraining, much in the same way that the current dominant gender ideologies expanded women's political influence while simultaneously containing it to the domestic realm.

Competing Gender Ideologies — From Rosie the Riveter to June Cleaver

The extremes characterizing this era resulted in mixed messages regarding the roles women should play and culminated in what some scholars regard as a backlash against women's presence in public and political life. The New Deal included measures to enhance legal protections for women and children and provided a platform for politically active women to become involved in policy making. Other New Deal policies discriminated against working women and limited women's control over the government policies affecting them by placing male bureaucrats in charge of the majority of New Deal programs. During the depression, when any form of income could determine whether a family survived or starved, women were encouraged—and at times forced—to leave the workforce in order to provide job opportunities for men. But when the United States entered World War II, women were recruited by the government to take on jobs created by the wartime industry and to fill positions left vacant by the men who went to war.[5] Following the war many women were once again forced out of the workplace and lost their jobs to returning soldiers; the same government that had recruited them for wartime work now entreated them to pursue careers as homemakers. A healthy economy and the postwar baby boom kept many women in the home throughout the 1950s. Yet in the following decade, these home-bound years would be considered the root of women's discontent.[6]

The gender ideologies competing to define American womanhood reflected the times, particularly the debate over spheres. The prevailing theme of each ideology was domesticity. Although the egalitarian spirit of the early suffrage movement persisted, it was overshadowed by so-called social or domestic feminism, which saw its ideals reflected in Roosevelt's New Deal. The depression and World War II, times of crisis that called for women's active involvement in the public sphere as well as in the home, created a climate in which both social feminism and republican motherhood flourished. The postwar years saw a retreat to suburbia and the promotion of domesticity and consumerism as powerful Cold War weapons. Following the war the true womanhood ideology, also known as the cult of domesticity, was a convenient way to promote women's return to the home and subsequent retreat from public and political life. However, within the domestic sphere, homemakers were empowered in ways that exceeded the moral authority of Victorian era true women. Particularly through their role as the primary consumers for the family, women exerted more authority within the home than they had in previous generations.[7]

Female leaders who had joined together in the fight for suffrage prior to 1920 went their separate ways soon after the passage of the Nineteenth Amendment, divided mainly by philosophical differences regarding gender. Alice Paul and the National Woman's Party, embracing an egalitarian viewpoint, focused their energies on the Equal Rights Amendment (ERA), first introduced in 1923. The ERA was opposed by the majority of women's groups, including the League of Women Voters (LWV), formerly the National American Woman Suffrage Association, and the National Women's Trade Union League (NWTUL). Members of groups such as the LWV and NWTUL, who came to be identified as social feminists, believed that women were inherently different from men and needed protective measures to improve their home lives and to prevent their being exploited in the workforce. Social feminists were the descendants of the new women of the progressive era, who argued that "their domestic duties gave women special moral qualities and a special claim to influence in American society." Both Eleanor Roosevelt and Frances Perkins, FDR's secretary of labor, aligned themselves with leading social feminists and fought for protective legislation.[8]

Republican motherhood was again invoked to justify women's growing political participation. Believing that women's lives were defined by their roles as wives and mothers, social feminists felt that women were obligated as citizens to work to secure political rights and protections for women and children, within both the home and the workplace. This philosophy reflected the republican motherhood notion that "a mother, committed to the service of her family and to the state, might serve a political purpose." Roosevelt often justified her active promotion of social reform by characterizing herself as a concerned mother, and most of the causes she supported were aimed at improving the lives of women, children, and families.[9]

Republican motherhood was also used to frame women's wartime roles. Throughout U.S. history, rules regarding proper female comportment have been "temporarily abandoned whenever the country needed women to do something they weren't supposed to do." Such was the case during World War II, when many middle-class white women, encouraged for the past decade to stay out of the workforce, were told it was their patriotic duty to take over for the men who were fighting the war overseas. The government created one of the most famous American images, Rosie the Riveter, as part of a campaign that made factory work both patriotic and feminine. Meanwhile women were reminded that it was also their duty to fight the war from the home front by submitting to rationing, buying war bonds, and volunteering at their local Red Cross or USO (United Service Organization) canteen. Women's magazines and advertisers constructed even the most basic of domestic duties as patriotic acts, integrating political values into women's domestic lives.[10]

When the war ended, however, the same government that had recruited women workers started campaigning almost immediately to get them out of the workforce. Government officials were worried there would not be enough jobs for returning servicemen and that another depression would occur. Women were then told it was their patriotic duty to give up their jobs to returning soldiers. Rather than relying solely on republican motherhood, the gender ideology of true womanhood was brought to the forefront again as a way to frame middle-class white women's return to the home.[11]

Following the war true womanhood and the cult of domesticity emerged as the dominant gender ideology, in the guise of the postwar homemaker. The fictional Betty Crocker and June Cleaver were the images of the "new" true woman, the ideal homemaker with her perfectly coiffed hair. Now "women seemed to have been catapulted back in time to the nineteenth century, to the cult of the True Woman and the corset that went with it."[12] The mythical ideal of the American family with the woman as devoted wife, mother, and homemaker dominated from the mid-1940s until the 1960s. In 1963 Betty Friedan argued, "In the fifteen years since World War II, this mystique of feminine fulfillment became the cherished and self-perpetuating core of contemporary American culture." She claimed that white women "had no thought for the unfeminine problems of the world outside the home; they wanted the men to make the major decisions. They glorified in their role as women, and wrote proudly on the census blank: 'Occupation: housewife.'" These middle-class white women were part of a large-scale domestic revival. The ideological shift used family and home as metaphors for America's identity and security during the Cold War.[13]

Some scholars view the resurgence of true womanhood as a backlash against advances made by middle-class white women during the depression and war years. This backlash was promoted largely by women's magazines, which "enjoined women to sacrifice their own ambitions for the sake of husband and children." For many white women this meant giving up jobs and lives they enjoyed outside the home. The backlash reflected earlier debates over women's changing roles, for the feminine mystique, a new take on the Victorian cult of true womanhood, first appeared after World War I, dominated through the depression, and then reappeared following World War II.[14]

But there was a positive element to the postwar backlash in that it sparked the women's liberation movement of the 1960s. The rebirth of feminism can be traced to the "family-centered years of the 1950s" when "cultural ideology defined the wife/mother role as both women's special duty and path to fulfillment." As Friedan found when she interviewed white middle-class housewives in the 1950s, many already wanted "something more than my husband and my children and my home." By the early 1960s, the question regarding the status of American women would be taken up by a presidential commission appointed by President Kennedy and chaired by former first lady Eleanor Roosevelt.[15]

Another positive aspect of this era's domestic ideology often overlooked by feminist scholars was the domestic empowerment that characterized the homemaker who played a vital role in American civic and cultural life. Particularly in women's magazines, "domestic" was not a narrow term referring simply to housekeeping. It encompassed family and social relationships, personal well-being and appearance, purchasing habits, school and neighborhood activities, recreation, and civic involvement. The term "domestic" in Cold War rhetoric also connoted all that was not foreign, thus linking home and family to national security. Women's magazines "included debates on the nature and significance of the homemaker's role that reveal the cultural fluidity of such concepts as *home* and *domestic* at mid-century."[16]

While a true woman exercised authority through her moral superiority to men, the homemaker's authority came largely from her buying power in the marketplace. Advertisers had begun to recognize women as the primary household consumers in the late nineteenth century, but the economic pressures of the depression and World War II now imbued women's consumerism with added significance. The homemaker enjoyed both agency and influence as she made decisions regarding the family spending, and this power expanded during the Cold War, when consumption represented "the superiority of the American way of life." Through their purchasing power, women joined the ranks of American cold warriors. Such domestic empowerment politicized the private sphere by linking it to the public marketplace and the political arena and can be viewed as an early articulation of the second-wave feminist mantra "the personal is political."[17]

The social conditions of the mid-century decades promoted this domestic ideal, which shaped definitions of womanhood in the same way true womanhood had once dictated the performance of gender roles. The postwar backlash and subsequent "domestic containment" of the Cold War limited definitions of women's proper roles, and by extension the performance of the first lady position. The same ideology also promoted a domestic empowerment that acknowledged the social significance of homemaking and the growing power of women.

Framing the First Lady at Mid-Century

The framing of the first lady institution between 1932 and 1961 accentuates the domesticity ideology while recognizing the first lady's own political contributions. Press coverage of the institution jumped dramatically, bringing attention to the contestation over women's roles, the competing gender ideologies, and the more prominent public roles of women. Roosevelt personified for the press the social feminist and the republican mother, while her successors embodied the Cold War homemaker. These ideologies were used as framing devices in articles assessing each first lady's performance of her various duties. The heavy press coverage of Roosevelt, Eisenhower, and Kennedy propelled them to celebrity status, positioning each woman as a role model for American womanhood.

EMBODYING DOMESTICITY—EMPOWERMENT AND CONTAINMENT

Throughout the history of the institution, journalists have presented the first lady as a model of American womanhood. However, there was now an increase in this type of framing, which mirrored the growing pervasiveness of domesticity as the dominant ideology. Both the individual women who held the position and the cultural climate of the era endorsed journalists' constructing first ladies as personifications of gender ideologies. Articles appearing in women's pages and magazines focused primarily on women's various domestic roles, infusing them with a sense of domestic empowerment that simultaneously contained their political influence. The first ladies of this era were more active than their predecessors in constructing their public image, either through their visibility or their evasion of the spotlight. However, through practices such as personification framing, journalists remained the primary filter through which the words and images of first ladies were disseminated throughout the public sphere.

Roosevelt personified for journalists the reformist spirit of the New Deal and social feminism not only through her actions but also through her words. She was the most active in respect to publicity; she held regular press conferences open only to women journalists, gave speeches on an almost daily basis, published a daily newspaper column, hosted radio programs, and wrote for various publications, all activities that garnered regular press coverage and expanded her exposure as a public woman.[18] Journalists often built their story around her quotes, positioning her as the physical embodiment of the ideals she promoted in her speeches. Sometimes journalists went as far as to use her name in the headlines of their stories, attributing the ideas in the story directly to her. For example, an article in the *New York Times*—"Housewives Entitled to Fixed Salaries, like Any Worker, Mrs. Roosevelt Holds"—opened with the following sentence: "The suggestion that wives who stay at home to look after the household should receive a definite salary for their work was advanced last night by Mrs. Franklin D. Roosevelt, wife of the President." The article then noted Roosevelt also supported protective legislation for working women and quoted her as saying, "a woman who works to give her children the necessities and some of the advantages of life should have her work day limited to eight hours."[19] Journalists framed such comments as representing the views of groups such as the NWTUL, of which Roosevelt was an active member. For reporters Roosevelt became the embodiment of social feminism for she gave voice to its ideological values and acted out its basic tenets.

Roosevelt's activism combined with her focus on domesticity positioned her at times as a personification of republican motherhood. Twentieth-century first ladies extended the republican motherhood ideology, resulting in the premise that "being a good first lady meant hailing, modeling, and promoting publicly the civic values that *good* mothers historically instilled." A 1933 *Washington Post* article featured a statement from Roosevelt telling her fellow homemakers they had a significant role to play in the country's economic recovery: "We women have to go about our daily task of home-making, no matter what may happen, and we needn't feel that ours is an unimportant part, for our courage and our willingness to sacrifice may well be the springboard from which recovery may come." This statement imbued homemaking with political purpose and empowered women to act as citizens, noting that their daily domestic duties have political consequences.[20]

Such sentiments of domestic empowerment were echoed in articles during World War II, when Roosevelt urged "the women of the country to do all in their power to help speed victory in the war" as homemakers and consumers. Under the headline "First Lady Decries Home-Front Complaints and Urges Women to Do Utmost to Aid War," a 1945 *New York Times* article stated, "Housewives of this country, she declared, should be able to take a ration stamp cut to distribute food supplies as equitably as possible without feeling that they are being badly treated."

According to the story, "The First Lady asserted that women had a responsibility as buyers to stick to essentials and to pass useful articles on to others when they ceased to need them." The article pointed out how Roosevelt exhibited women's home-front roles by overseeing White House rationing, providing a "model for American housewives." Such framing recalls the actions of revolutionary era republican mothers, who contributed to the war effort by caring for their farms and families and boycotting British goods. Although these stories conflate domesticity, consumerism, and patriotism, thereby defining women's citizenship in relation to their roles as homemakers, they also recognize the significant civic role played by homemakers, especially during times of crisis. Because women managed the households during this era, they were empowered to make decisions that impacted not only their own personal domestic spaces but the nation as well.[21]

Although social feminism and republican motherhood were both characterized by domestic discourse, these ideologies rarely appeared in the postwar era. They were replaced with a more fervent ideology of domesticity that dominated discussions of womanhood and the first lady institution. The Cold War incarnation of the cult of domesticity, later labeled "the feminine mystique" by Friedan, constructed women as "sexually attractive housewives and consumers under the American capital system." This "vision of domesticity," which conflated domesticity with both femininity and consumerism, was a powerful Cold War propaganda weapon.[22] For journalists, Mamie Eisenhower and Jacqueline Kennedy, and to a lesser extent Bess Truman, personified this "vision of domesticity."

For starters, the first ladies of the postwar era were the visual embodiments of femininity, each one looking the part of the average American woman. For postwar Americans, fashion represented femininity. Bess Furman of the *New York Times* reported that Truman was "as folksy in tone as is the Midwest itself," which matched her husband's "plain Midwestern democracy" image.[23] In Martha Weinman's review of first lady fashion, Truman was quoted as saying of the first lady, "Why should she look different from anyone else?" Reporters such as Weinman played on this, offering "homespun descriptions of her resemblance to 'your next-door neighbor.'" Eisenhower also personified the typical postwar housewife and came the closest to representing the American woman. Weinman wrote, "Mamie has, in effect, come closer to the ideal than any other first lady of memory. . . . In addition to difficult hair, she looks average, as most women do; she loves clothes, as most women do; she dresses a bit more youthfully than is warranted by Paris standards, as most American women do; and she has a guilt about unnecessary spending as, again, most women have." A "housewife" was even quoted as saying, "I've always sympathized with her because I've never been able to do anything with my hair, either." Eisenhower was "typical, and thus ideal," Weinman concluded. She argued that both Eisenhower and Truman embodied a shifting cultural perspective on the ideals of American womanhood: "The cozy conjunction of a White House wife who looks just like your neighbor roughly parallels Hollywood's abrupt shift in leading ladies from goddesses to girls-next-door and is infinitely better suited to these identification-conscious times than the grand-lady manner of Dolly Madison's day."[24] In a time when both print media and politicians were more focused on images, Truman and Eisenhower visually represented the average American housewife and Cold War femininity.[25] Such framing encouraged readers to identify with the first lady, making the "ideal" of womanhood more attainable by the "typical" woman, primarily through consumption.

The emphasis on representing the "average" housewife was so pervasive during the postwar era that in 1960 the first lady's image even became a campaign issue. Kennedy was more youthful and stylish than either her predecessors or the average American housewife and personified for the press both culture and sophistication. Kennedy's legacy "was an image of beauty, culture, and good taste that no woman could easily match."[26] But this young, sophisticated, smarter first lady image was not immediately embraced by the public. Kennedy was criticized as being "too chic," and some reporters argued that her cultured image alienated the "average American woman" and could cost her husband votes. Weinman claimed, "This fall, the question of style for a President's wife may be a Great issue. Can too much chic—or too little—mean votes?" Weinman suggested that "if Mrs. Kennedy could un-chic a bit, she would make an admirable fashion diplomat." Meanwhile the "conservative perfection" of Pat Nixon, Kennedy's "competition" for the first lady position, was critiqued as having a "consciously manipulated air that poses certain problems vis-à-vis the public." One observer stated that "Pat Nixon always looks too good to be true . . . [and] it irritates me." By not looking like the average housewife, both Kennedy and Nixon found themselves under fire. Weinman focused primarily on controversy surrounding Kennedy, including a report that she and her mother-in-law spent too much on clothes, "some $30,000 a year in Paris salons." Weinman claimed that "Mrs. Kennedy's coiffure seems to arouse even greater ire than her clothes. A picture of her that appeared recently in The Times engendered several comments, including one that reads, 'we have better-looking floor mops than the bouffant coiffure worn by your favorite Bobby-Soxer. (Signed) Twenty Iowa Homemakers.'" It was Kennedy's "devil-may-care chic," according to Weinman, that troubled American women, who could not identify as easily with the stylish socialite as they could with her predecessors.[27]

Kennedy's livid reaction to this criticism in the press also set her apart from Eisenhower and Truman, who had avoided expressing their opinions in public. Kennedy responded defensively to her critics a few days later, attacking Pat Nixon in the process. During an informal round of interviews with female reporters, which was supposed to focus on her new maternity wardrobe, Kennedy candidly spoke her mind concerning the press coverage of her fashion choices. Nan Robertson's front page article in the *New York Times* carried the headline "Mrs. Kennedy Defends Clothes; Is 'Sure' Mrs. Nixon Pays More." The article opened, "Mrs. John F. Kennedy, stung by reports that women resent her because she is 'too chic' and spends too much money on clothes, called her critics 'dreadfully unfair' yesterday." Robertson noted that Kennedy "expressed hurt and surprise at slurs on her avant-garde dressing habits" and quoted her as saying, "They're beginning to snipe at me about that as often as they attack Jack on Catholicism." She further stated, "A newspaper reported Sunday that I spend $30,000 a year buying Paris clothes and that women hate me for it. I couldn't spend that much unless I wore sable underwear." Kennedy's tone was both argumentative and flippant as she addressed her critics. Kennedy then attacked Pat Nixon, one of the first times a candidate's wife openly challenged her opponent in the press: "'I'm sure I spend less than Mrs. Nixon on clothes,' the 31-year-old wife of the Democratic candidate said. 'She gets hers at Elizabeth Arden, and nothing there costs less than $200 or $300.'"[28] By challenging her critics and Nixon, Kennedy violated the norm that prescribed against women assuming a more aggressive rhetorical style in public. However, because Kennedy defended her own spending habits by attacking Nixon's consumerism, she trivialized the debate by turning it into a competition between women rather than a matter of larger political significance.

The "fashion debate" highlights one of the problems of personification framing. Both Kennedy and Nixon were reduced to mere images focused on fashion, which failed to capture the complex personalities and interests of each woman. As Kennedy argued, such critiques were "dreadfully unfair" because they were based on incomplete and sometimes false information. Yet these journalists still used these limited public constructions in order to critique each woman—as did Kennedy when she attacked Nixon's clothing expenditures. Placing such high importance on the fashion choices of the candidates' wives also ignored the complexities of the first lady institution. Despite the "fashion debate," Kennedy went on to become the "first lady of American fashion," personifying a youthful yet sophisticated image and complimenting her husband's public image, which blended "Camelot and Catholicism, continental chic and touch football."[29]

Journalists continued to position the first lady as a model of American womanhood. Each woman personified domesticity, but in ways that matched the social conditions of their time and their personalities. For journalists, Roosevelt's advocacy represented social feminism and made manifest the spirit of her husband's New Deal. As the cultural climate shifted, first ladies personified the "domestic containment" of the postwar era with its focus on traditional gender roles and femininity. Truman, Eisenhower, and Kennedy represented different—but equally compelling and familiar—images of the ideal woman. Truman and Eisenhower looked like the typical American homemaker, whereas Kennedy resembled the movie stars in the fashion magazines read by the typical American woman. While Eisenhower represented the feminine mystique of the 1950s, Kennedy resembled the college-educated housewives of Friedan's study, who were becoming disillusioned with the domestic ideal and searching for other avenues of personal fulfillment. Changes in definitions of domesticity impacted how journalists framed their discussions of the first lady's duties.

THE TWO-PERSON CAREER—FRAMING THE PERFORMANCE OF THE FIRST LADY POSITION

Coverage of the first lady position between 1932 and 1961 showed a shift in the framing of the institution that reflected an expansion of the first lady's duties as well as the current domestic ideologies governing gender performance. The social feminism of the 1930s, seen in Eleanor Roosevelt's active performance of the position, slowly gave way to the cult of domesticity embraced by her successors. Both standpoints promoted a sense of domestic empowerment, albeit in different ways. Most articles focused on the presidency as a two-person career. This frame limited women to the traditional roles of wife and homemaker but also recognized that wives play significant roles in their husbands' careers. While the two-person career frame can be traced back to the parlor politics of the new republic and had been used by journalists over the years in their coverage of the first lady institution, during this era it came to dominate discussions of the first lady's duties. By this time journalists routinely covered the first lady as part of a presidential couple. In a 1960 article, the *Ladies' Home Journal* stated, "Politics today is a husband-wife partnership." But "such cooperation was seen not as a mark of liberation but as an appropriate extension of wifely duties." Thus, the two-person career frame was compatible with the domestic ideology employed to frame the performance of the first lady position.[30]

In discussing their roles journalists now continued to frame first ladies primarily as wives and mothers, recognizing that these women initially became public figures through marriage. The *New York Times* reported that Bess Truman was "devoted to her husband and daughter," while Mamie Eisenhower "cherish[ed] her role as wife and mother."[31] According to a 1952 *New York Times* article, Eisenhower was not "frightened" of her new job "because it would mean playing the role of a wife, entertaining and meeting people, which was no different from what she had always done." Most stories about Jacqueline Kennedy framed her as a "young wife and mother devoted to her husband and children."[32] Even Eleanor Roosevelt was lauded by *Good Housekeeping* for her commitment to her family: "despite her many outside activities, she is a fine and conscientious mother" and a "devoted and supportive wife." Karlyn Kohrs Campbell argues that, in two-person careers such as the presidency, "the division of labor will vary with the talents and attitudes of the partners and because the wife's role combines state and domestic duties."[33] Journalists recognized that, as devoted wives, these first ladies assumed various roles from the more traditional helpmate to public surrogate and political advisor.

As helpmates, wives were loyal supporters of their husbands' careers. In the first story written about new first lady Truman, the *New York Times* reported she was "on call twenty-four hours a day as her husband's helper," which implied that Truman's life revolved around her husband, echoing the subservience of the cult of domesticity. The notion of her being "on call" around the clock also indicated that her husband relied on her. Similarly, a 1956 profile of Eisenhower claimed, "Even as First Lady, Mrs. Eisenhower takes the feminine view. She sees her role, and lives it, as a husband-helper." In this case the reporter explicitly links the helpmate role to gender ideology by referring to it as the "feminine view." Despite the submissive tone, the language also implied that both Truman and Eisenhower were playing important roles in their husbands' lives, one that had them "on call" as their husband's "helper," which alluded to a spousal advisory role.[34]

According to the press, one way a wife can help her husband is by acting as his protector, an example of women's authority in the private sphere, and public statements of the first ladies encouraged the protector frame. According to the *New York Times,* Eisenhower believed that her primary job was "looking after Ike." A *New York Times* headline from 1952 proclaimed that "'Policeman for Ike' is wife's idea of her principal role in public life." According to reporter Laurie Johnston, Eisenhower stated that she could do more good for her husband by "playing policeman— seeing that he gets to bed on time and doesn't get irritated by small things" than by making speeches or commenting on political issues.[35] The image of Mamie ordering Ike to bed presents her as the authority figure within the home. Kennedy also assumed a protective role. Upon her husband's election, it was reported that "her greatest immediate desire was that 'Jack must get a month's rest, or else he won't be able to be a good president.'" Kennedy also insisted that her children were her first priority. She told Nan Robertson of the *New York Times*, "I'll do everything I can and should do in any official way. But I don't want my young children brought up by nurses and Secret Service men."[36] In this forceful statement Kennedy articulated that she would not allow the duties of the first lady to infringe on her home life, thus marking her control of the private domain. The framing of both Kennedy and Eisenhower as protectors of the family emphasized the role of women as nurturers whose lives were defined by the need to care for their families. By highlighting the protector role that these women assumed over their husbands, however, reporters imbued them with domestic authority. While such framing promoted domesticity, it also empowered each woman to make decisions to place limits on her public activities as first lady in favor of her private duties as wife and mother, as well as limiting the activities of her presidential husband.

The role of protector sometimes extended into the public sphere, when journalists applied the protective helpmate frame to first ladies who acted as presidential surrogates. Eisenhower took on many of the ceremonial public appearances formerly associated with the presidency. She was credited for having "taken from the President's shoulders much of the load of making personal appearances and being photographed for worthy causes," framing her as a helpmate and protective wife. According to the *New York Times,* many of Roosevelt's public appearances were an extension of her wifely helpmate role: "Since President Roosevelt's disability makes it difficult for him, in spite of his robust general health, to get around, Mrs. Roosevelt has relieved him of a host of social duties performed by his predecessors." Since Martha Washington's time, the surrogate role has helped justify a first lady's public activities; in Roosevelt's case, it allowed journalists to explain her expansion of the first lady's duties.[37]

The press often framed the Roosevelts' marital partnership as a fusion of the personal and the political. Roosevelt expanded the role of presidential surrogate by parlaying it into an advisory role; not only did she appear on the president's behalf, she also reported back to him the details of what she saw and heard, acting as his "eyes and ears." For example, her extensive traveling was viewed in part as a way of helping her husband compensate for his disability, which made it difficult for him to make informal public appearances. As her husband's emissary she toured numerous New Deal program sites and communities during the Depression. Rita S. Halle, in a 1933 *Good Housekeeping* article, described Roosevelt as a figurative extension of her husband: "If in this remarkable partnership she is, as it has been said, 'his ear to the ground,' it is a natural and not a calculated thing. Because she can go places he can't go, see people he can't see, and because of her rare gift of articulate expression, can bring back to him as no one else can, visualizations which result in benefit to you and to me and to all the masses of people who make up America." However, Halle tempered her framing of Roosevelt as advisor with a disclaimer: "I do not mean by this to give the impression that Mrs. Roosevelt interferes, or that she is solely responsible for the fine things that the President does. I want to show only that her attitude inevitably reflects itself in his actions, just as that of any wife who has earned respect for and faith in her views over the years, finds a response in the point of view of her husband."[38] This claim seems designed to defend Roosevelt from critics who asserted that she was abusing the "pillow talk" power of wives and overstepping the boundaries of the first lady position. It also reasserted that Roosevelt's political interests were simply an extension of her personal wifely duties, which were in part based on her husband's physical limitations that were well-known to members of the press yet seldom discussed.

Other articles clearly framed Roosevelt as one of her husband's most trusted political advisors, extending the two-person career from the home to the office. In a 1936 profile *New York Times* reporter Kathleen McLaughlin called Roosevelt an "aide and counselor to the President," asserting, "In many places and on varying occasions she has been the eyes and ears through which he has saw and heard. Each of her jaunts as a presidential deputy terminates with a report to him—orally, if there is time on their schedule, typed out in detail if there is not—on different phases of the project or community she has been delegated to inspect." McLaughlin described Roosevelt as a "keenly practical politician," noting that she "incorporates into these reports her impressions of trends and shifts in the public mind on major enterprises and policies of the administration. These the President peruses and sometimes quotes to his other counselors."[39] In this story Roosevelt's actions sound more like those of a staff member than a wife. By overtly framing Roosevelt as an advisor whose work was comparable to that of other presidential counselors, this story gives her actions more political meaning.

The two-person career frame was also used by journalists to explain the growing public, although not necessarily active, roles played by wives in their husbands' campaigns. Stories about the presence of wives on the campaign trail also made these women, even the publicity-shy Bess Truman, recognizable public figures. Both Harry Truman and Dwight Eisenhower recognized how important a high-profile wife could be on whistle-stop campaign trips. A *New York Times* article attested to this: "Important assets to Mr. Truman on this trip have been Mrs. Truman and their daughter, Margaret. . . . When the train stops at a station, Mr. Truman appears first, makes his little speech, then says he would like to introduce his family. First it is Mrs. Truman, then the daughter, and they get a big hand."[40] The press, though, sometimes framed Truman as a passive, and somewhat reluctant, campaigner. One article noted, "Mrs. Truman's role in the 1948 campaign will consist merely of accompanying her husband on trips." At a campaign stop in St. Louis, Truman was said to have "listened more passively" to her husband's speech than her daughter, who "smiled at the cutting thrusts of her father."[41] Despite being described as passive at times, Truman was mentioned in almost every article about her husband's campaign, which testifies to her constant presence on the campaign trail.

According to press constructions Eisenhower seemed genuinely to enjoy the social aspects of campaigning but was less interested in the political side.[42] One report said she was "the quintessential political wife, waving graciously and smiling at her husband's side." The *New York Times* said of Eisenhower, "To campaign crowds she showed a double-dimpled smile and a full-armed wave of greeting that reflected her liking for people. . . . Often the whistle-stop crowds yelled, 'We want Mamie,' until she appeared on the back platform."[43] Once again Truman and Eisenhower were both framed as their husbands' helpmates, supporting their careers by standing alongside them on the campaign platform. However, such appearances also furthered their status as public women.

Surprisingly, Roosevelt was also framed as a supportive wife in campaign stories. Roosevelt continually told the press she would not deliver campaign speeches, although her regular activities often had her speaking in support of her husband's policies. A 1936 story stated that Roosevelt "declined to make 'political speeches' on the grounds that she was sticking to a resolution to let the President talk politics for the family," a statement that sounds much like Eisenhower's claim in 1952 that "Ike speaks well enough for both of us."[44] These comments indicate that public speaking, especially on political issues, was still not a widely embraced activity for even publicly active women such as Roosevelt, who in fact was a prolific speaker. One notable exception was Roosevelt's speech at the Democratic National Convention in 1940, where she appeared as a surrogate for her husband.[45] Although she was hailed by the *New York Times* as "the first wife of a President or nominee ever to address a major political party conclave," there was little fanfare surrounding her speech. In fact, instead of focusing on the speech the headline proclaimed: "No Campaigning, First Lady States." Both the *Times* and the *Washington Post* published the full text of the speech, standard procedure in convention coverage, and the *Times* commended Roosevelt for "an impressively delivered appeal for a united country."[46] Despite the innovation of a first lady's addressing a nominating convention, the focus of the framing remained on Roosevelt as a supportive wife.

As in most two-person careers, homemaking and hostessing are the domain of presidential wives, making these a common frame in coverage of the first lady institution. Previous first ladies, when framed as hostesses, were generally lauded for their etiquette and social graces; in contrast, the first ladies of this period were constructed primarily as smart consumers and skilled hands-on managers, language that reflected the professionalization of homemaking. The first lady is the manager of the

White House and its enormous staff, overseeing everything from daily menus to planning state events to renovations of the historic home. Roosevelt embraced home economics, which "valiantly compared homemaking to nondomestic work, analyzed it with reference to its managerial and worker functions or its business and spiritual elements, and assimilated it to a professional model."[47] According to a *New York Times* article, "Mrs. Roosevelt has given practical expression of her faith in home economics by testing out in the White House menus prepared by Miss Flora Rose of Cornell University, in which science and economy were combined to afford a maximum of nourishment at a minimum cost." This was part of Roosevelt's plan to "cut down expenses at least 25 percent" in accordance with her husband's policy that all government departments cut back on expenses.[48] Truman was described as "a housewife who does her own marketing and cooking" and who "takes her housekeeping duties seriously." According to the *Washington Post*, "Her object is to provide a pleasant setting for her family, and to keep the budget down."[49] Similarly, a close friend of Eisenhower was quoted as saying, "Mamie is a very good housekeeper. She knows what's going on and how the money is being spent. She wants an orderly house." After moving into the White House, Eisenhower "took a firm hand in the housekeeping, mastering the complexities of the major operation quickly and imbuing it with the warmth of her personality."[50] Such press accounts assured the American public that, despite the existence of a trained White House staff, these first ladies were actively involved in managing the executive mansion's household budget and operations. Such framing highlights the domestic empowerment of the first lady, who exercised complete control over the home much like any workplace manager, thus promoting homemaking as a career that took on extreme importance in an era marked by the depression and fears of a possible postwar economic slump.[51]

Marital partnership and the various roles played by wives in a two-person career were the dominant themes of coverage of the first lady institution during this era. Although individual interpretations of those roles varied, domesticity permeated the framing of each first lady's performance of the position. Coverage of the institution evidences that "the idea of the presidential couple as a construct began to emerge. Politicians, reporters, and citizens began looking at the president and his wife as a team."[52] Although the partnership frame had appeared in earlier stories, it had not dominated discussions of the institution as it did during this period. The social, political, and economic conditions—from the paternalism of the New Deal to the domestic containment of the Cold War—provided a context for reporters to focus on presidential couples. Such coverage intensified the spotlight on first ladies' performance, turning women such as Roosevelt, Eisenhower, and Kennedy into media celebrities for they regularly appeared in newspapers and magazines. However, gender continued to dictate the press framing of these women, to the extent that they were constructed by journalists as role models for American womanhood.

Emergence of the First Lady as Political Celebrity

A residual effect of the heightened publicity surrounding the first lady institution is the construction of certain first ladies as political celebrities. The technologies of this era—particularly the development of radio and television, and print's mounting use of photographs—placed a greater emphasis on the projection of image and personality, which has been tied to the creation of a "celebrity culture."[53] The first lady's emergence as public woman allowed for her development as celebrity. As Roosevelt, Eisenhower, and Kennedy became more visible and vocal, through the attention given them in the mass media, they achieved celebrity status. Yet their celebrity was always connected with gender performance. Their individuality often disappeared as the press constructed them as representatives of gender ideologies and role models for American women. Thus, coverage of first ladies as political celebrities grew out of the previous era's press practice of personification framing and the legitimization of the first lady as public woman. It also represented a press phenomenon where women journalists, empowered in their role as writers, constructed first ladies as important political figures.

The names of Roosevelt, Eisenhower, and Kennedy became synonymous with a particular vision of American womanhood during their tenures. Roosevelt achieved celebrity status through her unprecedented activity and activism as first lady. For reporters, she represented the expansion of women's, and the first lady's, political roles during the Depression and wartime era. Her successors embodied the "domestic containment" of the Cold War and its focus on women's civic contributions as housewives and consumers. Eisenhower and Kennedy acquired celebrity largely through the images they projected of femininity. Their styles and fashions came to represent the 1950s and early 1960s. Through the treatment of the first ladies as celebrities, journalists presented them as role models worthy of emulation by American women.

Roosevelt became a celebrity through her unparalleled activity as first lady. She was viewed by many, including the women journalists who covered her, as the personification of women's progress and the expansion of the first lady position. *Good Housekeeping* writer Rita Halle stated, "No other First Lady did one half the things Mrs. Roosevelt has done, broke precedent the way she has broken it, or was in the limelight of the news so much or so often. . . . She breaks precedent by doing things, not by failing to do them. The difference between her and the other First Ladies is not in the things she leaves undone, but in those she adds to what others have done." Roosevelt's precedents contributed to her celebrity, which she achieved independent of her husband. According to Elizabeth Gertrude Stein of the *New York Times,* "Roosevelt is the first to be a public figure and personage in her own right. Mistress of the White House, lecturer, a writer, civic leader, she is unique in the long line to which she belongs." In 1936 reporter Kathleen McLaughlin claimed that, "whatever may be said of her in this controversial period, [Roosevelt] will at least go on record as having made articulate that lay figure, the presidential wife, who from the era of George Washington had been officially mute." McLaughlin wrote again about Roosevelt in a 1944 profile: "She is no whit different from the energetic, indefatigable speaker, organizer, and executive who kept the public gasping during her first months in the White House. She still tosses off incredible numbers of tasks in any working day, still covers challenging distances, still accepts and discharges an imposing number of engagements, still extends hospitality to individuals, prominent and obscure." Such positive framing of Roosevelt's political activities not only constructed her as a political celebrity but also gave tacit approval to the expansion of the first lady's duties.[54]

Reporters also positioned Roosevelt as a role model for women's expanding public activity, political advocacy, and individual agency. Women were encouraged to emulate Roosevelt by becoming more politically active. Throughout her tenure Roosevelt persuaded women to get involved in political organizations, to run for political office, and to use their political power both through the ballot and by working in their communities. She entreated women to support labor unions and women workers by refusing to purchase garments made in sweatshops.[55] Roosevelt went as far as crediting her accomplishments to the expanding roles of American women. Upon receiving an award as "America's best-known woman broadcaster" from the National Association of Broadcasters in 1945, Roosevelt stated, "I couldn't have done anything as the wife of the President unless the women were accepting responsibilities and playing a great part in a great period."[56] Roosevelt's political celebrity was viewed as exceptional, particularly by a press corps composed predominantly of women, whom Roosevelt had empowered through her press conferences. These journalists consistently noted that Roosevelt's activities were unique, not only for women but for first ladies also. Such coverage extended the boundaries of women's political activism, showing more positive consequences of a first lady's achieved celebrity status.

Eisenhower and Kennedy were also positioned by the press as political celebrities, but they were framed quite differently. For the press and public Eisenhower exemplified Cold War domesticity, to the point that the mere mention of the name Mamie conjured a particular image for Americans in the 1950s. Eisenhower "embodied the traditional role expected of most American women during the 1950s—to be, above all, a devoted wife." For the most part, "Mrs. Eisenhower was portrayed by the press as a personification of the feminine mystique." An example comes from Nona B. Brown's article about the 1956 campaign, in which Eisenhower was constructed as the personification of domesticity: "Mrs. Eisenhower has generated a popular picture of herself as a warm, generous, friendly woman who devotes herself to her husband and family. This is a first lady stereotype that is immensely popular, so Mamie has merely to appear with Ike, even if only on a television screen, to evoke the warmest kind of response." The Eisenhowers used Mamie's popularity and celebrity status to their advantage throughout their eight years in the White House.[57]

Eisenhower's celebrity was tied largely to her fashionable appearance, and stories focused on how she personified Cold War consumption. According to the *New York Times,* "'Mamie' is an affectionately regarded and familiar image to millions—with the little hats with matching gloves, bags, and shoes; the costume jewelry chosen for the right touch and the charm bracelets jangling with the symbols of her husband's career."[58] Some designers "sniffed at Mamie's relish for dyed-to-match shoes and colored stockings, mink coats, charm bracelets and bangs. In the end, however, what she called 'looking high class'—adorning a basic style with marks of familial success and individuality—came to be known as 'the Mamie look.'" Meanwhile "Mamie's fetish for pink," widely publicized through the press, "may have helped to confirm the ultimate feminization of the color." By 1955 "Mamie Pink" was a popular color for everything from dresses and hats to dishware and linoleum flooring.[59] In 1957 Eisenhower wore pale yellow at the inaugural ball, and a reporter predicted that, "as a result this color will be showing up in clothing, home furnishings, paints, plastics, and automobiles."[60] The plethora of products associated with Eisenhower in this article was representative of the postwar focus on consumerism. Eisenhower's celebrity was linked to her personification of commodification as she embodied style and fashion and in turn promoted the products associated with her.

Eisenhower's celebrity was attributed to consumption; her image was dependent on products, from hats to minks to charms, which in turn inspired the creation of more consumer goods that were tied, however loosely, to that image of the 1950s woman. A *New York Times* story gave Eisenhower credit for shaping her image: "She has carefully considered her own stage presence, never appearing at any event without being 'turned out' for the occasion." This statement credits Eisenhower with carefully cultivating an image personifying the feminine ideal promoted by her husband's administration and representing many "depression-weary Americans [who] were eager to put the disruptions and hardships of war behind them and enjoy the abundance at home." Like TV's June Cleaver and Donna Reed, "Mamie" became synonymous with white middle-class women in the 1950s.[61]

Kennedy was something of an idol in the early 1960s, projecting a very different image from Eisenhower's and representing a younger generation of American housewives. Kennedy's celebrity, like that of her predecessor, was associated mainly with consumption, however. Kennedy's fashions were treated by the press not so much as an expression of her personality but as a visible indicator of the shifting cultural climate. According to a *New York Times* article, "'Fantastically chic' was the phrase most often applied to her." The story went on to say that Kennedy was "a pace-setter who has worn sausage-skin pants, streaked hair, chemise dresses and sleeveless tunics long before they became popular currency. At 30, she has the tall, slender, and rather muscular figure that seems to inspire creative American designers and the younger crop of Parisian couturiers."[62]

Kennedy's celebrity and image were appropriated by retailers looking to sell the "Jackie look" to American women seeking to emulate the first lady. The *Washington Post* noted that "the entire fashion industry from wholesale to retail is discovering that the 'Jackie Kennedy look' is the hottest merchandising gimmick since Shirley Temple dolls." The article stated that the pillbox hat, which has become associated with Kennedy in collective memory, was one of the top trends of 1961: "Pillbox hats are moving off millinery counters like soda pop at a Fourth of July picnic. Bonwit Teller, which advertised the pillbox sketched on a model who looked like a twin of the President-elect's wife, has found that customers are asking for 'the Kennedy hat.'"[63] Kennedy's style came to define her to such an extent that an entire museum exhibit featuring her fashions and accessories was developed in 2001. According to curator Hamish Bowles, Kennedy "was at once a paradigm of old-fashioned dignity, sharing with her husband a love of history and a keen appreciation of ceremony, and a reluctant pop-culture icon, who like John F. Kennedy, had an intuitive understanding of the power of image in an age when television was becoming a potent medium."[64] As they had with "Mamie" before her, reporters used "Jackie" as shorthand, in this case for the youthful and sophisticated style that Kennedy embodied. Despite her dislike of public life Kennedy became an international celebrity who still represents the ideal of American womanhood in the early 1960s.

Celebrity can be both empowering and constraining. Celebrity status empowers women, and first ladies, by normalizing the presence of women as celebrated individuals in the public sphere. Roosevelt, Eisenhower, and Kennedy each represented a different performance of American womanhood, reflecting the changes in women's lives during these years. Roosevelt embodied the feminist ideal of women's political activity, while Eisenhower and Kennedy promoted women's role as Cold War consumers. Such framing, in stories featured both on the front pages as well as in women's publications, was instrumental in perpetuating the political celebrity of first ladies.

Through the media and their own image-making activities, these first ladies became celebritized public women, alleviating the stigma once associated with public womanhood, publicity, and women's agency. Roosevelt, in particular, represented women's potential as political leaders. Her constant claims that she was not different from the average American woman equated her accomplishments with the achievements of all women and elevated the contributions women made to civic life. Treating first ladies as celebrities recognizes the important role played by these women in American culture and celebrates the power and influence of women, even when that power is tied to traditionally feminine activities such as shopping. Particularly when celebrity is linked to domesticity, the roles that women play in both public and private are elevated, once again indicating a sense of "domestic empowerment," which characterized much of the coverage of first ladies during this era.

Celebrity, however, can also be limiting. One danger is that celebrity "articulates the individual as commodity," reducing a person to an image that can then be sold in the public sphere.[65] Such was the case with Eisenhower and Kennedy, whose individual agency was often lost in the process. By linking women with consumption, women's power was confined to more gendered and thus less threatening activities within the male public sphere. Whereas emulating Roosevelt required women to become politically active individuals, imitating Eisenhower or Kennedy called on women to consume, to limit their public power to buying a toaster in "Mamie pink" or wearing a "Jackie pillbox." Certainly the positive coverage given to Roosevelt expanded the political boundaries for women, yet the prevalent focus on consumption then reduced first ladies' influence. Rather than being positioned as models of American citizenship, their public performances were treated as representing mere consumption, which yielded visions of limited political influence for American women.

Conclusion

In 1936 writer Fannie Hurst proclaimed, "As for the one who follows [Roosevelt] into the White House, I say, God help her. I'm confident there will be no going back to the pastel tradition" of former first ladies.[66] The position quickly reverted to the "pastel traditions" that Hurst decried, however, and the White House was dominated by "Mamie Pink" throughout the 1950s. An examination of press coverage of the institution reveals a common theme defining these years. This was an ideology of domesticity that simultaneously empowered and restrained American women, including first ladies.

The first ladies of this era personified the various incarnations of the domestic ideal, from the maternalism of social feminism and republican motherhood to Cold War domesticity with its domestic containment and empowerment of the homemaker. This era has largely been dismissed in feminist histories because it did not feature an active woman's movement. When this "in-between" period is mentioned, it is usually derided for its focus on domesticity and the so-called feminine mystique, considered the source of "the problem with no name" in the 1960s. If press coverage of the first lady is any indication, however, the homemaker was not as powerless as Friedan made her appear. The homemaker was recognized by the press as exerting authority over her domestic space, particularly through her role as consumer, which tied her activities also to the public and political spheres during times of both economic crisis and prosperity. This acknowledgment of the political efficacy of women's traditional roles can be viewed as an important first step in creating a feminist consciousness recognizing that "the personal is political." Meanwhile, by positioning first ladies as role models for American women, the press normalized women's presence in public life and women's burgeoning political involvement, which would set the stage for the emergence of the woman's movement of the following era. The voices of first ladies were more frequently featured in the press through direct quotes, and their images as publicly active women were widely circulated. These women assumed a much more active role in the construction of their own image, though their voices and images were still filtered by the press, albeit one made up in part by other women acting outside the private sphere. By recognizing the roles these first ladies played both as individuals and in their husband's campaigns and careers, journalists validated women's experiences as significant and newsworthy.

The first ladies of this era were viewed by the press as part of a marital partnership, and press framing of the first lady's duties focused primarily on her part in the two-person career. Such framing simultaneously reinforced traditional gender roles while imbuing wifely duties with political significance. The personal and public activities of these presidential wives became political, from appearing as supportive wives on the campaign trail, acting as presidential surrogates, or managing the White House. As one author notes, "No First Lady since Eleanor Roosevelt—including Bess Truman and Mamie Eisenhower—could avoid involvement in the politi-

cal fray. Each presidency since the Roosevelts has thus been, to one extent or another, a co-presidency," focused mainly on "joint image-making,
not power-sharing."[67] Press framing of the first lady's duties supports this
statement as the activities of most first ladies were consistently framed as
extensions of their role as presidents' wives, thus reinforcing the gendered performance of the position. Nevertheless, first ladies, like American women in general, were recognized as now playing a larger role as
citizens. They may have been cast as wives and mothers with their main
stage being the home, but nonetheless they were also recognized by the
press as important players in the nation's political drama.

One of the most notable changes in this period was the elevation of
certain first ladies from public women to celebrity status. The development of the first lady as public woman in the modern era coupled with
the journalistic practice of personification framing led to the establishment of Roosevelt, Eisenhower, and Kennedy as gendered celebrities.
These women were each recognized as a public figure in her own right,
which granted them a level of agency often denied to previous first ladies
and to women in general. Roosevelt, in particular, was lauded for her individual political accomplishments and her contributions to both women's
progress and the expansion of the first lady institution. Her successors
were among the most recognizable figures of this era, and their styles and
fashions were enthusiastically copied by American women. By positioning these first ladies as role models, journalists recognized women's growing public influence on American politics and culture. Even when their civic
contributions were limited to consumption, women were recognized as contributing to the postwar economy, which thereby imbued their actions with
a sense of political efficacy. Such a focus on consumption reveals how
women's public and political role was contained ideologically. Centering
women's agency in shopping for self and family reduces the chance of their
rallying against political oppression at a time when women's public and political influence began to grow.

The coverage of the first lady institution during this era evidences a
period of mounting political activity for women and an ongoing debate
over women's roles in American society. These stories are instructive to
today's scholars who seek to contest the notion that the struggle for
women's rights was limited to the historical periods referred to as the first
and second waves of feminism. The pervasiveness of domesticity in the
framing of the first lady institution and the growing celebrity of first
ladies would be challenged by the social and political upheaval and
changing cultural norms of the following decades. Press coverage would
focus on the quandary of the next generation of first ladies: whether to
question or accept domesticity as a defining quality of both the first lady
institution and American womanhood.

The First Lady as Political Activist, 1964–1977

*I*n the March 1964 issue of *Ladies' Home Journal* Katie Louchheim observed that the "evolution of the role of First Lady in America during the past half century has been . . . almost as dramatic and sweeping as the expansion of the role of the Chief Executive." The most significant development was the power acquired by the first lady through her position as a public figure: "Regardless of how much distaste the First Lady may possess for public life, her role can no longer be a private one; she acquires indirect power when her husband takes the oath of office as President of the United States. This power, or influence, a complex and delicate mixture of various social, political, and moral forces, bears upon nearly every important situation and tradition in our national life." Louchheim recognized the influence that accompanies celebrity status in American culture. Even the title of the article, "The Spotlight Shifts in Washington: A New First Lady Moves to Center Stage," indicated the celebrity associated with the first lady position and the evolution of her influence, as she moved from public woman to political celebrity.[1]

The gendering of the first ladies' celebrity continued as the press constructed these presidential wives as role models for American women. The article said of Jacqueline Kennedy: "Her grace and charm as a White House hostess, her quiet pride in her family life, and her heroism in the face of a senseless tragedy have been brought to Americans in hundreds of pictures and articles." Kennedy was framed as hostess, mother, and wife, all traditional feminine roles, even though her performance of those roles occurred on the most public of stages. Gendered frames were also used to describe her successor, Lady Bird Johnson, but with different results. Louchheim stated, "It would never do for a well-bred Southern lady to admit to possession of the tools of the intellect. Lady Bird's deceptively feminine demeanor serves as a suitable disguise for a woman of stature and substance."[2] This article not only highlights the performative aspects of both gender and the first lady position but also foreshadows a shift toward a more politically savvy, and active, first lady.

By the 1960s every first lady "was a political wife and a veteran of campaign and public life."[3] During this thirteen-year period four political wives held the first lady position, though three of them served incomplete terms. Claudia Taylor "Lady Bird" Johnson (1963–1969) assumed the role following the assassination of President Kennedy. (Thelma) Patricia Ryan Nixon (1969–1974) left the White House upon her husband's resignation in the wake of Watergate, which promoted Betty Bloomer Ford (1974–1977) to the first lady position. Only Rosalynn Smith Carter (1977–1980) served an uninterrupted full tenure in the White House. These women played active roles in their husbands' political careers, although their approaches differed because of their personalities and interests. When their husbands were elected to or assumed prestigious government positions, these women found themselves in the public spotlight, faced with both the benefits and the constraints of celebrity.

As in earlier eras, journalistic framing of first ladies from 1964 to 1977 mirrored the cultural climate, especially in relation to women's place in society. In the past, true womanhood was a prevailing gender ideology; during this period second-wave feminism dominated the discourse. The perception of domesticity as "the feminine mystique" gave the "true woman" ideology a negative connotation.[4] The ideals of feminism and domesticity were often viewed as opposites, particularly after the antifeminist movement embraced domesticity as women's "true" nature. It is somewhat surprising that the biggest shift in the dominant discourse was seen in women's magazines, which tended to promote domesticity. "Women's lib" now became a major issue for these publications. Articles celebrated the new "liberated" (albeit white) woman and encouraged their readers to expand their interests beyond the home. The first ladies of the era found themselves caught up in this second wave of feminism. Johnson, Ford, and Carter personified the "contemporary woman," successfully balancing career and family. In contrast Nixon embodied the Cold War domesticity of the previous era, which was often criticized during the height of feminist activity.

The women's liberation movement influenced how journalists framed the duties of the first lady position also. Journalists compared these activities to women's growing activism, and the different first ladies' various performances were viewed as an expansion of women's roles beyond the domestic sphere. Journalists indicated that being "just a wife" was no longer enough for the first lady. Instead they accentuated her various political roles such as presidential advisor, campaigner, surrogate, and independent advocate. This framing infused the first lady institution with power and gave rise to the first lady as political activist. Rather than mere helpmates, activist first ladies such as Johnson, Ford, and Carter were seen as playing an influential role in the "co-career" they shared with their husbands; conversely Nixon was framed as a more traditional political wife and thus considered a less influential first lady.

The political activism, or lack thereof, of first ladies also impacted press constructions of these women as political celebrities. The rise of a more adversarial relationship between politicians and the press during this era resulted in a more critical reporting style, which impacted the first lady coverage also. Journalists concentrated on gauging the expanding political influence of these first ladies, scrutinizing their performance of the position and comparing them to former first ladies who had achieved iconic status. Such reporting led to critiques regarding the extent of their influence, which sometimes resulted in double binds, often perpetuated by women's leaders, women's magazines, and at times women journalists, who simultaneously both promoted first ladies as political activists and challenged the appropriateness of their power. Such framing established the notion that first ladies were central to women's culture, with their expertise related primarily to women's issues. Yet women's issues were still marginal to the male political sphere. And when these first ladies expanded their interests beyond women's issues, critiques of their actions increased. The result was a no-win situation for activist first ladies when their influence extended too far beyond women's designated space for political activities. On the other hand Nixon's lack of activity was also criticized, which resulted in a no-win situation for her as well. Thus, coverage of first ladies in the 1960s and 1970s in many ways reflected the paradoxes of women's lives that were addressed by second-wave feminism.

Competing Gender Ideologies — Liberating Women from the Feminine Mystique

The social and political unrest of the 1960s and 1970s provided a fertile environment for the so-called rebirth of feminism. Feminism had never really disappeared from the cultural landscape, but the lack of an active feminist movement coupled with the dominance of the domestic discourse overshadowed the feminist activity of the post-suffrage era. Thus, the revival of an organized social movement in the 1960s has been referred to as the "second wave" of feminism. The contradictions then developing in women's lives coupled with the constraints of the home-maker role during the Cold War era played an important part in the resurgence of a feminist movement in the 1960s. As women began to evaluate their lives, the "old feminist calls for economic and political equality, and a new emphasis on control over reproduction, resonated deeply across generations, classes, and races."[5] But the "new" feminism did not resonate with all Americans. The movement faced ridicule from many men, women, and media outlets, as well as vigorous attacks from well-organized opponents who embraced women's traditional domestic roles. Despite these challenges, however, the call for women's liberation was successful in generating widespread discussions of gender roles.

The emergence of twentieth-century first ladies as public women and political celebrities evidenced women's spreading presence in the political sphere and laid the groundwork for women's political activism. By "going public" through the press in the earlier part of the century, first ladies had alleviated the stigma surrounding female publicity and normalized women's roles as public figures in their own right. As some of the most prominent political women, first ladies represented for journalists women's growing influence, whether as social activists or as consumers. Although gendered framing continued to characterize first ladies' activities as extensions of women's traditional domestic roles, which alternately served to justify, contain, and depoliticize women's power, the steady expansion of news coverage of the first lady institution throughout the century helped justify women as news makers and women's issues and activities as newsworthy. Both the social feminism of women such as Eleanor Roosevelt and the domestic empowerment and containment of the Cold War consumer set the stage for the reemergence of an active women's movement in the 1960s.

A handful of events in the early 1960s are often credited with prompting the development of a social movement focusing specifically on women's rights. The formation of the 1961 President's Commission on the Status of Women, chaired by Eleanor Roosevelt, was one such precipitous act. The commission's report *American Women,* released in 1963, outlined discrimination against women in all facets of American life and particularly in the workplace, where women earned up to 40 percent less than their male counterparts. Members of the president's commission lobbied for the Equal Pay Act, passed in June 1963, which mandated "equal pay for equal work." It was the first federal legislation to prohibit sexual discrimination. The following year, Title VII of the 1964 Civil Rights Act barred discrimination in employment on the basis of "race, color, religion, sex, or national origin." This established the Equal Employment Opportunity Commission (EEOC) to field complaints regarding bias in the workplace. When it became clear that the EEOC was not enforcing the ban on sex discrimination, a group of delegates to the 1966 Conference of the Commissions on the Status of Women came together with activists such as Betty Friedan to form the National Organization for

Women (NOW), which quickly became the leading organization in the burgeoning women's liberation movement.[6]

Friedan's *Feminine Mystique*, published in 1963, often receives credit for providing the ideological foundation for second-wave feminism. Friedan's book "generated the kind of attention that made feminism a popular topic of conversation once again." Friedan claimed that countless American women, deprived of the chance to develop their own identity, were suffering from a growing discontent with their roles as housewives and mothers. She argued that the so-called feminine mystique "makes the housewife-mother, who never had a chance to be anything else, the model for all women." Friedan's solution was for women to reject the feminine mystique and develop lives of their own, primarily through education and careers. Although her analysis was heavily biased toward the experiences of white middle- or upper-class women, the popularity of the book began a cultural debate concerning women's roles. Even if readers disagreed with Friedan's conclusions, "they could not help but to reexamine their own lives in light of the questions it raised."[7]

Although "radical" feminists were some of the earliest women's rights activists of this period, "liberal" feminists represented for the media the mainstream of the women's movement. Groups such as NOW and the National Women's Political Caucus (formed in 1971) had identifiable leaders such as Betty Friedan, Gloria Steinem, and congresswoman Bella Abzug—willing representatives who were experienced in dealing with the media. Liberal feminists tackled a number of issues, from abortion rights to equal pay and the Equal Rights Amendment (ERA). The "Women's Strike for Equality" on August 26, 1970, commemorated the fiftieth anniversary of the passage of the Nineteenth Amendment and marked the beginning of women's liberation as a mass movement. The strike also marked a milestone in media coverage of the movement. The strike received front-page coverage in national newspapers including the *New York Times* and led the evening newscasts on all three networks. For the first time women's liberation activity reached the status of "hard news."[8]

The women's liberation movement continued to make headlines, as feminists claimed a number of key legislative victories in the 1970s. Record numbers of women charged employers with sexual discrimination in hiring and promotion, including female employees at major magazines such as *Newsweek, Time,* and the *Ladies' Home Journal,* where over one hundred feminists staged an eleven-hour sit-in. In 1972 the Supreme Court began applying the Fourteenth Amendment to cases of alleged sexual discrimination. In 1973 the Court handed down the landmark *Roe v. Wade* decision legalizing abortion. Among those bills passed in 1972 alone were Title IX of the Higher Education Act, the Equal Opportunity Act, and the ERA. The latter was overwhelmingly approved by Congress on March 22, 1972, and sent to the states for ratification. Despite continued efforts in support of a number of issues, the ERA and its ratification became the mobilizing issue for feminist activism in the late 1970s and often dominated discussions of the women's movement, especially in the media.[9]

Congressional passage of the ERA then crystallized an organized movement that directly challenged feminism by promoting traditional gender roles. In 1972 Phyllis Schlafly established the National Committee to Stop ERA. As Susan Douglas put it, Schlafly "became a media celebrity, and the media became her most powerful weapon." Schlafly stumped across the United States arguing that women would be deprived of their rights as wives and mothers and that the ERA would lead to a variety of problems, from the drafting of women into the military to unisex bathrooms. While liberal feminists argued that the separate spheres philosophy should be eradicated, Schlafly and her supporters countered with the claim that women and men were biologically different and that the domestic sphere should be protected. The highly publicized protest activities of Schlafly and the anti-ERA movement receive much of the credit or blame for defeating the constitutional amendment and certainly contributed to the backlash against feminism in the 1980s.[10]

Despite the failure to ratify the ERA, feminists claimed a number of victories in the 1960s and 1970s. The "second wave" of feminism brought more women into public and political life than ever before, from the rising number of working women to the housewives who joined Schlafly's Stop ERA movement. One of the most important contributions of the second wave of feminism was "the redefinition of the political to include both public and private realms, both male and female concerns," which extended the work done by earlier public women including first ladies.[11] Women's issues once considered private such as abortion or breast cancer were being discussed in public forums and were making front-page news. The widespread social discussion regarding gender roles prompted by second-wave feminism heightened the salience of women's issues for the press. Through the press, the first ladies were now among countless Americans engaging in public debate over women's changing roles.

Framing the First Lady during the Second Wave

Press framing of the first lady institution between 1964 and 1977 mirrored the cultural conversation regarding women's roles sparked by second-wave feminist activity. Coverage focused heavily on the public and political activities of the first ladies. Johnson, Ford, and Carter personified for journalists the "contemporary woman" who balanced traditional roles with feminist activism. In contrast Nixon embodied Cold War domesticity.

While her public activity was on a par with that of her contemporaries, she was often criticized for her lack of activism and was characterized as a throwback to the previous era. The result of such framing was the emergence of the first lady as political activist. However, as the period wore on, journalists questioned the extent, the limitations, and the appropriateness of first ladies' political influence.

PERSONIFYING THE CONTEMPORARY WOMAN OF THE SECOND WAVE

Just as domesticity had defined women's roles in the previous era, second-wave feminist ideals pervaded discussions of American womanhood during the 1960s and 1970s. Women's magazines such as the *Ladies' Home Journal* praised "the power of a woman," proclaiming in the September 1969 issue, "The contemporary woman—better-educated, longer-lived, more involved in her community and the world—has a greater opportunity to improve and change the society around her."[12] The expanding public and political activities of the first ladies now encouraged journalists to draw parallels between the activism of the first ladies and the activism of American women. For the press, particularly women's magazines, Johnson, Ford, and Carter were fitting role models for American women, in part because they supported feminist ideals without rejecting women's traditional roles. While Nixon personified the more traditional political wife, she was still recognized as a public figure in her own right, but in some cases Nixon represented the limitations of the "feminine mystique" so widely praised just a decade earlier.

The ideal contemporary woman, according to journalists, was now able to move beyond the confines of the domestic sphere without abandoning her family, or her femininity. In introducing their "Women of the Year" in 1976, for example, *Ladies' Home Journal* stressed that their awardees, who included scientists, educators, and leaders from various feminist, civil rights, and women's groups, "do not mark down the woman who moves in a smaller sphere—the wife, mother, and homemaker who expresses herself in the creation of a home and family. (Indeed, many of these women have played that role.) Instead, their example proves that women today have many options, many talents, many goals."[13] Thus, the contemporary women of the second wave balanced domestic duties with careers, civic responsibilities, and interests independent of their husbands and children, embodying both the activist spirit of second-wave feminism and the domesticity of traditional homemakers. This "superwomanly" ideal, which had first appeared during the modern era, would become synonymous with second-wave feminism's contention that women could "have it all."[14]

For journalists, the first ladies of this era often personified contemporary womanhood, serving as role models for women who sought to balance their many private and public responsibilities. In a 1965 *Good Housekeeping* profile, anthropologist Margaret Mead defined Lady Bird Johnson as "a model for any responsible American woman, whoever she may be and wherever she may live." Mead noted, "In her picture of contemporary women Mrs. Johnson includes married and unmarried women, career women and volunteers, all of whom she calls on in one sweeping challenge to be responsible individuals." Drawing on Friedan's work, Mead claimed that Johnson was "not troubled by what has been called the 'feminine mystique.' In her own life she has combined home and children and career, hard, exacting, successful activities for which she has taken full responsibility, and happy cooperation with her husband." Ruth Montgomery, in another *Good Housekeeping* article, similarly noted that Johnson "proved herself not only a devoted wife and mother, but also a canny business executive and a seasoned political trouper." Christine Sadler's profile of Johnson in *McCall's* referred to Friedan's work, albeit indirectly, observing, "Not surprisingly, fancy treatises examining the status of women as an abstruse problem amuse her; but her interest in encouraging projects begun by women, or encouraging their broader education could hardly be more real." Johnson frequently spoke to audiences of young women, persuading them to become public women. According to a 1964 *New York Times* article, she told an audience that "women must take their place in public life as well as in home life," stating, "Women can no longer afford to concern themselves only with the hearth—any more than men can afford to concern themselves only with their job." Mead concluded that by giving "new dignity to the role of wife, as one facet in the life of a 'total woman,'" Johnson was a model of "what other American women can do and be in the mid-20th century." For reporters, then, Johnson's actions and ideals embodied the spirit of the contemporary woman who balanced family, career, and civic responsibilities. Johnson also reflected the ideals of the developing women's liberation movement by encouraging women to expand their horizons beyond the domestic sphere.[15]

The ability to balance femininity and feminism was another essential characteristic of the contemporary woman. According to reporters, both Johnson and Rosalynn Carter managed to attain this balance. Montgomery's *Good Housekeeping* profile of Johnson claimed that "behind her mild Southern manner is a remarkably capable and energetic executive. . . . In addition to being competent, the new First Lady is friendly, good-looking, intelligent and faultlessly groomed." Johnson's feminine manner and appearance are paired with references to her intelligence and abilities. William V. Shannon of the *New York Times* similarly proclaimed that, in

Carter, "the nation's women have acquired an articulate and attractive spokeswoman, one who is a loving wife and devoted mother and also a strong, independent personality in her own right." By describing Carter as both articulate and attractive, a wife and mother and also a "strong, independent personality," Shannon highlighted the required balance of feminine and feminist characteristics. Several stories highlighted the femininity of Johnson and Carter by drawing on their southern heritage. Elizabeth Janeway of *Ladies' Home Journal* said of Johnson, "Her voice is Deep South . . . but Lady Bird Johnson is neither a Southern Belle nor a Southern Bigot. People who have begun to listen to her words instead of her accent find that her speech is tangy, terse, and individual."[16] Carter was often referred to as a "steel magnolia," a phrase associated with southern women's mix of gentility and strength.[17] A *New York Times Magazine* feature maintained, "After only two months in the White House, the 'steel magnolia' with the soft drawl promises to be the most active First Lady in decades." According to the same story, she handled an appearance on *Meet the Press* "with the aplomb of Scarlet O'Hara," referencing fiction's archetypal steel magnolia.[18] Such framing feminized these women, particularly their voice, by once again balancing their political acumen with aspects of femininity.

The balancing act performed by contemporary women was viewed by some reporters as an embodiment of the feminist mantra "the personal is political." By sharing the most intimate details of her life with the press, Betty Ford personified how the personal was inseparable from the political, particularly for first ladies. Known for her outspokenness Ford freely admitted "to smoking, being divorced, seeing a psychiatrist, taking tranquilizers, drinking with her husband and—heaven forbid—sleeping with him," making her someone that women could identify with. Myra MacPherson in the *Washington Post* noted that Ford "was able to play many different roles and that left the public with the notion that she was a completely modern female." This article highlighted the idea that contemporary women could support women's liberation without rejecting traditional domestic roles. In 1976 Ford was named one of *Ladies' Home Journal's* "Women of the Year" for her "inspirational leadership" in making public her personal health crisis. Ford was lauded for "her courage and outspoken candor in her battle with breast cancer" and for being "an inspiration to women everywhere." By publicizing her experience with breast cancer Ford raised awareness of an important women's health issue at a time when breast cancer was rarely discussed even within families, let alone in public.[19]

The contemporary woman, who often now ventured beyond the domestic sphere, was viewed as distinct from the Cold War homemaker, whose devotion to domesticity was derided by feminists as the "feminine mystique." For journalists Pat Nixon symbolized the feminine mystique, and she was often framed as being out of step with the times. For example, *Washington Post* reporter Dorothy McCardle called Nixon "a dutiful wife in the old-time sense." Susanna McBee in a 1970 *McCall's* profile described Nixon as "the paradigm of the proper, dutiful wife, and the proper, dutiful wife always defers to her husband, especially a husband whose career is politics." Elaine Tyler May wrote, "Women of the fifties, constrained by tremendous cultural and economic pressures to conform to domestic containment, gave up their independence and personal ambitions." Nixon was framed as one of those women whose spirit, as Lenore Hershey observed, had been "submerged forever in her relentlessly ambitious husband's career." In a July 1968 *Good Housekeeping* article, Flora Rheta Schreiber described Nixon as "selfless," noting that "her husband's career has always come first." When reporters constructed Nixon as the dutiful wife, their tone was often negative, even mocking the domestic ideal that had dominated news framing of women through the early 1960s.[20]

During the second-wave feminism, journalists' practice of personification framing drew the first lady into the cultural debate over women's changing roles. By personifying the contemporary woman or the feminine mystique, the first ladies of this period called attention to the women's movement.[21] By linking first ladies, treated as role models for American women, to the women's movement, journalists legitimized feminist ideology as an acceptable way to define American womanhood. This type of framing appeared most frequently in women's magazines, which embraced the women's liberation movement while still touting domesticity. For these publications in particular, Johnson, Ford, and Carter each represented the superwoman, managing to balance her public and private roles and illustrating that women could be both contemporary and traditional. Such personification framing led to a focus on the role of first ladies as political activists.

THE EMERGENCE OF FIRST LADY AS POLITICAL ACTIVIST

Coverage of the first lady institution during the 1960s and 1970s concentrated primarily on the public and political activities of these women, often framing them as their husbands' political partners. Even profiles in women's magazines, which traditionally highlighted their domestic roles, focused more on the political aspects of the first lady position. The first lady as political activist was an extension of the first lady as public woman and political celebrity as well as an outgrowth of the second-wave personification framing's focus on women's activism. Like their predecessors these first ladies played various political roles, including presidential advisor, campaigner, and social advocate. They took advantage of their celebrity status and recognized that their power rested chiefly in the publicity associated with the first lady position.

Her public activity was an overarching frame throughout this era in stories about the first lady's performance. For journalists the terms "activity" and "activism" were often conflated, which influenced their discussions of the first lady's duties. Johnson, Ford, and Carter were all defined, by the press and by themselves, as "active" first ladies. Johnson was frequently referred to as a "can-do woman." Mead in *Good Housekeeping* stated that Johnson "defined her role as one whose significance must 'emerge in deeds, not words.'" Her numerous travels across the United States—campaigning for her husband, his "Great Society" programs, and her cause of beautification—supported this statement. Ford, during her first news conference, told the press she intended to be "an active first lady," working on behalf of the ERA and promoting the arts as well as programs for children and the elderly. Likewise, a *New York Times* headline proclaimed, "Mrs. Carter Planning Active Role in Capitol," and Carter's press secretary, Mary Finch Hoyt, predicted that "Rosalynn will be more active and effective than any First Lady in years." Like Johnson, Carter traveled extensively, representing her husband both at home and abroad. And like Ford, she lobbied for the ERA, while also acting as an advocate for mental health and the elderly and advising her husband on those issues and others. However, the rise of first ladies' political activism remained gendered, as these women focused their energies primarily on causes associated with women, children, and beautification.[22]

Nixon was the exception within this group. The level of her activity was similar to that of her contemporaries, but in terms of trips at home and abroad, campaigning, and public appearances, her performance of the role was judged as more passive because she was less political than her counterparts. McBee observed in her *McCall's* profile of Nixon, "She wants to be an active First Lady. She wants to urge people to work voluntarily in their communities, but she seems to think that visiting a few projects and making a report will achieve that purpose." McBee speculated, "I believe that Mrs. Nixon does indeed want to do inspiring things as First Lady, but she has been the docile wife for so long that it is hard now to shift gears."[23] Nixon's failure to politicize her efforts in an era defined by women's political activism often made her the target of criticism.

While many first ladies throughout history functioned as close political advisors to their husbands, the activist first ladies of this era were more frequently framed this way by the press. A 1964 article in *Good Housekeeping* argued that Johnson "has always considered herself—and been considered—her husband's partner in all his affairs," while a profile in *McCall's* claimed, "she and the President are a team and always have been." Johnson was quoted by the *Washington Post* as saying that her husband accorded her "the fine compliment of thinking I have good judgment and he also knows that I will tell him as I see it." She routinely helped her husband prepare his speeches, and he often consulted her regarding his "Great Society" programs. According to a *New York Times* article about Johnson's mail, the public recognized her advisory role: "There are more 'tell-it-to-the-president' letters to the First Lady than there have been in Administrations back to Franklin D. Roosevelt." According to an aide, "Mrs. Johnson is so interested in anything having to do with legislation that people are writing in encouraging her to prod the President a little bit on different legislative matters, or telling her to commend him on various stands, such as the war on poverty."[24] Like Johnson, Carter was framed by the press as one of her husband's closest advisors. The *New York Times* pointed out that "Mr. Carter has described his wife as his 'best friend and chief advisor.'" Carter said, "Jimmy respects my judgment on things, that's all. I think I have some influence on him." Carter became famous for sitting in on cabinet meetings and for advising her husband on political appointments, which were viewed as very political acts.[25]

The advisory role of first ladies has largely been played behind the scenes. In Ford's case reporters emphasized the personal nature of her political influence. An article in *McCall's* stated, "While she has not invaded the Oval Office, Mrs. Ford gets her views across when she and the President are alone; she calls it 'pillow talk.'" According to this story, Ford "claimed credit for the appointment of HUD Secretary Carla Hills. 'I got a woman into the cabinet. I never give up. Now I'm working on getting a woman on the Supreme Court as soon as possible.'"[26] In a rare presidential interview with a women's magazine, Gerald Ford told the *Ladies' Home Journal,* "As a political partner, she is a prime asset." He credited his wife with persuading him to support the ERA: "She convinced me that women's rights have to be protected and guaranteed by law, just as the rights of racial and religious minorities, if there is to be genuine equality." He also admitted that she advised him on his economic program by telling him to "think about the millions of American women shopping each day for their families."[27] Whether the first ladies' persuasive influence occurred in public or in private, their advisory role was framed by journalists as overwhelmingly political, which highlighted how these women contributed to their husband's political careers.

The wives' campaign roles were also now framed as more political than before, for these women, as independent political actors, were stumping solo in support of their husbands. Johnson campaigned actively, making unaccompanied trips to many areas that were solidly Republican.[28] Her ride through eight southern states in October 1964 aboard the "Lady Bird Special" was "the first whistle-stop campaign journey ever taken by a President's wife on her own." Johnson's press secretary, Liz Carpenter, called the whistle-stop tour "a salvage operation in the wake of the Civil Rights Act of 1964."[29] Johnson made speeches at forty-seven stops over the four-day period, drawing large mixed crowds that included many African Americans as well as small groups of heckling Goldwater supporters "yelling 'nigger-lover Johnson' and 'What about Vietnam?'" Nan Robertson of the *New York Times* observed that, "throughout Mrs. Johnson's trip, the outstanding visual impression by the sides of the railroad tracks was of black hands waving Johnson posters and white hands holding posters for both presidential candidates," thus framing the trip within the context of civil rights, a major campaign issue in 1964.[30] Claude Sitton of the *New York Times* credited the "Lady Bird Special" with garnering several firm endorsements from Southern Democratic leaders, tapping "new sources of active support, financial and otherwise," and arousing "enthusiasm for the campaign that had been sorely missing." Robertson assessed the success of Johnson's trip: "On the trip, the President's wife has spoken to tens of thousands of persons at rallies and from the rear of her observation car. But, perhaps more important, she has also been on the job constantly between stops, talking to a steady stream of politicians and party workers."[31] The "Lady Bird Special" capitalized on Johnson's celebrity, using her popularity to reach out to southern voters who were deeply divided over civil rights. When her husband carried four of the eight Southern states in the election, the "Lady Bird Special" received much of the credit.

To see the first lady campaigning independently of her husband became commonplace during this era. Carter—who spent nearly two years on the road answering the question "Jimmy who?"—was framed by the press as an active solo campaigner. A *New York Times* article stated, "Unlike most candidates' wives of the past, Mrs. Carter . . . campaigned on her own rather than with her husband in the Carters' attempt to reach as many voters as possible." According to a Carter aide, "She didn't do only women's teas. She showed up at factories at 4 in the morning, at Democratic meetings, at church gatherings, shopping centers and public festivals— she held her own news conferences and did television interviews." Reporters praised her ability to "speak without notes" and to connect with audiences from the stump. By highlighting that Carter, an effective public speaker, spoke to promiscuous audiences and campaigned alone, these comments evidence that women's presence in the political sphere was still considered somewhat unusual.[32] Carter's son Jack told *McCall's* that "it was like having two candidates, equally attractive. It meant we could travel twice as far and meet twice the number of people. I think that won it for us," foreshadowing the concept of a "co-presidency" and the "two-for-one" mantra that appeared as framing devices in later news coverage. Carter became so well-known for her campaign efforts that in June 1977 Megan Rosenfeld of the *Washington Post* referred to the mounting presence of wives on the campaign trail as "the Rosalynn Carter phenomenon."[33] Ford also campaigned actively in 1976, representing her husband at several Republican state conventions during his tough primary race with Ronald Reagan. Indeed, upon his loss to Jimmy Carter in the general election, his wife literally spoke for her husband (he had lost his voice), reading his concession telegram to the press and thanking Ford supporters.[34]

Nixon was a regular feature on the campaign trail, though both she and the press downplayed the political importance of her campaign presence. She was framed primarily as a liaison to women voters, a more traditional campaign role for political wives. The *New York Times* stated in 1968, "This year, as in 22 of her 56 years, Mrs. Nixon is out on the campaign trail. She modestly calls herself 'a volunteer for Nixon—his eyes and ears with the women voters.'" Nixon announced in a press conference that she would play "an active role" in the 1968 campaign. According to the *New York Times,* "She said she would spend her time consulting volunteer groups and visiting women's organizations, meeting with the ladies of the press and making television appearances." However, Robertson, in another article, claimed "Mrs. Nixon said she had never spoken on the issues" and quoted her as saying, "I think women do like to see women, but sometimes they don't like to listen to them. I think women would rather hear the candidate speak than have the wife speak for him."[35] Her comments devalued women's speech, even to a non-promiscuous audience, and reflected the negative connotation that had long been associated with women's publicity and political activism. For reporters such a statement served as insight into Nixon's gendered performance of the first lady role and also marked a sharp contrast between her and Johnson, her activist predecessor.

Another role of the activist first lady was as presidential surrogate. Throughout their tenures Johnson and Carter used their campaigning skills and celebrity to garner support and publicity for their husbands' programs. A *Good Housekeeping* profile said that Johnson was "clearly more steeped in practical politics than any other First Lady, except perhaps Eleanor Roosevelt in her later years. Clearly, when Mrs. Johnson says she plans to help her husband in every way possible, she is uttering no platitude." One of the ways she helped was by traveling around the country promoting her husband's programs, particularly his "war on poverty" projects such as Head Start and VISTA. She made front-page news when she visited a "poverty pocket" coal town in Pennsylvania, where she told the crowd, "Last Wednesday I sat in the gallery of the Congress and heard my husband declare war on poverty in this country. Today, I feel as if I have been standing on the first battlefield of that war." She viewed her role as going "behind the cold statistics to the human needs, problems, and hopes" of impoverished Americans, thus acting (much like Eleanor Roosevelt did for the New Deal) as a human link between her husband's programs and the people.[36] After being named the honorary chair of Project Head Start, Johnson garnered publicity for the program by touring project sites and holding "poverty project teas" with leaders of national women's organizations, making the most of her celebrity.[37]

Like Johnson, Carter was framed as a surrogate for her husband, but her trips also took her abroad. Her most notable excursion was a "12-day tour of the Caribbean and Latin America," which made daily headlines in both the United States and abroad.[38] She told reporters that her visit was "on behalf of the President to express his friendship and good will and to conduct substantive talks with the leaders of these nations on issues of bilateral, regional, and global importance." As the first president's wife to undertake such an important political assignment abroad, she often found herself defending her trip. Her response was, "I think that I am the person closest to the President of the United States, and if I can help him understand the countries of the world, that's what I want to do." To prepare, Carter "took Spanish lessons three times a week" and was "briefed by 40 experts on Latin America in 13 sessions lasting [from] two to five hours each."[39] David Vidal of the *New York Times* noted that, before the trip, "there was widespread skepticism that it could produce any results," particularly since Carter was visiting a region "dominated by a male culture" and "would be unable to gain the ear of male leaders, often military men, on issues as varied and complex as nuclear proliferation, commodity prices, arms sales, trade and third-world development problems and, of course, human rights." However, Vidal concluded, "Mrs. Carter has achieved a personal and diplomatic success that goes far beyond the modest expectations of both her foreign policy tutors at the State Department and her hosts."[40] Carter's adding the role of diplomat to the first lady's duties heightened the political influence of the first lady position.

Press coverage of first lady activism and advocacy during this era helped to institutionalize the expectation that all first ladies actively champion a social cause they are invested in personally. In some cases advocacy also led to a first lady's involvement in policy making. As in the past, however, such activism was often gendered, which both justified and limited the first lady's influence. Johnson's primary personal project was "beautification." Like Ellen Wilson and Eleanor Roosevelt before her, she took a particular interest in improving living conditions in Washington, D.C.[41] Johnson formed the Committee for a More Beautiful Capital with interior secretary Stewart L. Udall, for the dual purpose of making the Washington Mall more attractive and "beautifying Washington's drabber and more squalid residential areas and downtown sections." At a publicity event Johnson "performed some symbolic gestures by planting a few pansies" but also "took the committee to a former slum area in southwest Washington where luxury apartments and public housing structures are now intermingled." Johnson lobbied on behalf of the 1965 Highway Beautification Act, dubbed "Lady Bird's bill," and continued to call attention to conservation and environmental protection throughout her tenure. The label of "beautification" still gendered Johnson's advocacy, however, and overshadowed the more political aspects of her environmentalism.[42]

As political celebrities, first ladies were often positioned by the press as spokespersons for women's issues, such as Ford for breast cancer awareness after she underwent a radical mastectomy just a few weeks after she moved into the White House.[43] An editorial in the *New York Times* said, "Mrs. Ford has set an admirable example in dealing forthrightly with an area still frequently beclouded by irrational flights from reality." She herself wrote about her experience in *McCall's* a few months after her surgery: "Nobody used to talk about it years ago and, even now, few women will admit to having had a mastectomy. One of the things I'm most proud of is that we did talk about it openly and as a result I didn't feel ashamed or 'dirty' because I had cancer." Ford hoped that, "if I as First Lady could talk about it candidly and without embarrassment, many other people would be able to do so as well. I also wanted to feel that something good would come from my ordeal."[44] Within a few weeks of her surgery, the *New York Times* reported that "thousands of women across the country have been rushing to seek breast cancer examinations." In 1976 Ford was recognized by the American Cancer Society for her "candid and optimistic response to the disease" and for her continued efforts to educate women about the benefits of early detection.[45] Recognizing the power of the publicity surrounding the first lady, Ford successfully used her position to raise awareness and to alleviate the stigma associated with breast cancer.

Similarly, Carter used her position to bring attention to her two primary issues: mental health and aging. Her appointment as the honorary chair of the President's Commission on Mental Health garnered coverage of the commission's efforts.[46] She also chaired a "White House Conference on Aging" in order to "help 'personally spotlight' the problems of old people in America." As spokeswoman for these issues, Carter was viewed as representing women everywhere who were caring for mentally ill or elderly family members.[47] These stories reveal the power of political celebrity, but such gendered framing also contained the influence of both Ford and Carter to women's issues, traditionally undervalued within the male political sphere. Thus, while these activist first ladies were positioned as key players in women's political culture, they remained on the fringes of U.S. political culture, finding their political influence both gendered and limited.

The women's liberation movement also benefited from the first lady media spotlight thanks to Ford's and Carter's lobbying on behalf of the Equal Rights Amendment. MacPherson in *McCall's* declared that Ford's "increasing feminism and courage to speak out on issues has brought a totally unexpected bonus to those who prefer activism after years of silence from First Ladies." Similarly, the *Ladies' Home Journal* asserted that "her championing of the women's rights movement—and specifically the Equal Rights Amendment—has meant much to its supporters." According to an article in the *New York Times* in February 1975, Ford was "making telephone calls and writing to legislators in several states where the amendment has recently come up for action, including Illinois, Missouri, North Dakota, Arizona, and Nevada." Ford described her lobbying as a "very soft sell" and explained to MacPherson of *McCall's* that she "merely asked that the amendment be allowed to get to the floor and to let the people vote their conscience."[48] Carter followed Ford's example, making phone calls to legislators and urging their support of the ERA. A headline on the front page of the *Washington Post* on January 19, 1977, proclaimed, "Indiana Ratifies the ERA—With Rosalynn Carter's Aid." According to the article, Carter "called Democratic state Sen. Wayne Townsend, known to be wavering in the caucus, and persuaded him to switch his vote," making Indiana the "35th state to ratify the Equal Rights Amendment."[49] Later that month, after Virginia failed to ratify the amendment by one vote, Carter was reportedly "working to change votes" by "calling several state legislators."[50] The press considered such activism by first ladies on behalf of an active feminist movement unprecedented, even though their actions were extensions of previous first ladies' social reform efforts. By publicly using the power of the first lady position to lobby for feminist legislation, Ford and Carter both provoked a mixture of praise and criticism that often played out in the press.

During this era, the media spotlight focused primarily on first ladies' activities outside of the White House. There was a noticeable decrease in the number of stories about hostessing and White House homemaking, usually a staple of first lady coverage in both newspapers and women's magazines. When these stories did appear, they often now reflected the first ladies' activism. Johnson held a series of "women doers" luncheons, for example, to honor women "who had achieved distinction in many fields," while Carter turned "a White House tea for Jihan Sadat of Egypt into an open forum . . . on a variety of social issues confronting both the United States and Egypt."[51] Because the focus was on these first ladies' public activities, their activities within the White House were sometimes overlooked. Dorothy McCardle of the *Washington Post* said of Nixon, "I don't think she gets enough credit for what she does. There's been very little fanfare about the way she's enlarged the Americana collection at the White House and restored the authentic nineteenth-century spirit."[52] Once again Nixon suffered as a result of her perceived political inactivity, failing to garner the positive publicity that had been granted by the press to the domestic activities of first ladies just a decade earlier.

An outgrowth of first ladies' escalating political activism during this period was the recognition, by first ladies and journalists, of the growing power of their position. A 1975 *McCall's* profile observed that Ford "revels in the power the position holds and has learned to use that power for causes she espouses." Ford stated, "I have learned over the past few months the positiveness of the position—which I hadn't realized before. I have come to realize the power of being able to help." The same article pointed out that Ford "mentions the word 'power' more than once and speaks with pride, for example, of the clout her name now brings."[53] Carter made a similar comment about the power of the position. According to the *Washington Post* in 1977, she told an audience of twenty-two hundred Democratic women, "One thing I've had to adjust to is that my influence, no matter what I say, goes across the country."[54] Such comments point to the fact that the power of first ladies was largely tied to their celebrity status and the press coverage accorded to them. As celebrity political activists whose performances occurred in very public mediated spaces, these first ladies normalized women's political activism and made significant contributions to the idea of a public, political woman. Because their celebrity, and hence their power, was being felt routinely in the political sphere as never before, however, these first ladies faced questions about the extent—and potential abuses—of their influence as non-elected officials. Thus, as the activism and perceived power of the first lady position increased, so did the press scrutiny of the first lady institution.

Assessing the Influence of the First Lady as Political Activist

While press framing during this era celebrated first ladies as political activists, news coverage also critiqued these women's growing influence. The resulting coverage represented the ideological contestation over women's changing roles. As MacPherson's story in *McCall's* proclaimed, "While there is a loss of privacy and anonymity as First Lady, there is also direction, a well-defined role, an exalted status and a chance to influence public opinion that is unparalleled for any other woman in this country." MacPherson reflected on the first lady's evolution from public woman to political celebrity to political activist. The activist first ladies of this era used their celebrity to "go public" and gained the opportunity to influence public opinion on a variety of subjects, from the ERA to breast cancer to their husbands' economic and health agendas. In doing so they also witnessed the limits of their celebrity, at least in the estimation of journalists, who at times challenged their growing public and political influence. Such coverage now started to mark the boundaries of "proper" first lady performance. Drawing on the collective memory of the institution, some journalists sought to put the activism of these first ladies into historical perspective, comparing them to iconic predecessors who represented a particular performance of the first lady position. Other reporters used gender prescriptions to judge the various levels of first lady activism. The ways that journalists critiqued first lady influence in this era created a series of double binds that were ultimately used to question, and to contain, the first lady's growing political power.[55]

PRESS MEMORY AND ICONIC FIRST LADIES

During an era characterized by women's changing roles and first ladies' political activism, reporters began to ask the question, "What should a first lady's role be, anyway?" To answer, press coverage drew upon the collective memory of the first lady institution, comparing current first ladies to a handful of their predecessors who, in journalists' estimation, had achieved iconic status. These iconic first ladies personified a historical gendered performance of the position that could be used to gauge the activities of present and future first ladies. These mediated memories were sometimes problematic, however, because they reduced former first ladies to representations of a single role or ideological perspective. Eleanor Roosevelt, for reporters, became an activist icon while Jacqueline Kennedy was reduced to a fashion icon, constructions that ignored Roosevelt's focus on domesticity and Kennedy's accomplishments as first lady.[56]

Roosevelt and Kennedy personified contrasting performances of the first lady position, with other former first ladies thrown in as points of comparison. Mead claimed in her *Good Housekeeping* profile of Johnson that "before Eleanor Roosevelt and Jacqueline Kennedy, the role of the First Lady was usually played in such a low key that it might be said it was hardly played at all." Mead discussed the impact of celebrity, noting that women "were inspired" and "roused to action" by Roosevelt while they were "frankly delighted" by Kennedy's style. Other reporters offered similar assessments of former first ladies. In her 1971 profile of Nixon, West asserted, "We have had First Ladies who fitted easily into familiar categories. Bess Truman and Mamie Eisenhower were round-faced mothers and housewives. Eleanor Roosevelt was the homely, intelligent humanitarian." In contrast, West described Kennedy as "beautiful, glittering and lavish as a star. She hated politics; she was high-handed, and she accompanied her husband only when she felt like it." McBee offered similar descriptions in a 1970 article, claiming that a first lady had two models to follow: "She may, if she wishes, be like that nice Army wife Mamie Eisenhower, or that social anonymity before her, Bess Truman, and do little more than go to luncheons." Or she could "pattern herself after such social or political or intellectual arbiters as Abigail Adams or Dolley Madison or Eleanor Roosevelt."[57] Such constructions reduced the complexities of the performance of the first lady position to a series of binaries—public or private, active or passive, political or nonpolitical—that mirrored the double binds now used to critique each woman's performance. These constructs also established a sense of competition between first ladies by highlighting their differences rather than focusing on their similarities.

The activist first ladies were, not surprisingly, frequently compared to Roosevelt, the activist icon, and contrasted with their less political predecessors. For journalists, Roosevelt set the standard by which her successors were measured. One story proclaimed that Johnson would be "the first First Lady since Eleanor Roosevelt to make speeches on world conditions," for example, while another article noted that, "unlike Jacqueline Kennedy, Mamie Eisenhower, and Bess Truman, Lady Bird Johnson has been and continues to be deeply involved in her husband's political life."[58] Similarly, a *New York Times* article about Carter said, "Neither Bess Truman nor Mamie Eisenhower involved themselves in their husband's political lives." In contrast, Carter was described as her husband's "'political partner,' a definition that might have applied to Mrs. Roosevelt and, to a degree, to Lady Bird Johnson but to few other president's wives." One reporter called Carter "more determinedly activist than any First Lady since Eleanor Roosevelt, who is said to be her heroine and model," and suggested that she "may become the most influential First Lady since Eleanor Roosevelt."[59] MacPherson reported Ford was "flattered" that people called her "the most outspoken First Lady since Eleanor Roosevelt" and remarked that "Mrs. Kennedy beautified the White House and Mrs. Johnson beautified the country, but issues were taboo. Mrs. Ford has invested her position with a sense of purpose not seen since Eleanor Roosevelt."[60] Journalists claimed that Nixon disliked being compared to previous first ladies, but this did not stop reporters from doing so. When asked by one reporter, "How are you different from Dolley Madison? Or Eleanor Roosevelt? Or Grace Coolidge—with whom you've been compared?" Nixon's response was "Does it matter?" Another profile noted, "She had to find her own unique style: not Lady Bird's, not Jacqueline's, not Mamie's, but her own."[61] In these stories the mere mention of a former first lady's name carried with it a specific, albeit limited, memory regarding a particular performance of the position. Although they were celebrities in their own time, for some such as Eisenhower their celebrity faded once they left the media spotlight, reflecting the historical amnesia of the press.

Comparisons usually oversimplified these first ladies' performance, evidencing the limitations of iconic framing and media memory. During this activist period, for example, the performances of Truman, Eisenhower, and even Kennedy served as models of political inactivity, a criticism based on current standards that did not accurately represent how these women were framed during their tenures. Johnson, Ford, and Carter were viewed as following in Roosevelt's activist tradition. Their travels and public speaking were thus legitimized, as was their involvement in policy making and playing the role of presidential advisor. Unlike Roosevelt, however, these women did not have to justify their activity as being an extension of their wifely role. Thanks to the influence of feminism on the gendered framing of the era and the activities of former first ladies, women's political activism was not only accepted, it was expected. On the other hand the growing political influence of first ladies was now questioned, particularly because of the gendered nature of their power.

CHALLENGING FIRST LADIES' POLITICAL ACTIVISM

The heightened publicity led to more frequent critiques of the first ladies' influence, demonstrating the double binds historically faced by public women. Through their political activism, or lack thereof, the first ladies now prompted journalists to "reconsider the relationship between presidential spouses in order to infer the extent and character of a form of influence exerted largely outside public scrutiny."[62] Journalists took it as their job to capture the extent of these women's influence. This reaction to her political activism evidenced the limits of a first lady's celebrity and represented a backlash against the increased political power of the first lady specifically and of women in general.

Some of the backlash was generated by the anti-feminist movement in reaction to the first ladies' support of women's liberation, coverage of which pitted women against each other. Ford and Carter were both frequent targets of anti-ERA groups. In February 1975 the *Washington Post* reported that Ford's response was to "keep lobbying for the Equal Rights Amendment in spite of heavy criticism from opponents of the measure who picketed the White House" with placards reading "Stop ERA" and "Happiness Is Stopping ERA." Ford viewed the protests as a badge of honor, telling a reporter, "I'm the only First Lady to ever have a march organized against her."[63] Ford publicly defended the ERA and its supporters. When asked by an interviewer from *McCall's* "if she would debate Phyllis Schlafly, the high priestess of status quo for women and chief opponent of the Equal Rights Amendment. Said the First Lady, who has vociferously lobbied for the amendment, 'I wouldn't waste my time.'" Ford challenged anti-ERA arguments in the press, however, saying, "You get all this silly business about co-ed facilities as an argument against the amendment. Think about it: how many campuses have sexually integrated dorms and are perfectly accepted?" She also took on Stop ERA leader Schlafly, saying, "Phyllis Schlafly has her great motherhood thing. I've been through motherhood. I think it's marvelous. But I'm not so sure mothers shouldn't have *rights*."[64]

Ford's vocal support of the ERA generated criticism. At first, White House mail was "running 3 to 1 against her outspoken support of passage of the Equal Rights Amendment."[65] One of the letters asserted, "What right do you have as a representative of all women to contact the legislators and put pressure on them to pass the hated E.R.A.?" Ford responded in an article written by MacPherson in *McCall's*, saying, "I see no reason why as First Lady I cannot go right ahead like any other woman." A 1975 profile in *Ladies' Home Journal* claimed, "She has stood by her support of the Equal Rights Amendment, provoking some criticism, but making many proud that a First Lady would campaign so forcefully for women's rights."[66]

The anti-ERA movement criticized Carter's lobbying efforts on behalf of the ERA also, and such criticism was highlighted in the press. Schlafly organized a White House protest against Carter, following her calls to Indiana and Virginia legislators regarding the ERA. Schlafly told the *Washington Post* that "state legislators around the country resent this improper White House pressure." The 150 demonstrators carried signs that read, "Rosalynn Carter—if my daughter is ever drafted it will be your fault!" and "Mrs. Carter, you have no right to lobby ERA!" Carter declined comment, but her press secretary said she would "continue to work in support of ERA." Following the protest and a "surge of critical calls," Carter "stopped announcing all of her activities on behalf of the E.R.A.," although she continued to lobby on its behalf.[67] Unlike Ford who, despite criticism, publicly challenged her detractors, Carter responded to the pressure from her critics by silencing the publicity surrounding her activism. In both cases, however, supporting the ERA pitted Ford and Carter against other women, which undermined the feminist notion of "sisterhood" and characterized the debate over women's rights as little more than a "political catfight."[68]

Coverage of these first ladies reflected the ideological contestations over—and cultural ambivalences toward—women's equality that characterized this period. While the press praised the activist first ladies for their political influence, journalists also accused them of overstepping the invisible gendered boundaries that constrain the first lady position. Johnson was criticized by congressmen and lobbyists for her lobbying on behalf of the Highway Beautification Act. Johnson's press secretary Liz Carpenter said, "We never were happy with that name (beautification)," a more gendered term than "conservation" that did not reflect the controversy Johnson stirred up especially "from national billboard lobbyists who tried, and sometimes succeeded, in getting the press to laugh at the tree planting and flower-spreading." Such gendered framing was used deliberately to depoliticize her advocacy and undermine her political influence. Johnson's efforts were caught in a form of the femininity-or-competence bind, which devalues certain issues by labeling them "feminine" and therefore unworthy of attention from male politicians.[69]

Ford was often praised by journalists for her "candor" and subsequently was accused of being too outspoken, which prompted one article to ask, "How much should a first lady say?" Trude B. Feldman in the *Ladies' Home Journal* claimed, "Betty Ford has won a reputation for speaking out on thorny issues, touching off the kind of controversy that some observers say has hurt her husband."[70] For example, when she told Morley Safer of the CBS news program *60 Minutes* that she "wouldn't be surprised" if her eighteen-year-old daughter, Susan, told her she was having an affair and engaging in premarital sex, Ford's comments generated "a breathless front page tempest for days" and led to a flood of mail to the White House. The *Ladies' Home Journal* carried an article about "the Answer that rocked a nation," featuring reactions from "famous mothers" such as Betty Friedan and Phyllis Schlafly, again pitting women against women, and tying Ford's response to the debate over women's liberation.[71] Ford was criticized also for her statements on legalized abortion, particularly when she asserted she was glad to see abortion "brought out of the backwoods and put in the hospitals where it belongs." She maintained her pro-choice position despite "a rash of criticism from Right-to-Lifers."[72] Criticism of Ford's public statements on sexual issues was not at all surprising given the long-standing negative connotations associated with public women, women's speech, and sexuality. By speaking her mind Ford challenged these taboos, but she also invited critics' sexualization of her comments, thus violating the double bind of silence or shame used to constrain women's speech.[73]

Journalists' gendered critiques of Carter's influence represented efforts to impose limitations on the first lady's power as a celebrity. Reporters speculated whether she had too much political power for a first lady. Kandy Stroud characterized her as "a tough, shrewd power-behind-the-throne, ambitious both for herself and her husband." Similar comments were made by Meg Greenfield, who claimed there were many "downsides" of a politically active wife: "She is variously regarded as the seductress, the bewitcher, the mysterious power behind the throne, the possessor of unfair advantage and the wielder of undue influence." These remarks sexualized public womanhood, harking back to the days when a woman who dared to enter the public sphere was called Jezebel, the biblical wife who exercised "undue influence" on her husband.[74] Carter's Latin American trip sparked editorials discussing the appropriateness of the first lady's assuming a diplomatic role. The *New York Times* questioned "whether it was somehow insulting to send the First Lady if the President and Vice President were too busy with other countries," implying that both her gender and her unofficial position might be an issue. The editorial concluded, however, that "it is the quality of her ambassadorship that should concern us, not the range of subjects on which the President might wish to exploit her prestige and proximity." Greenfield, in a *Washington Post* op-ed, disagreed, claiming that "the question raised by her Latin American trip is not whether Rosalynn Carter is capable of serving as an agent of her husband's government, but rather whether she should." Greenfield asserted, "If Mrs. Carter is going to conduct diplomatic discussions abroad and enter into policy matters in a systematic way at home, her efforts and her influence are going to have to be judged as those of an ordinary professional." She concluded that "before it's over, Mrs. Carter—a remarkable woman—will have demonstrated whether or not a political wife who comes out of the kitchen can stand the heat."[75] For Greenfield the issue was accountability. However, her final comment regarding political wives coming "out of the kitchen" unnecessarily gendered the question of Carter's political activism.[76] It is interesting to note that much of the gendered criticism came from women journalists and appeared in both newspapers and women's magazines.

Nixon represented the other extreme, a political wife who was not active or outspoken enough, and was positioned by journalists as a model of what not to be. Female reporters, in particular, criticized Nixon for viewing herself as a wife first and an individual second. McBee described Nixon as a follower of "the traditional rules" in relation to her performance of the position: "Be an extension of your husband, not a public figure in your own right; avoid all public comments and controversy, for a misstatement may damage his career. Mrs. Nixon has been a political prop for so long that, at 58, she is having great trouble becoming anything more."[77] Stroud (the first to call Nixon "Plastic Pat") assessed her image: "I think she lost that spontaneity when she played to the hilt the consummate politician's wife. Because she had to be inconspicuous and keep in the background, she lost her individuality and much of her confidence."[78] For these journalists, Nixon personified the ways that the feminine mystique deprived women of self-fulfillment, making her a disappointing role model in an era of feminist activism.

Nixon was criticized also for failing to exploit the power of the first lady position. In keeping with her more traditional performance, she chose volunteerism as her cause; promoting "volunteerism," however, was viewed as "safe," if not downright dull, by reporters. *Washington Post* reporter Marie Smith said, "Both Mrs. Johnson and Mrs. Kennedy had definite interests and promoted them effectively. Mrs. Nixon doesn't." McBee offered the example of Nixon's tour of West Coast volunteer projects in 1968: "Every place she went was 'fun' or 'exciting' or 'marvelous,' and often all three. Such comments are polite, but they don't really say much about innovative ways that private citizens can constructively change their communities—a goal Mrs. Nixon has embraced." McBee concluded that Nixon's "impact outside Washington has been so small it can be measured in millimeters."[79]

Some reporters criticized Nixon's lack of political activity and avoidance of issues on the campaign trail. In a 1972 article titled "Mrs. Nixon, on Seven-State Tour, Shuns Politics," Robertson of the *New York Times* pointed out that Nixon "made no speeches" and "never, never talked politics." Reporters, frustrated with the lack of "newsworthy" activities, pressed Nixon during her only news conference, a press briefing in Chicago where, Robertson noted, she was "forced to tackle, or at least parry, the issues. . . . She turned tense and anxious as she was asked about the war, abortion, amnesty, the Watergate bugging, equal rights . . . and other thorny topics. It was, everyone who has followed Mrs. Nixon for years agreed, the toughest grilling she has ever undergone."[80] Nixon's silence on political issues ended up hurting her, as she found herself forced by the press to address such issues, only to be critiqued for her responses, in some cases by women reporters who wanted more from a second-wave first lady.

The first ladies of this period found themselves ensnared in double binds reflecting both the ideological contestation over women's roles and the limitations of their celebrity. While the public and press called on the first lady to be more active, she was warned not to overstep her boundaries or abuse her power. However if, like Nixon, she was not active enough then she was criticized for this as well, setting up a classic no-win situation. In a 1977 *Washington Post* feature on "First Families," MacPherson quoted historian Joseph P. Lash as saying, "A President's wife who undertakes a specific job in the government faces double jeopardy; she is without real authority, yet she is expected to perform miracles. When she dares to assert leadership, it is resented and resisted and if she does not, officials try to anticipate what she wants done."[81] Such double binds served to contain the first lady's power. While her celebrity gave her the necessary publicity to break down barriers for women's political activism, it was not powerful enough to overcome obstacles questioning the appropriateness of women's place in the male political sphere. In certain instances, women journalists both promoted first ladies' political power and yet also worked to limit it.

Conclusion

While some, such as Winifred D. Wandersee, believed that the first ladies were prevented from moving "beyond the confinement of an exceedingly demanding, yet rigidly defined role. . . . Their lives were truly appendages to their husbands."[82] Press coverage of the first ladies of this era contradicts her statement. These women were routinely presented as influential and active public figures in their own right, traveling extensively and routinely speaking with the press as they campaigned independently for their husbands and also advocated their own social causes. Even Nixon, the most traditional public wife of the period, was recognized for her individual achievements. Her problem, according to her press critics, was that she was not politically active enough. During an era of active feminist protest, Nixon had the misfortune of embodying the very ideology feminists were rallying against, the "feminine mystique." Despite being described as "warm" and "friendly" by reporters, Nixon often found herself under fire for being a "traditional political wife," the role she had been expected to perform throughout her public life.

Gendered framing also impacted the media memories of former first ladies. When former first ladies are framed as icons, their performances are further reduced to the personification of ideologies or roles. However, the memory they are reduced to reflects the legacy of press framing as well as the politics of the second wave as much if not more than it does the first ladies' lived performances. Iconic framing reflects the limits of collective memory, particularly the problem of forgetting.[83] The focus on the first lady's activism during second-wave feminism impacted which first ladies were remembered and how their images circulated as those of political celebrities. In the process some first ladies' activities, which garnered significant press coverage during their eras, were almost completely forgotten. The result is that, with the exception of a few iconic first ladies such as Eleanor Roosevelt and Jacqueline Kennedy, political celebrity for most first ladies is short-lived, further evidencing the limitations of both celebrity and the media's historical memory.

The first ladies of this era became sites of ideological contestation generated by second-wave feminism. Since feminism was often constructed by the press as a competition between women, it devalued the significance of feminist issues and upheld the patriarchal stronghold within U.S. political culture. The most notable feature of the press coverage of this period was a more critical tone as journalists developed a more adversarial approach to reporting. Most journalists "realize that they must meet organizational, occupational, and audience expectations. In addition, the news organizations within which they work are influenced by societal and cultural environments." Thus journalists are influenced by the gender ideologies that shape U.S. culture and their organizational culture, which in this era required them to challenge political officials, including politically active first ladies. Furthermore, "Given these layers of influences, it is not too surprising that the individual characteristics of journalists do not correlate strongly with the kinds of news content they produce." Despite such cultural influences, "it would be a mistake to think that individual journalists have no freedom to select and shape news stories."[84] Given the tensions between journalism's adversarial culture and the politics of individual journalists (particularly women reporters who supported women's liberation), it is not surprising that the same journalists who praised the political activists as contemporary superwomen who could balance both feminist ideals and traditional domestic roles also critiqued these women's performance of the first lady position, questioning whether they were becoming too politically active.

A consequence of such ambivalent reporting was a series of double binds that left first ladies in a perpetual no-win situation. As MacPherson of the *Washington Post* pointed out: "The capacity for accomplishment is great, but an activist First Lady is assured of not only rewards and heady personal power, but criticism and frustration as well," evidencing the double binds that were associated with an active performance of the position during this period.[85] Conversely, Nixon was disparaged for being an "old-fashioned" political wife and judged as being too passive. The result was a number of critical articles, rare in earlier twentieth-century coverage, but that would carry over into the next period. The empowerment and limitations of first ladies' celebrity witnessed during this period would be exacerbated as the feminist backlash gained momentum in the 1980s.

The First Lady as Political Interloper,
1980–2001

*I*n a 2000 *New York Times* editorial, Jan Jarboe Russell noted the quandary that first ladies have faced over the years: "From the beginning, Americans have not known quite what to do with the wives of presidents. Those who spoke their minds, like Mary Lincoln, Eleanor Roosevelt and Hillary Clinton, were vilified for meddling in the nation's business. Those who failed to assert themselves as individuals, like Mamie Eisenhower and Pat Nixon, were derided as female furniture." Russell noted that the latest contenders for the position, Laura Bush and Tipper Gore, were hoping to avoid this trap by taking a more "traditional" approach to the role than their predecessor, Hillary Rodham Clinton, had done. "If Mrs. Bush or Mrs. Gore wants to be a stay-at-home wife, fine. However, let's not expect her to do anything substantial about raising literacy rates or improving our mental health. And let us not have a first lady answer to any title that begins with 'co': co-partner, co-conspirator, co-president."[1] This article evidences the dilemma facing first ladies: how to be a model of American womanhood while performing one of the most publicly visible and influential, yet undefined and unelected, positions in American culture.

At the end of the twentieth century the first lady institution continued to serve as a site of ideological contestation over women's roles, with the debate over gender performance arguably more heated than ever. The first ladies of the previous era had mirrored the activism of the period and were judged in large part against the cultural backdrop of second-wave feminism. With the exception of Nixon, the Cold War homemaker, the first ladies of the second-wave era were framed as political activists. However, their increased influence was met with heightened criticism concerning the power of the first lady position, evidencing the feminist backlash that swelled in the 1980s and 1990s. During the final decades of the twentieth century, journalists were preoccupied with assessing the first lady's influence and questioning her "proper place" in American politics and culture. At the turn of the twenty-first century, "vestiges of gentility persist, the Victorian ideal still survives. This anachronistic post remains rooted in the leadership models of the late-nineteenth-century America in the public role of genteel matron."[2] The final three of the twentieth century and the first to hold the position in the new millennium were faced with negotiating the boundaries defining and containing the performances of the first lady position. Two of these women, Nancy Davis Reagan (1981–1989) and Barbara Pierce Bush (1989–1993), represented the Cold War generation. They were followed by the first baby boomers, Hillary Rodham Clinton (1993–2001) and Laura Welch Bush (2001–2009). As always these women were at the center of the cultural debate over women's roles.

Press coverage from 1980 through 2001, a period characterized by the so-called postfeminist backlash, reflected the larger cultural debate. Personification framing drew upon and helped to perpetuate the conflicts between the "traditional" domestic ideal and the feminist "superwoman." Reagan and Barbara Bush represented the Cold War domestic ideal, while baby boomer Laura Bush embodied the "new traditionalism," which emerged as an answer to the feminist superwoman personified by Clinton. The result was competitive framing, which pitted these women one against another and reduced the complexities of gender performance to a series of dichotomies: feminine or feminist, submissive or independent, committed to family or committed to career.

Journalists also used gendered framing to judge these women's performance of the institution's various roles, in the process setting boundaries for the "proper" performance of the first lady position. Helpmate, protector, and volunteer were framed as proper first lady duties while advising, policy making, and advocacy sometimes crossed the boundaries and extended these women's influence too far into the male political sphere. Stemming in part from the expanded political activism of the previous era, questions regarding the first lady's political influence became a defining issue of this period. Reflecting the legacy of "the personal is political," journalists expressed concerns over the "hidden power" of first ladies, whether in the form of private influence over their husband or personal political ambitions. Reagan and Clinton served as examples of women who sought to overextend or misuse the power of their position.

Well-established media frames were influential in defining the boundaries of the first lady position, with the primary focus being on containing her perceived power. Drawing on media memory, journalists used iconic first ladies as boundary markers, noting historical limitations on the position. When the first lady was perceived as overstepping the boundaries and straying too far into the male political sphere, she was characterized by the press as a political interloper, framing that sought to contain her "improper" influence. Meanwhile the debate over women's place became a central campaign issue, casting candidates' wives as key players as each side sought to define "family values." Once again women were treated as opponents in a no-win contest, portrayed by the press as a political catfight. All of the attention given first lady institution caused journalists (female reporters and editorialists in particular) to question the expectations and double binds concerning the position.

Competing Gender Ideologies—Feminism and Domesticity in a Postfeminist Era

On the verge of a new millennium Americans were still debating women's "proper" place in society. The 1980s and 1990s were character-ized by the conflict between the ideals of second-wave feminism and the feminist backlash, resulting in what some scholars and journalists have called the "postfeminist" era. The concepts of a feminist backlash and a post-feminist ideology are not new. Similar "'backlashes' to women's advancement" have occurred in other periods of U.S. history, "triggered by the perception— accurate or not—that women are making great strides."[3] Thus the backlash of the 1980s resembled the reactions to women's more public roles in the early 1900s as well as during the Depression and World War II eras.

After the social movements of the previous decades, it is no surprise "the New Right emerged in the 1970s and 1980s as a powerful political force with the dual aims of reviving the Cold War and reasserting the ide-ology of domesticity."[4] The New Right played on the perceived genera-tion gap between the activist baby boomers and their more conservative parents. The anti-ERA and anti-abortion movements, embracing the do-mestic ideal, were part of the New Right's efforts to counter liberal poli-tics, including feminism. Their pro-family movement sought to bring back the middle-class family model of breadwinning men supporting homemaking wives and their children. The New Right was most success-ful "in defining 'family' in a manner that made it seem like the exclusive domain of conservatives—particularly those who claimed to espouse what they called 'family values.'" Since the 1980s, "family values" has been a rallying cry for conservatives.[5]

The rise of the New Right and the election of Ronald Reagan in 1980 brought the backlash against feminism to the political foreground. Susan Faludi contends, "Just as Reaganism shifted political discourse far to the right and demonized liberalism, so the backlash convinced the public that women's 'liberation' was the true contemporary American scourge—

the source of an endless laundry list of personal, social, and economic problems." Topping the list was the disintegration of the nuclear family, a primary argument of the New Right. At the end of the twentieth century, feminism had become a symbolic lightning rod for the problems of modern family life. The media continued to present feminism as an extreme ideology, even though many of the advances sought by both the first and second waves of the women's movement, especially women's rights to pursue education and employment, had been embraced by U.S. culture.[6]

The result of the 1980s backlash, according to the news media and some scholars, was the era of postfeminism, a term used by some journalists to indicate the so-called death of the women's movement. Judith Stacey has defined postfeminism as "the simultaneous incorporation, revision, and depoliticization of many of the goals of second-wave feminism." She argues that "the diffusion of postfeminist consciousness signifies both the achievements of, and challenges for, modern feminist politics."[7] The primary claims of postfeminism are that a collective feminist movement is no longer needed because the "playing field" has been leveled and women now have the freedom to make individual choices regarding their lives. The depoliticization of second-wave feminism often reduces feminist social goals to individual lifestyle choices, which can lead to the commodification of feminism. This is similar to what happened during the 1920s backlash when the media represented the individualistic flapper lifestyle as the "independence" fought for by first-wave feminists. Postfeminism is useful in describing the attitudes of many women toward feminism today, particularly the ways in which many feminist ideals are embraced while the "feminist" label is rejected. Often called the "I'm not a feminist, but . . ." phenomenon, postfeminism reflects the ambivalence of the woman (usually white and middle- or upper-class) who "is torn between a philosophy that seeks to improve her lot in life and a desire not to pay too dearly for endorsing that philosophy."[8]

The "superwoman" is important in both postfeminism and the feminist backlash. She is a woman who tries to "have it all" by balancing her public-sphere activity with traditional domestic-sphere duties. The superwoman ideal, and press criticism of it, dates back to first-wave feminism. During periods of backlash, feminism has historically been blamed for the unhappiness supposedly caused by the superwoman ideal, which tells women they can have it all yet does not explain the sacrifices they must make in order to do so. In the postfeminist period, feminism is blamed for giving women "unrealistic expectations" that they can have it all, yet many of the rights that first- and second-wave feminists fought for, such as access to higher education and the workplace, are taken for granted. It can be argued that social inequities such as the wage gap, lack of affordable day care, and the "second shift" at home are more likely than feminism to be at the root of women's dissatisfaction, even for middle- and upper-class white women. For the New Right and the media, feminism and its superwoman ideal were more convenient scapegoats.[9]

In the 1980s "New Traditionalism" emerged as the salvation of stressed-out superwomen. This was a revamped version of the Cold War feminine mystique created by advertisers and targeted to baby boomers. The new traditionalist was "little more than a resurgence of the 1950s 'back-to-the-home movement,' itself a creation of advertisers and, in turn, a recycled version of the Victorian fantasy that a new 'cult of domesticity' was bringing droves of women home." The new traditionalist, as described in an advertising campaign for *Good Housekeeping* magazine, "found her identity" in serving home, husband, and children.[10] Thus new traditionalism, in the spirit of postfeminism, advocated a lifestyle for women that involved exchanging their careers for the fulfillment of family life and promoted consumerism as a source of domestic power. Many women and men found such pro-family ideologies appealing in the wake of the antifeminist backlash. However, the economic necessity of a two-paycheck household made the new traditionalist an unobtainable ideal for many American women, even if they wanted to give up their job.[11]

The media's juxtaposition of second-wave feminism with new traditionalism during this backlash created a dichotomy of feminism versus femininity, of nontraditional versus traditional, and of career versus family, which created often competing and contradictory prescriptions for women's behavior. In some respects postfeminism represents the middle ground where women attempt to "both retain and depoliticize the egalitarian family and work ideals of the second wave."[12] While most scholars contend that the news media generally promoted new traditionalism's vilification of feminism, journalists also reflected the ambivalence of postfeminism simply by taking many of the advances of feminism for granted and by promoting the superwoman ideal. As visible in press frames, such ideological contestation played out through first ladies' performance of "family values."

Framing the First Lady in the Postfeminist Era

Journalists' framing of the performances of both gender and the first lady position during the final decades of the twentieth century reflected the ambivalence of postfeminism, pitted feminism against traditionalism, and reduced women's lives to a series of personal choices regarding the roles they played. Once again, growing coverage of first ladies was coupled with more intense scrutiny of the position, as the institution functioned as a site of contestation over women's place and power. By the end of the century the role of the first lady, particularly as a model of American womanhood, was a hotly contested topic, which resulted in numerous newspaper and magazine articles assessing the institution and the women who held the position.

FEMINIST VERSUS TRADITIONALIST—PERSONIFICATION FRAMING AND POSTFEMINISM

The last two decades of the twentieth century were in many ways a culmination of one hundred years of debate over women's proper place in American society. After the active feminist movement of the 1970s, women were exercising new legal rights and taking advantage of expanded opportunities in the public and political spheres. But like their early twentieth century counterparts, women were also dealing with questions concerning how to balance their new public roles with their traditional domestic concerns. At the same time, the Cold War domestic ideal resurfaced, and its focus on the nuclear family and women's primary roles as homemakers and consumers was at odds with second-wave feminism's promotion of women's careers. New traditionalism was a repackaging of Cold War domesticity for the baby boom generation and was presented as an alternative to the superwoman expectation. At the same time the specter of "radical" feminism—based largely on negative constructions by both conservatives and the media—continued to haunt professional women. During this period the women who were in the running for the office of first lady were positioned by many, including journalists, as personifications of these competing ideologies.

The 1980 election of the Reagan-Bush ticket reflected the new era of conservative politics rooted in Cold War ideals, including a renewed emphasis on the traditional gender roles of male breadwinners and female homemakers. For journalists, Nancy Reagan and Barbara Bush represented Cold War domesticity. Reagan embodied the affluent homemaker; she was routinely framed as a "devoted" and "adoring" wife. Lally Weymouth, in an article in the *New York Times Magazine,* called Reagan "part of the Him Generation—a woman who, in the words of the Tammy Wynette song, stands by her man." Enid Nemy, in the same paper, said that Reagan "was brought up in a traditional style, and she knows how to be a wife and run a home."[13] Barbara Bush, whose "grandmotherly image" was frequently mentioned in stories, symbolized the average homemaker of her generation. A *New York Times* article referred to her as "an icon of an older generation of wives who stayed home" while another story reported that "conservative Republicans hold Mrs. Bush up as a symbol of traditional wifeliness."[14] According to a *Ladies' Home Journal* profile, "She's raised five children, lived in twenty-eight homes in seventeen cities, and been a grandmother ten times over, and has spent forty-three years cooking, carpooling, and, as she says, 'keeping the bathrooms clean.'" In the Bush household, the division of labor remained along traditional lines. She asserted, "I don't fool around with his office and he doesn't fool around with my household." This remark reinforced her framing as a traditional homemaker and echoed the domestic empowerment of the Cold War era, which granted women control over private matters concerning home and family.[15]

The return of the domestic ideal was part of the larger backlash against second-wave feminism. Journalists framed comments by both Reagan and Bush as representing conservative arguments that the women's liberation movement undermined the nuclear family and devalued women's roles as wives and mothers. Profiles of Reagan noted that she opposed "abortion on demand" and the ERA, the two defining issues of second-wave feminism. Reagan stated she was "for equal pay if both men and women are equally qualified" but chided feminists for "knocking family life," telling *Ladies' Home Journal*, "I'm not for marches or placard waving. I think if we stopped giving all movements a 'stage' on TV, there would be fewer 'performances.'"[16] Meanwhile, Barbara Bush defended homemaking as a career. *McCall's* reported, "She genuinely enjoys her role as wife, mother and grandmother. Asked whether she regrets not having graduated from Smith College (she left after less than two years to marry George Bush) and pursuing a professional career, she put it this way: 'Why, I have had my own career as a homemaker. I chose my life and I have no regrets.'" In another interview, she blamed second-wave feminism for steering women away from the homemaker role. Bush told the *New York Times* that "women's lib has made it very hard for some women to stay home; the payoff if you do stay home is enormous." Speaking out against feminist activism and in defense of the homemaker role contributed to the press framing of Reagan and Bush as embodiments of the feminist backlash.[17]

Journalists often juxtaposed images of the traditional homemaker of the Cold War generation with the careerism of feminist baby boomers. For journalists, Hillary Rodham Clinton personified the feminist superwoman, the "working mother who does it all and has it all" and represented the "professional women" of the baby boom generation.[18] The *New York Times* noted that Clinton had "come to symbolize the strong, independent woman of the late 20th century." Sally Quinn, in a *Washington Post* article, dubbed Clinton "the very model of the modern working women," noting that "like most American women, Hillary Clinton has to struggle to balance the many facets of her life." According to a 1992 *Ladies' Home Journal* profile, Clinton saw herself as "a working mother trying to balance all these responsibilities, very much like those that are faced by millions of American homes."[19] In a 1993 article looking at Clinton's first hundred days as first lady, she was cast "as a woman trying to balance work and home, able to work round the clock on health care yet manage to make scrambled eggs for a sick Chelsea." The superwoman framing continued in the 1996 campaign. One editorial called Clinton a "Supermom" who "packs an appeal as a mother as well as a loyal wife and professional balancing her obligations on a high wire."[20]

In the wake of the feminist backlash, Clinton also personified what many conservative critics deemed the negative aspects of second-wave feminism. In a *New York Times* editorial, Susan Faludi contended that Clinton was positioned as "an emblem of the modern women's movement," threatening conservatives with "her professionalism, her role in her husband's career, her feminist views, her failure to produce a brood of young 'uns and last, but not at all least, her financial independence."[21] Throughout the 1992 campaign Clinton was portrayed as "a hard-edged careerist," or "a radical feminist in demure Talbot's clothing," or "an un-wifely feminist with undue influence on her husband's policy-making—Gloria Steinem with the claws of Madame Nhu."[22] Her comments that she was "not some little woman standing by her man like Tammy Wynette" and that she could have "stayed home, baked cookies and had teas," remarks often repeated during the campaign, were interpreted as showing contempt for homemakers.[23] At the Republican National Convention, she came "under full-scale attack as the Republicans try to turn her into a symbol of anti-family values."[24] Although conservatives were credited with creating these negative constructions, journalists promoted these backlash images by using them repeatedly to frame their discussions of Clinton.

New traditionalism provided a useful framing device for journalists and conservatives. It bridged the generational divide by encouraging baby boomer women to embrace the Cold War domestic ideal and reject the careerism of second-wave feminists such as Clinton. New traditionalism took center stage in 1992 when Marilyn Quayle—"wife of the vice president and everything, she implied in a speech, that Hillary Clinton is not"—addressed the Republican National Convention. The *New York Times* called Quayle a "self-sacrificing 90s Supermom" who served as "the campaign's generational foil to Mrs. Clinton." Another article claimed Quayle "was the model baby boomer conservative: a career woman who for all but a few years of her adult life had refrained from actually practicing her career." The *New York Times* editorial "A Word from the Wives" asserted that Quayle's thinly veiled attacks on Clinton were also a challenge to the superwoman ideal: "That her law career never had a chance to bloom, as Hillary Clinton's has, doesn't mean she's any less of an intellect —and makes her more of a wife and a mother. Take that, all you women who've fought to have it both ways—balancing careers with loving care of your families." The most quoted line of Quayle's speech—"Most women do not wish to be liberated from their essential natures as women"—was interpreted as support for "talented women who are not threatened by giving up their careers to stay home with the kids."[25]

Tipper Gore was also framed as a new traditionalist who "balances out Hillary Clinton" on the 1992 Democratic ticket. One profile described her as a "perfect baby boomer wife who . . . had chosen to stay home with her children while her husband plunged into politics." In the 2000 presidential race Gore was often compared to fellow new traditionalist Laura Bush, who was consistently framed by journalists as a "loyal wife" and a "fiercely devoted mother." According to Lois Romano in the *Washington Post*, "Bush came of age in the '60s, but, as was the case with her husband, the cultural revolution passed her by." The same story also noted, however, that "while she had the 'luxury' of staying home to raise the twins, she nonetheless considered herself a 'contemporary' woman," who had married late (aged thirty-one), earned a master's degree, and worked a decade in Texas public schools "before settling down" and willingly "trading her career for motherhood." As a news frame, new traditionalism was presented as a "choice" made by these postfeminist women, an alternative to the careerism promoted by second-wave liberal feminism and personified by Clinton.[26]

The contestation over women's changing roles still played out in press coverage of the first lady institution. Candidates' wives were positioned by reporters as models of American womanhood, personifying the ideals of Cold War domesticity, second-wave feminism, or new traditionalism. However, such personification framing severely downplayed the intricacies of gender performance by reducing each woman to a single ideology and ignoring the complexity of their individual lives. Some journalists recognized the reductive aspects of gendered framing. For example, Marjorie Williams of the *Washington Post* wrote, "Barbara Bush, Hillary Clinton, Tipper Gore, and Marilyn Quayle all represent some rough attributes of their various generations, ideologies and backgrounds. . . . But for the three younger women in the race, there has been tension between their expectations as post-feminist baby boomers and the traditions of politics." Williams argued that all three were "grouping toward some uneasy amalgam of autonomy and sublimation—in which their own legitimate ambitions and careerist personae are melded into their husband's career. . . . At least Barbara Bush spares us the maddening fiction of the new woman embedded in the old family."[27] The performance of gender for even "traditional" political wives such as Barbara Bush and Nancy Reagan, particularly in their duties as first lady, was far more complex than Williams and her colleagues often recognized.

THE EMERGENCE OF FIRST LADY AS POLITICAL INTERLOPER

Coverage of the first lady institution now reflected the juxtaposition of traditionalism and feminism in the gender debate, with reporters viewing some roles as falling within the boundaries of "proper" first lady performance while others were framed as crossing such boundaries. According to press coverage, proper first lady comportment included acting as her husband's helpmate and concerning herself primarily with traditional women's public activities. In contrast, using the "hidden power" of the position to advance her own personal or political agenda, whether as advisor, policy maker, or independent advocate, was considered to be overstepping the boundaries of first lady performance. When these boundaries were violated, journalists framed these women as political interlopers, trespassing into the male political sphere. By highlighting these actions as inappropriate, such framing assumed that the first lady's influence should be contained to women's issues, which limited the power of this unelected position.

The frame of helpmate, which journalists used frequently throughout the first half of the twentieth century to describe first ladies' duties, now reappeared. Nancy Reagan, Barbara Bush, and Laura Bush were all framed as helpmates. Reporter Maureen Dowd claimed that Reagan's "greatest role was that of supportive wife"; John Corry observed that "she wants only to help her husband." Beth Weinhouse of the *Ladies' Home Journal* wrote, "She's proved that there's still a place for the old-fashioned wife whose main function is helping her husband." Reagan told Charlotte Curtis of the *Ladies' Home Journal*, "I know it's old fashioned, but my first duty is to be the best wife I can be."[28]

Barbara Bush was viewed similarly. Bernard Weinraub of the *New York Times* declared that Bush was "the quintessential traditional political wife—deferential to her husband and ambitious for him, determined to remain uncontroversial, deeply involved with her family." Donnie Radcliffe in a *Washington Post* profile called her "a steadfast helpmate, tending her family's needs while her husband worked his way to the presidency."[29] Similarly, Laura Bush was described primarily as a helpmate for her husband. Ann Gerhart, in a *Washington Post* profile, quoted him as saying, "I have the best wife for the line of work I'm in. She doesn't try to steal the limelight." During rallies, Alison Mitchell in the *New York Times* noted that "Mrs. [Laura] Bush leads the George Bush cheering section." In another article, Bruni described Laura as "an integral part of her husband's success, not because she is a second engine of his ambition, but because she is a shock absorber, keeping him calm, keeping him steady and, occasionally, keeping his mischievous and arrogant streaks in check." During campaigns Laura frequently traveled with her husband because, according to Lois Romano in the *Washington Post,* "the governor functions better when his wife is with him . . . she's a calming presence." The helpmate frame simultaneously constrained and empowered both Barbara and Laura Bush. By framing their influence as wifely concerns, their contributions were confined to the private sphere, yet still important to their husbands' successes.[30]

The frame of protector, an extension of the helpmate role that had been prevalent in the Cold War era, reemerged during this period. Reagan was frequently framed as her husband's "chief protector."[31] During the 1980 campaign, Reagan "came out swinging" over what she called "a character assassination" of her husband. She said in a campaign advertisement that she resented President Carter's "vicious" attacks on her husband "as a wife and a mother and a woman." The *New York Times* noted that, as first lady, she kept track of "Mr. Reagan's schedule and anything that she considers might be harmful to his political or personal interests."[32]

The protector frame was applied to Barbara Bush also. Dowd of the *New York Times* stated in 1989, "Just as Nancy Reagan protected her husband's stately persona, challenging advisers when her Ronnie was being overstuffed with facts or overbooked for public appearances, so Barbara Bush keeps a tigress's eye on people who make her husband look bad." A White House official said Bush "feels protective of the man and the office. And if she feels her man or the Presidency is being trivialized, she will certainly let you know." According to Alison Cook in the *Ladies' Home Journal,* Bush "insisted" she never lobbied her husband, because "the President needs a respite from the pressures of the office. 'I love my husband too much,' she says, 'to add to his burdens.'"[33]

As with earlier first ladies, the protector frame served as a form of domestic empowerment in its recognition of these women's power within the private sphere. However, because their protection sometimes extended into political affairs, this domestic empowerment was scrutinized to a greater extent than it had been for their predecessors. Reagan was criticized harshly for having too much power over her husband's schedule, for example, whereas Mamie Eisenhower, who as protector also kept a close eye on her husband's activities, did not face the same level of press questioning.[34]

Criticism of Reagan's private influence evidenced how fears of the "hidden power" of first ladies intensified during this era.[35] Speculation regarding their hidden power appeared most often in stories framing these first ladies as presidential advisors. Articles about both Reagan and Clinton constructed them as influential presidential advisors, which often led to the charge that they were "the power behind the throne."[36] Reagan's influence was seen as stemming from her close relationship with her husband. According to a *New York Times Magazine* profile by Weymouth in 1980, "She is constantly by her husband's side, and he considers her his best friend. She often attends staff meetings, and her husband uses her as a sounding board, discussing with her almost every important decision he makes." Weinraub in the *New York Times* in 1985 assessed Reagan's "evolving and growing role," which combined "what her friends call a powerful protective streak for her husband and her own input in the day-to-day workings of the Administration."[37] Reporters questioned the level of her influence, especially when she appeared to prompt her husband's answer to a question about talks with the Soviet Union. Accounts of her role in dismissing key aides throughout her husband's political life, particularly chief of staff Donald Regan, also "contributed to the image of Nancy Reagan as a behind-the-scenes manipulator" and thus a political interloper.[38]

The response from both Reagan and her husband to such charges was to downplay her influence. A 1984 *Washington Post* article noted that her husband "was clearly annoyed by reports that she is 'the power behind the throne, directing me or something.'" Another story stated, "Denying that her influence is pervasive, Mrs. Reagan said: 'I read that I make decisions and I'm the power behind the throne, and that I get people fired. I don't get people fired.'"[39] But after years of such denials, Reagan finally "acknowledged wielding power over her husband on some personnel decisions, and added, 'In no way do I apologize for it.'" According to a *New York Times* article that appeared after the 1988 election, she claimed she felt "compelled to exert influence in President Reagan's eight years in office because she did not believe that his staff generally served him well."[40] The timing of the article indicates that Reagan felt safe to admit her influence only after it was politically expedient and such comments could not be used against the Republican ticket in the election. It also suggests that the politicization of the first lady's power was so feared that Reagan wielded it far away from the media spotlight.

Journalists speculated that Clinton, on the other hand, was not just the "power behind the throne" but a usurper interested in personal political power. The Clinton campaign's claim that voters would get "two for the price of one" raised fears of a first lady as "co-president," which became a dominant theme in the framing of Clinton as a political interloper. Clinton's husband regarded her as "a political and policy adviser" and promised she would play a prominent role in his administration. According to *Ladies' Home Journal*, "When a reporter asked him who would be his Robert Kennedy—his most trusted policy advisor and confidant—Clinton answered without hesitation that it would be his wife." Fears of "undue influence" of an "unelected individual" became a common topic of reporters' stories and a central campaign issue.[41] Gwen Ifill of the *New York Times* in 1992 stated, "Many people who are uncomfortable with the notion that she might act as an unelected co-president have been quick to revive the phrase Mrs. Clinton used early in the campaign: 'If you vote for him, you get me.'" Alessandra Stanley, also of the *Times,* noted that "the couple's 'buy-one-get-one-free' approach soured when voters began viewing Mrs. Clinton as a hardheaded careerist who dominated her mate and seemed contemptuous of ordinary housewives." According to a 1992 *Ladies' Home Journal* profile, Clinton's critics saw her as a "tactlessly outspoken, driven woman who is using her husband as a surrogate for her own ambition."[42] One article reported that some voters found Clinton "pushy, strident, too independent," while another said she "was seen as tough, aggressive, angry, humorless, power hungry."[43] The perception in other reports was "of a woman who wants power for herself," and campaign researchers discovered that "more than Nancy Reagan, she is seen as running the show."[44] These descriptions suggest that a woman's ambition, when unchecked, is a dangerous threat. Clinton inadvertently "played into one of the conceptual frames by which news of women is defined: She confirmed male fears of a too-powerful woman who doesn't mind her proper place." As such she was framed as a political interloper who sought to advance into the political realm by way of the bedroom. Such negative perceptions, tied to the framing of her in the press, prompted an image makeover that then downplayed her role as presidential advisor and instead presented her in the more traditional first lady roles of "loyal helpmate and attentive mother."[45]

Scrutiny of Clinton's advisory role continued when she assumed the role of policy maker. The press noted she was going beyond the boundaries of first lady performance when she was appointed to "the most powerful official post ever assigned to a First Lady" and chaired a committee "to prepare legislation for overhauling the nation's health-care system." Reporters highlighted the unusualness of a first lady venturing so far into traditionally masculine political territory. Robert Pear in the *New York Times* reported, "Breaking decades of tradition, Hillary Rodham Clinton will set up shop in the West Wing of the White House, alongside the President's senior staff members, where she will help formulate policy on health care and other domestic issues." She made front-page news when she traveled to Capitol Hill for a "closed-door policy discussion with leaders from both parties." Calling the visit a "vivid display of her clout," Michael Kelly of the *New York Times* claimed that the trip, "extraordinary for a First Lady, was the latest manifestation of her influence" and that "on a symbolic level" the meeting underscored the importance "of Mrs. Clinton within the power structure of Washington." The language in these articles underscores the boundary-violating aspects of Clinton's role. By tying her visits to her "influence" and "power" rather than framing them as a routine part of her position as a task force chair, journalists implied that her actions were atypical for a first lady.[46]

After the failure of health care reform, Clinton "retreated" from taking the lead in shaping policy and played a "less public" role, according to press reports.[47] James Bennet in the *New York Times* in 1997 stated, "Scorched by the fallout after Mrs. Clinton's leadership in seeking universal health care coverage, the White House has labored to play down her influence, describing a conversion from policy-maker to speech-maker, helpmate, and goodwill ambassador." Another article claimed that her "failed attempt" at reforming health care "taught" Clinton the limitations of the first lady position.[48]

By characterizing both Reagan and Clinton as the "power behind the throne," journalists questioned the extent of their influence as presidential advisors, often implying that these women wielded too much political power. Both women were compared to Lady Macbeth. Robin Toner in the *New York Times* wrote that "at least 20 articles in major publications this year involved some comparison between Mrs. Clinton and a grim role model for political wives: Lady Macbeth."[49] Such negative constructions of Clinton and Reagan as public women were reminiscent of press framing from the earliest decades of this country's history, when presidents' wives such as Dolley Madison and Rachel Jackson were labeled Jezebels. Lady Macbeth now replaced Jezebel as the epitaph for a political wife who sought to use her husband to achieve her own ends. Like the biblical Jezebel, Lady Macbeth exercised "undue influence" on her husband, leading to his downfall.[50] By casting Reagan and Clinton each as a modern-day Lady Macbeth, critics constructed them as political interlopers to be feared for their refusal to remain contained as well as for the potential consequences of women's unchecked power in the male political reserve.

Following the critical press coverage of Reagan and Clinton as political interlopers, their successors were often framed as avoiding advisory or policy-making roles. Both Barbara and Laura Bush claimed to be uninvolved in their husbands' work. A *Ladies' Home Journal* article, indirectly referencing Reagan, noted that Barbara Bush "does not wish to be seen as the power behind the throne. Her political instincts, she insists, are 'around zero.'" The *Washington Post* echoed this theme, claiming that Barbara Bush "does not seek an active political or policy role."[51] Stories about Laura Bush's disinterest in presidential advising made direct references to Clinton. Laura Bush was "not involved in the mechanics of her husband's career in the mode of Hillary Clinton." Bruni in the *New York Times* said, "Mrs. Bush made it clear that her interest was in helping him, not promoting herself, and that she was not offering voters two for the price of one." Marian Burros wrote that Bush claimed she was "not that knowledgeable about most issues" and as first lady "declared policy questions off limits."[52]

While these women did not generate the same level of criticism as their predecessors, journalists remained skeptical about their efforts to downplay their political influence. Barbara Bush's evasion of an advisory role was viewed by some journalists as a calculated attempt to avoid criticism. McLellan in a *Ladies' Home Journal* article noted that Bush "won't even hint at substance in public. Some might call her self-imposed silence muzzling; to others it's simple wisdom." Radcliffe of the *Washington Post* asserted that "behind the non-threatening white hair and wrinkles ticks the mind of a politically shrewd woman who choreographs her moves as carefully as her husband does his own," thus highlighting Bush's "hidden power."[53] Reporters were quick to note occasional cracks in her façade. In 1989 when she made an "off-the-cuff" remark on gun control that was at odds with her husband's views, her press secretary announced she would "stop talking publicly about controversial issues." However, she "made a sharp break with her practice of not speaking out on policy matters" when she told reporters during the 1992 campaign that abortion was "a personal thing" and should not be included in the GOP platform. According to Stanley in the *New York Times*, Bush quickly silenced herself and "retreated from the fuss she created, insisting that she had no place in policy-making" and telling reporters, "I'm through with abortion. I'm not running for President. George Bush is." This remark implied that she recognized her status as political interloper and had quickly retreated in order to quell criticism. Such coverage also indicated that journalists continued to be suspicious about the extent of her political interest and private influence.[54]

The coverage of these women reflects the assertion that "presidential wives raise the more problematic issue of the relationship between women, *sexuality*, and power," a relationship that had come under considerable scrutiny during the previous era. Williams, in her 1992 article, echoed this view: "All First Ladies influence their husbands to some degree. . . . Voters can live with this influence, as long as it's relatively subtle and can fall under the rubric of a wife looking after her husband's interest."[55] For journalists the Bush women usually fell safely under that rubric. Reagan and Clinton, on the other hand, were charged with overstepping the boundaries, evidencing a greater concern over the private power of first ladies during this era.

The first ladies of this era concentrated their efforts on helping women and children, leading journalists to frame their advocacy almost exclusively as an extension of their role as mothers. Barbara Bush's support of numerous causes was framed as "noblesse oblige." David S. Broder of the *Washington Post* said, "She comes from a tradition that says those who are favored with wealth and power thereby acquire reciprocal obligations to those who lack any advantages."[56] One article by Sarah Booth Conroy claimed that Bush "has always been noted for her lady bountiful, noblesse oblige attitude toward capital causes." Conroy in another article stated that, "for the last four years, every benefit has had Barbara Bush as an honorary chairman," recognizing the power of her name. Bush demonstrated the "compassion" promoted by her husband's administration when she "cradled an infant, kissed a toddler and hugged an adult AIDS victim" at a hospice for AIDS-infected infants.[57] An AIDS activist told Lois Romano of the *Washington Post*, "You can't imagine what one hug from the first lady is worth. . . . [T]hat's worth more than a thousand public service announcements."[58]

Bush's primary cause was literacy, though, which reinforced the maternal aspects of her volunteerism. And like her mother-in-law, Laura Bush devoted herself to literacy as well as to other educational issues. In a story about Laura Bush's plans to recruit new teachers and promote early childhood learning, Gerhart of the *Washington Post* called her "a high-profile cheerleader for public education" who could "back up her rhetoric with a remarkable talent for reading upside down while showing a picture book to students." Gerhart noted that Bush had "taken care to showcase herself as an informed supporter of her husband rather than a policy advocate." Such gendering of Bush's advocacy, by both herself and through Gerhart's framing, depoliticized her efforts.[59]

Advocacy efforts rehabilitated the public images of both Reagan and Clinton by containing their influence to women's issues. Reagan's "Just Say No" to drugs program aimed at children and teenagers was credited with "bringing her popularity to an all-time high."[60] Following the failure of health care reform, Clinton's policy making and advising were characterized largely as advocacy efforts on behalf of women and children, a change in framing that contained her power and limited her influence to gender-appropriate issues. In 2000 *McCall's* listed "extending health care to children" and "helping to change the adoption and foster care system" as Clinton's principle advocacy accomplishments as first lady. Clinton, as "the most traveled first lady in history," also acted as an advocate for women internationally. In a story about her 1997 tour of Africa, Victoria Falls, in the *Washington Post,* called Clinton an "international feminist . . . urging 'solidarity' among women of the world," noting that, "as in her other trips, she has convened round-table discussions at nearly every stop in Africa to talk with local women's leaders about the challenges facing them in their home countries, from family planning to education and economic advancement to domestic violence."[61] She promoted the same causes domestically, including family planning, early childhood education, and start-up aid for small businesses.[62] James Bennet of the *New York Times* observed in 1997 that, "while the White House may lump her various causes under the anodyne rubric of 'children's issues,' Mrs. Clinton is still pursuing a far broader agenda of causes—including foreign development, immunization in the inner cities and expanding financial credit for women—than almost any predecessor in the undefined role of First Lady." By acting as advocates for women and children, first ladies "helped to define the parameters of women's political space" and in many ways "reified the nineteenth-century assumption that women's political space was somehow different from men's." Their more traditional gender performances also diffused press criticism of their advocacy.[63]

Throughout this period, gender continued to define the performance of the first lady position in ways that increasingly constrained these women's actions—to a greater extent than their predecessors. It was as if the first lady position, particularly under Reagan and Clinton, had exceeded its limits in influence both privately (Reagan) and publicly (Clinton). Any exercise or perception of power, even in the private sphere, was now scrutinized intensely by journalists. The resulting coverage focused on conflicts, contrasts, and criticisms of the women who held the first lady position.

Exploring the Boundaries of First Ladies' Political Influence

The first lady institution has always served as a site of contestation regarding women's "proper" place. The women who held the position became powerful symbols of women's roles through the journalistic practice of personification framing, and the image used to present them evolved from that of public women to political celebrities to political activists. By treating first ladies as public figures functioning within the political sphere, journalists covering them in the news normalized women's public participation and political efficacy. However, because their performances were judged in relation to the prevailing gender ideologies of their times, the press consistently restricted their influence to make them serve as role models for American women or champions of women's issues only. The performance of the first lady position has often been viewed as relevant to women only, instead of all citizens, furthering the assumption that women and women's issues remain less central to U.S. political culture. Press coverage of women in politics "is an artifact of this country's age-old but unresolved debate over women citizens' proper roles versus 'proper women's' place."[64]

By the end of the twentieth century, the performance of gender roles and the subsequent performance of the first lady position were the subject of a heated debate. Through their gendered framing of first ladies, journalists created boundaries of empowerment and containment that marked the "proper" performance of the first lady position. Iconic first ladies and gendered prescriptions were used as boundary markers, to delineate the elasticity and limitations of first lady performance. When a first lady was suspected of straying too far into the male political sphere, the press framed her as a political interloper, evidencing a discourse of containment regarding first ladies' political activities as well as the cultural fears over women's power and place within U.S. political culture.

ICONIC FIRST LADIES AS HISTORICAL BOUNDARY MARKERS

Journalists continued to compare and critique first ladies past and present as they sought to define the "proper" role of the contemporary first lady.

Reporters looked more frequently to the legacy of the first lady institution in an effort to contextualize (albeit in a limited way) current coverage of presidents' wives. In such newspaper and magazine stories, iconic first ladies represented an amalgam of gender and role performance and functioned as boundary markers, delineating the historical limits of the first lady position. These icons were used by journalists to frame their contemporary counterparts, evidencing the historical extent and limits of gendered celebrity as well as the consequences of press framing.

The activist icons were often used by journalists to establish the boundaries of the first lady's political influence, particularly in relation to their role as advisor. For example, Gwen Ifill of the *New York Times* said in 1992, "The role of the President's wife has always been a subject for debate, particularly during the years of such close Presidential confidantes as Abigail Adams, Eleanor Roosevelt, Rosalynn Carter and Nancy Reagan. But Mrs. Clinton's much more publicly acknowledged influence has raised new questions." Because Clinton's influence seemed to extend beyond that of any of her predecessors, she was viewed as exerting too much power. Reagan's and Clinton's political influence was often measured in comparison to that of Eleanor Roosevelt or Rosalynn Carter, who represented the extremes of the first lady's advisory role. Concerning Reagan's influence, one profile asserted, "Nancy Reagan is a modern political wife, far more involved in the political process than, say, Mamie Eisenhower was, but she should not be compared to Rosalynn Carter, a very active First Lady." Dowd in the *New York Times* in 1984 stated that Reagan was "careful not to appear too influential." The article quoted an aide as saying, "She doesn't want to come across as an Eleanor Roosevelt or a Rosalynn Carter." Yet, despite these efforts to distance herself from the activist icons, Reagan was judged by journalists to be a more powerful "hidden hand" advisor in some respects than either Roosevelt or Carter, evidencing the anxieties over the first lady's private power in the post-second-wave period.[65]

Because she overstepped the boundaries of first lady performance, journalists lumped Reagan in with activist icons Roosevelt and Carter in their coverage of Clinton. In a *New York Times* article in 1992, Stanley said that Reagan was remembered "as a behind-the-scenes manipulator who was the real power behind a pliant husband." In some articles Reagan was mentioned in tandem with Carter, as in a *Washington Post* story that referred to Reagan and Carter as "objects of continual controversy."[66] Next to Reagan, Clinton was most frequently compared to Roosevelt, whom she routinely cited as one of the women she most admired. According to a *Washington Post* article by Kurtz, "many liberal women have elevated Hillary Clinton to Eleanor Roosevelt status."[67] Clinton frequently noted that, like herself, Roosevelt had been criticized by the press even before she moved into the White House; Clinton said she often pondered what Roosevelt would do in certain situations.[68] In these stories, activist icons marked the extremes of a first lady's influence. Articles noted that such first ladies regularly generated controversy and criticism by being "too influential," "very active," or "the real power." Rather than acting as positive models for first lady performance, the activist icons served primarily as cautionary tales, warning of the consequences of overstepping boundaries, and thus creating limitations on the political influence of the first lady advisory role.

Activist icons also served as contrasts to more traditional first ladies. Barbara Bush "cautioned reporters that she disliked comparisons to Eleanor Roosevelt, who was not as beloved in the Republican household where Barbara Bush was reared as in many other Depression-era homes." Patricia Leigh Brown, in a profile of Bush in the *New York Times,* claimed, "Unlike Nancy Reagan or Rosalynn Carter, she professes not to have much interest in her husband's business." Elaine Sciolino used Clinton's activism to frame Laura Bush as a "more traditional" first lady. In the *New York Times* Sciolino stated, "Mrs. Bush has made it clear that she will not be a policy-making first lady in the mold of Mrs. Clinton, an ambitious, outspoken, high-profile lawyer who alienated much of official Washington and many Americans with her determination to be a player on hot-button issues like health care."[69] Such contrasts reassured readers that these first ladies had no plans to overstep the boundaries of their position as their activist predecessors had done, evidencing the reification of such gendered restrictions that press coverage promulgated.

To assess current first ladies, journalists also used references to iconic political wives, who were remembered primarily for their more passive performance of the first lady position. *Ladies' Home Journal* proclaimed Barbara Bush "the most popular first lady in years—arguably the most beloved since Bess Truman," an assessment echoed by first ladies scholar Betty Boyd Caroli, who told the *Washington Post,* "She reminds me of Bess Truman."[70] A *New York Times* story likened Bush "to Jacqueline Kennedy for her skill at molding her public persona and for her upper-class savoir-faire." Bush cited Pat Nixon as a role model, calling her "courageous, loyal" and "down-to-earth."[71] These comparisons to the more traditional political wives implied that Bush was personally disinterested in politics, which in turn contributed to her popularity. Similar framing was used with Laura Bush. According to a *New York Times* profile, "Some historians predict that the first lady she may come to resemble most is Mamie Eisenhower." The article quotes first ladies scholar Gil Troy, "Laura Bush is most like Mamie Eisenhower in that she will resolutely in public refuse to appear to be interested at all in wielding power in any way. Like Mamie, you'll get that traditional, reassuring feminine presence."[72] These articles reinforced journalists' framing of Barbara Bush and Laura Bush as "more traditional" first ladies, whose performance of the first lady position did not court controversy because it remained safely within the boundaries of appropriate feminine activity. Within this context Truman, Eisenhower, Kennedy, and Nixon were remembered for distancing themselves from politics, a major shift from the previous era of feminist and first lady activism, when these women were judged more critically for their very lack of political activity.

First lady as fashion icon frequently appeared as a frame in discussions of the first lady's cultural influence. When it came to fashion, reporters repeatedly measured Reagan against the memory of Jacqueline Kennedy. The *New York Times* stated that "no one could compete with Mrs. Kennedy for stylishness until Mrs. Reagan came along with her high-fashion wardrobe." Radcliffe in the *Washington Post* surmised that "not since Jacqueline Kennedy have a first lady's clothes, figure, friends, family life and age aroused such interest." The *Ladies' Home Journal* declared, "Her taste and style have the fashion industry declaring that this First Lady is doing more for American clothing than anybody since Jacqueline Kennedy."[73] Through such favorable comparisons to Kennedy, reporters elevated Reagan to the status of fashion icon; just as Kennedy symbolized "the exciting early sixties," Reagan represented "the high-living eighties." As Radcliffe of the *Washington Post* asserted, Reagan "symbolized conspicuous affluence," providing journalists with a real-life version of the opulence represented in television shows such as *Dynasty*. According to a story by Leslie Bennetts about the 1981 inaugural, "Limousines, white tie and $10,000 ball gowns are in . . . as Nancy Reagan sweeps from fete to fete in a glittering full-length Maximilian mink."[74]

Reagan also faced criticism for her extravagant tastes, however. Bennetts in the *New York Times* claimed in 1981 that Reagan was "being hailed by some as a glamorous paragon of chic and criticized by others for exercising her opulent tastes in an economy that is inflicting hardship on so many." Anne-Marie Schiro pointed out that Reagan's coverage was reminiscent of the criticism faced by Kennedy for reportedly "spending thousands of dollars on clothing from Paris designers," although critiques of Reagan were much more consistent—and negative—than those of Kennedy.[75] For journalists Reagan violated the boundaries of feminine celebrity by being too out of touch with the average woman, a critique that had been leveled also against Kennedy at times. Because Reagan's extravagant tastes were difficult to emulate, she failed to serve the first lady's function as a role model for American women, further revealing the ways in which positioning first ladies as icons worked to contain contemporary performances of first lady roles.

During this period journalists used iconic first ladies to mark the boundaries of the first lady's celebrity. Previously Eleanor Roosevelt and Jacqueline Kennedy had anchored the extremes of first lady celebrity and ideological performance, for Roosevelt represented the political influence of activist icons and Kennedy signified the cultural influence of fashion icons. Barbara Bush and Laura Bush played it safe within the appropriate boundary markers, but Reagan and Clinton were frequently framed as ignoring and going beyond the boundaries, by being either too political or too extravagant. Such framing delineated historical boundaries of feminine performance, which were used by reporters to critique the performance of contemporary first ladies.

BOUNDARIES OF EMPOWERMENT AND CONTAINMENT

By defining what was deemed a proper or improper performance of the first lady position, journalists created many of the invisible boundaries that first ladies were subsequently accused of trespassing. The age-old question of women's "proper" sphere of influence was still a hot topic in the 1990s. Women's roles in families, in the workforce, and in politics formed a central issue of the 1992 campaign. As Judy Mann of the *Washington Post* put it: "The domestic debate in this year's election is going to be about the proper role of women in society. This is why Hillary Clinton is such a flashpoint. It is why Barbara Bush is not." Williams in the *Washington Post Magazine* contended that the 1992 election represented "a symbolic referendum on all America's conflicted feelings about feminism, family and child-rearing," claiming that "both the warring campaigns and the news media have found these four women irresistible as manipulable symbols of some of the most powerful themes in Americans' lives." For Tamar Lewin in the *New York Times,* the strategy was "to paint Mrs. Clinton as a radical feminist, in contrast with her Republican counterparts: Barbara Bush, quintessential grandmother, and Marilyn Quayle, who, like Mrs. Clinton, is a lawyer but has put aside her own career to support her husband's." Mann argued that the two major parties were offering opposing images of women's place, with the Democrats "welcoming women into the public sphere and starring them as candidates who wield power on behalf of other women," and the Republicans "playing the Barbara card, playing to the themes of family values and family protection, more code words for pushing women out of the public sphere and enshrining them in the private sphere where they can shine as nurturers, mothers, and support players." Such constructions promoted the domestic empowerment of women over private family matters, evidencing the legacy of ideologies such as true womanhood and republican motherhood, yet contained women's influence to the home, thus relegating women to the fringes of political culture and implying that women's "proper" place was still the domestic sphere. The resulting "family values" debate was framed primarily as a competition between the wives.[76]

When "family values" took center stage as a campaign issue in 1992, so too did the more "traditional" candidates' wives, who were empowered by strategists, pundits, and the press as embodiments of their husbands' "family values." Barbara Bush was so frequently referred to as her husband's "secret weapon" that one story called her the "un-secret weapon" and "the worst-kept secret of the 1992 campaign."[77] According to Stanley of the *New York Times,* "Her political mettle, backed by favorability ratings in public opinion polls that are nearly three times higher than her husband's, scares Democrats." Both the traditionalist Bush and new traditionalist Quayle were featured speakers at the 1992 Republican National Convention. The *Washington Post* reported, "Barbara Bush and her family values message—both in carefully chosen words and unmistakable image—have made it to center stage this year, casting her in a more visible campaign role than she has ever played before." The Republicans pitted Bush's popular grandmother image against the feminist careerism of Clinton, framing Bush with a rhetoric of familial, and thus political, empowerment.[78]

Clinton was consigned to the background at the Democratic convention, "listening to her husband speak and wearing the traditional gaze of the political spouse." As Anna Quindlen noted in a *New York Times* editorial, Clinton would have caused "an uproar" if she had taken the podium at the DNC: "People would have said she was ambitious and power mad." For Mann the "retro-mom and retro-granny combo" of Quayle and Bush avoided such criticism: "Unlike Hillary Clinton, Barbara Bush and Marilyn Quayle are support players. Hillary Clinton is a player, and there's the rub."[79] Traditional gender framing was used to justify Bush and Quayle's political participation, as with many of their predecessors, whereas Clinton's ostensible interloper status was used as a justification for her political containment. Catherine Manegold of the *New York Times* claimed that, "after hailing Hillary Clinton as a model new woman able to balance a family and a thriving law practice, Democrats retreated in the face of stinging criticism" and changed Clinton's image to "a presumably kinder, quieter wife and mother who beams incessantly at her man." Similarly, Karen Lehrman in a *Times* editorial said, "She's softened her hair, wardrobe and makeup, and even seems to have abandoned her yuppie headband—all with the none-too-subtle intent of making her appear more maternal, domestic, average, likeable."[80] Hence, Clinton was put in her "proper" (gendered) place, and her alleged quest for personal power was contained, at least for the moment. However, the press remained suspicious of Clinton and viewed her image makeover as a possible ruse to mask her political ambitions.

These women were pitted against each other as personifications of gender ideologies, a point that was made by several female journalists. Manegold concluded that the result was little more than a "political cat-fight" pitting "'good mom' versus 'bad mom'" while ignoring the real political issues.[81] Similar comments were made by Amy E. Schwartz of the *Washington Post,* who argued that both the campaign and the media were "pitting women against one another, Marilyn vs. Hillary, Barbara vs. Hillary, even, in some earlier coverage, Tipper vs. Hillary—is an old-fashioned way to replace a straightforward policy fight with a presumably more entertaining catfight." These remarks support Susan Douglas's contention that "the catfight remains an extremely popular way for the news media to represent women's struggles for equality and power."[82] According to Schwartz, "The notion that women owe the family some specific amount, which can be measured and therefore judged, is intertwined with the idea that one woman can be contrasted to another in a good girl/bad girl scenario." She concluded that "there is something morally disgusting about the spectacle of politicians, candidates, and commentators sitting around and calibrating the exact amount of personal sacrifice by women . . . that qualifies as upholding 'family values,' and damning certain women's self-sacrifice or self-subordination as inadequate." The result, as Williams observed, was that "our conversation about women's responsibilities and women's lives is artificially polarized by the two options of professional self-fulfillment and children" rather than reflecting the true complexities of women's lives.[83] While these female journalists pointed out how the "catfight" frame served politically to contain and devalue these women and the family values debate, they failed to note that many of the articles pitting these women against each other were in fact written by women or appeared in women's publications, demonstrating women journalists' complicity in creating such containment boundaries.

The debate over the "proper" roles of women and first ladies resulted in a no-win situation and a series of unattainable ideals. Gerhart, in a *Washington Post* profile of Laura Bush in 2000, pointed out the tendency of journalists to create such "either-or" double binds: "In this Age of Celebrity, how we love to stereotype public personalities to fit our mood of the moment. We are so eager to take all of the 'ands' of a complex personality and replace every single one with an 'or.'" Gerhart offered the example of Clinton, who "stars as the Neo Feminazi Witch or the Fully Actualized Modern Female, depending on which type is doing the typing." In the case of Bush, Gerhart claimed, reporters were obsessed with questions such as "Is Laura Bush a '50s retro wife? Or a thoroughly modern woman? Whatever that means. Is she publicly genteel and privately tart? Is she a stealth adviser, influential behind the scenes, or a dutiful helpmate, fading into the background?"[84] Similar comments were made in a story about Barbara Bush in 1992. Previewing her convention speech, a *Washington Post* article asked "which Barbara Bush will be speaking? The devoted wife, loving mother, down-to-earth grandmother. . . . Or the cagey political partner, who will capitalize on her image as the most popular first lady in decades, to keep her man in the White House?" According to Quinn of the *Washington Post,* Reagan "got criticized no matter what she did. She played the adoring, supportive wife and got killed for it—especially for 'the Gaze.'"[85] Such frames worked to contain the first lady's influence, but because the boundaries of woman's performance were so confining, the result was a no-win situation, not just for the first lady herself but for all women.

Female journalists, in particular, recognized that unrealistic expectations of the first lady role created double binds, many of which developed in the second-wave era as a reaction to the activist first ladies. Quinn concluded "it is a thankless and confusing role—you are damned if you do and damned if you don't. The First Lady (the title itself is hopelessly outdated) has always been in limbo, in a twilight zone." Joyce Purnick in a 1992 *New York Times* editorial asserted, "Even as the public learns to accept flawed candidates, it persists in demanding some idealized, elusive perfection from political wives. And just whose perfection is it anyway?" This ideal, for Purnick, forces first ladies to walk a tightrope between "too much" and "not enough," resulting in criticism stemming from such double binds: "Eleanor Roosevelt was too independent. Jacqueline Kennedy too passive. Nancy Reagan too controlling. Barbara Bush too gray. Hillary Clinton . . . too independent." Purnick wondered "what it is in the American psyche that wants its political wives to be Stepford Wives, fantasy femininity?" Quindlen made a similar observation, noting that "the remarkable thing about how long the fantasy of the adoring and apolitical First Lady has endured is how few occupants of the job have conformed to it." Williams urged journalists, politicians, and the public to put an "end to the phony family politics that now turn political wives into Rorschach images" and "role models" when their lives are actually "fantastically distorted by the practice of politics." By pointing out the boundaries containing the performance of the first lady, these women journalists, like many of their predecessors, defended the political activities of first ladies. Yet they also reified the boundaries by normalizing the first lady role as a no-win situation, particularly by referencing the truncated mediated memories of iconic first ladies to bolster their claims.[86]

Conclusion

A 2000 *New York Times* editorial posed the question, "Does it still make sense to have a first lady who is not hired, elected or paid by anyone, but is treated like knockoff royalty and held to archaic standards of behavior?"[87] As more women run for political office and have careers of their own, reporters increasingly question what to make of political wives, who garner power through marriage yet play an important role in a two-person career such as politics. Journalists themselves are facing a double bind:

how to cover a position that is both traditional and nontraditional. This would force them to abandon the false dichotomies and competitive frames that make for entertaining and easy-to-write stories. It would also require them to rethink the boundaries of performance and containment they helped create and sustain in the first place.

Journalists' use of gender framing in this era limited representations of female performance. The conflicting gender ideologies of feminism and traditionalism were frequently juxtaposed, with political wives personifying either one or the other, a reductive and simplistic form of framing that ignores the complexities of gender performance and first ladies' lives. For example, Barbara Bush told Christine Reinhardt of *McCall's* in 1992, "You know, I don't sit home and bake cookies all day long. I'm a little tired of that [impression]." While coverage generally praised traditionalism, some journalists were critical of this return to constructions of women they viewed as constraining and limited. Quinn concluded that Clinton, "and not someone like Barbara Bush, truly represents the majority of American women today." Thus, these women ended up in a no-win situation, constantly facing both praise and criticism.[88]

Such gendered framing carried over into discussions of the first lady role. When these women acted as helpmates and advocated causes benefiting women and children, they were deemed to be acting within the "proper" boundaries of first lady performance and their coverage was more positive, often reflecting the domestic empowerment of previous eras. However, when first ladies were perceived to have too much power, either in public like Clinton or in private like Reagan, their coverage was critical. Both Reagan and Clinton represented political interlopers who abused the power of the position, whether by acting as the "power behind the throne" or by embodying personal political ambition like Lady Macbeth.

Hence, the framing of the first lady institution from 1980 to 2001 focused largely on the gender debate over the "proper" place and power of women in general and of the first lady in particular. Over two hundred years of gendered framing culminated in the creation of boundaries that served alternately to define, empower, and contain the gendered performance and political influence of the first lady position. Journalists used iconic first ladies to mark the historical boundaries of first lady performances, naturalizing the limitations for first ladies. These boundaries were subsequently used to define proper comportment for contemporary first ladies. The women who embraced domesticity were pitted against political interlopers such as Reagan and Clinton. Even at the end of the century, journalists were still pondering the "proper" place of women and the "proper" role of the first lady, coming no closer to a resolution than their predecessors had done, yet still using many of the same frames rooted in the gendered prescriptions of the early nineteenth century to assess the performance of the first lady position.

A Century of Press Framing

A

Washington Post story on Laura Bush from the 2004 campaign observed, "First ladies seem to be publicly defined in relation to one another. Is a first lady or a prospective first lady like Jackie Kennedy or Nancy Reagan? It's like descriptions of hail—is it the size of a marble or a golf ball?—as if first ladies exist as some kind of environmental phenomena that come in a handful of predetermined sizes." According to this story, Bush believes that "the American public actually has broad and nuanced perceptions of first ladies. But the media are inclined to use a shorthand. 'It's easier to put people in a box, let it be either/or.'"[1] Despite pointing out the limitations of media framing, this article used the same framing formula. This is an example of the complexities of first lady press coverage, which often recognizes the challenges of the position while still holding first ladies to a high standard that journalists created. Many aspects of media coverage have changed since *Harper's Bazaar* offered "A Comparison" of Ida McKinley and Mary Bryan in August 1900, but there are still some striking similarities between now and then, particularly when it comes to the gendered framing of the first lady institution.[2]

The object of this study was to examine how journalists framed stories about the first ladies throughout the twentieth century and to assess specific implications of such framing practices. This process was necessarily selective and interpretive, given the scope and the wealth of press coverage. I have been particularly sensitive to cultural patterns and recurring frames shaping this coverage, especially the ways in which it reflected gender, publicity, and power during each historical period. Through journalistic personification framing, first ladies have always served as sites of ideological contestation over women's roles. First ladies have been routinely positioned by the press to be role models for American women, which resulted in their emergence as public women, political celebrities, political activists, or political interlopers. Such publicity made first ladies some of the earliest and most visible public women, which legitimized ordinary women's political activity and influence. However, while their status as public women and political celebrities resulted in both access to and influence within U.S. political culture, first ladies remained on the fringes, with their influence limited largely to domestic matters and women's issues. When their influence seemed to trespass into the male political reserve, the media coverage exhibited a rhetoric of containment that suggested the political activities of certain first ladies violated the gendered boundaries that the press erected. There are five key themes that emerge from this analysis.

Gender Ideologies and Press Framing

First, my analysis identifies the journalistic practice of personification framing, whereby an individual is positioned as the embodiment of an ideological performance, in order to render the complexities of that performance more quickly and easily comprehensible. Framing each first lady as a personification of one of the dominant and competing gender ideologies reflects the contestation of women's roles within the limited narrative framework of a single story. Examining how she functions as an embodiment of a gender ideology reveals media texts serving as sites of cultural conflict over women and politics.

The gender ideologies that compete to define American womanhood are often based on the concept of separate spheres. Tensions exist between ideologies that promote the domestic sphere as women's primary place and those that extend women's roles into the public and political spheres. True womanhood was a Victorian ideal that dominated gender prescriptions at the turn of the twentieth century. It prized women's domesticity and viewed the home as women's proper place. Throughout the century true womanhood's focus on domesticity continued to influence gender prescriptions. It encouraged the domestic ideal of the Cold War homemaker as well as the "return to the home" promoted by new traditionalism. Even feminism, with its call for expanded rights for women, at times reflected the tenets of true womanhood. Early twentieth-century social feminism and the ideology of the new woman shared the true woman's belief in the moral superiority of women, using such expediency arguments to justify women's social reform and political activities, which were seen as a necessary extension of women's domestic roles. Similarly, the ideology of republican motherhood validated women's civic participation and was frequently used to frame women's volunteerism. Political activism, though, was the hallmark of second-wave feminism. The women's movement sought to improve women's political, economic, and legal standing within U.S. culture. The feminist mantra became "the personal is political," which helped justify women's empowerment by blurring the boundaries between private and public spheres. Many women throughout the years (first ladies in particular) found themselves balancing domestic duties with growing roles outside the home, which prompted the notion of the "superwoman" who moved successfully between the different spheres.

Press coverage of first ladies reflected these competing gender ideologies, often symbolizing both traditional and modern ideals of womanhood and serving as a site of contestation over women's roles. Ida McKinley and Edith Roosevelt personified true womanhood at the turn of the twentieth century. Their modern-era successors were viewed as balancing the domesticity of true womanhood with the civic engagement of the new woman and republican motherhood. Public women were still viewed as suspect, however, and the first ladies' increased political activity sometimes raised questions. For journalists, gender ideologies could explain women's participation in social and political reform. The maternalism of social feminism and republican motherhood, for example, helped justify the advocacy efforts of Ellen Axson Wilson, Florence Harding, and Eleanor Roosevelt. By characterizing these activities as mere extensions of their roles as wives and mothers, press framing aided in quelling criticism of first ladies' political activities and normalized other women's presence, albeit limited, in the political sphere.

The locus of women's political power shifted primarily to the private sphere during the postwar period. Bess Truman, Mamie Eisenhower, Jacqueline Kennedy, and Pat Nixon all personified the domestic ideal of women as homemakers, helpmates, and Cold War consumers. Even Eleanor Roosevelt's efforts were often constructed as extensions of her home duties. Such framing imbued women's roles with a sense of domestic empowerment but simultaneously contained women's political influence to matters concerning only home and family.

By the time Nixon became first lady, the ideals of second-wave feminism were influencing press discussions of women's roles, and the Cold War domestic ideal was widely derided as the "feminine mystique." Nixon was criticized as a throwback to the previous era, while her counterparts were framed as contemporary women who, like many of their modern-era predecessors, embraced the political activism and independence promoted by second-wave feminism without rejecting their roles as wives and mothers. An adversarial press culture flourished during this era, which led journalists to critique the activism of Lady Bird Johnson, Betty Ford, and Rosalynn Carter and to question women's growing political influence. Such ambivalent coverage caught the first ladies in a double bind by simultaneously praising and critiquing their political influence, framing some first ladies as too political and others such as Nixon not political enough.

Second-wave feminism inspired a backlash at the end of the twentieth century, which perpetuated the double binds presented in media coverage of first ladies' performance of gender. This period saw the return to the domestic ideal (embodied in Nancy Reagan, Barbara Bush, and Laura Bush), which was pitted against second-wave feminism (personified by Hillary Rodham Clinton). Such framing created a competition between these women that reflected the larger cultural debate over women's roles. Personification framing was able to capture the contention over women's roles in various eras. But too often such framing reduced the complexities of these women's lives by using gender ideologies as shortcuts that often oversimplified discussions of gender performance.

Empowerment and Containment in Press Framing

The second theme concerns the role played by media framing in deciding the "proper" performances of the first lady institution. By reporting on the various duties of first ladies, journalists legitimized these duties as part of the first lady institution. Stories about the increasing public and political activities of presidents' wives expanded the boundaries of first lady performance and positioned first ladies as public women, political celebrities, and political activists, all of which empowered women as citizens to varying degrees.

The press positions first ladies as public women and political celebrities and as role models for American women. This empowerment of their celebrity helps elevate women's status in U.S. political culture. The celebrity that comes from press coverage made many first ladies prominent public figures in their own right, placed at the center of women's public culture. Some first ladies represented the domestic empowerment of women, particularly as consumers. Both Harding and Roosevelt, for example, promoted women's consumerism as an act of citizenship. Other first ladies such as Eisenhower, Kennedy, and Reagan endorsed Cold War consumption through their personal styles, which the press encouraged American women to emulate.

First ladies have also used their status as celebrities and political activists to work on behalf of women and children's issues. Wilson, Roosevelt, and Johnson all promoted housing reform in Washington, D.C. Ford's candor regarding her personal battle with breast cancer alleviated the stigma associated with the disease. Both Barbara Bush and Laura Bush promoted literacy and educational programs. Clinton worked to reform not only health care but also the foster care and adoption systems in the United States. Clinton and Laura Bush used their celebrity abroad to support programs benefiting women and children around the world. By lending their names to causes and by advocating social reform, first ladies expanded upon the tradition of upper-class women's volunteerism.

Coverage of first ladies' public activities both normalized women's place in the public sphere yet also worked to establish boundaries that restricted women's political influence to domestic matters. Problems existed, for example, when first ladies overstepped certain boundaries. The result was the framing of these women as political interlopers, which functions as a rhetoric of containment, and the results are visible in certain cases. Carter, for example, stopped releasing information regarding her lobbying efforts on behalf of the Equal Rights Amendment after being accused by ERA opponents of overstepping the boundaries of first lady political influence. Reagan repeatedly refuted claims that she wielded hidden-hand influence over her husband during his tenure, only admitting to the press the extent of her influence as she prepared to leave the White House. Barbara Bush publicly denied having any interest in political matters. If she violated private-sphere boundaries by speaking out on issues, she quickly censured herself and claimed her personal opinions were of no political importance. Most striking, Clinton underwent an image makeover during the 1992 campaign, following the failure of her health care reform efforts. She took on the more traditional role of helpmate in order to counter the frame that she was a political interloper whose personal political ambitions included serving as "co-president," a frame that dominated her press coverage. All of these first ladies were charged at some point with being "the power behind the throne," itself a sexualized discourse that has long been used to critique and contain women's political influence. Thus, gendered media frames function as boundaries alternating between empowerment and containment, giving journalists extraordinary power to define and assess the performance of the first lady position.

These boundaries have implications for both first ladies and all women within U.S. culture. The gendering of their status as political celebrities impacted the first ladies' ability to extend their influence beyond issues tied to the domestic sphere. If first ladies ventured into the male political sphere they found their actions contested, often through press coverage characterizing these activities as violations of proper first lady comportment. The press coverage of first ladies as role models and prominent political women implies that women, while influential in regards to domestic and maternal matters, should remain on the fringes of the larger U.S. political culture, which is primarily a male domain.

Framing of the first lady institution throughout the twentieth century evidences the power that journalists wield in shaping social reality. Framing perpetuates "certain routine and persistent ways of making sense of the social world, as found through specific and significant frames" that "find their way into media discourse, and are thus available to guide public life."[3] Journalists' gendered framing of first ladies has defined the boundaries of both gender and institutional role performance, categorizing these women according to their private and public activities as well as their political influence. By positioning them as role models for American women, journalists have promoted ideologies that delineate the boundaries of gender performance and seek to define women's "proper" place in U.S. political culture. Thus journalists play a significant role in shaping both cultural and political norms. Because of the cultural significance attributed to the first lady institution (largely by the press), the ways in which media frames empowered and contained first ladies as political women helped make sense of women's presence in the public and political spheres and have guided public expectations regarding women's performance of their various social roles.

Iconic First Ladies and Press Framing

Evidencing the role of collective memory in press framing, iconic first ladies function as key boundary markers in press assessments of the first lady position. Journalists "create a repertoire of past events that is used as a standard for judging contemporary action."[4] In this case journalists elevate a select group of first ladies to iconic status, positioning them as representatives of a particular gendered performance of the position. These mediated memories then set both historical and contemporary standards for judging current and future first ladies. These iconic first ladies, though, can function differently according to the historical context in which they are being used. The press practice of comparing and contrasting first ladies past and present employs a competitive framework that often highlights their differences rather than their similarities, reflecting the press memory of their performances and limiting their potential influence.

Stories that feature iconic first ladies offer mini-history lessons to their readers, highlighting memories of certain first ladies that the press created by writing the first draft of history. Over time whole chapters of history are reduced to a single remembrance or mere captions. The number of articles referencing iconic first ladies has grown considerably since the 1960s, evidencing the celebrity status of first ladies such as Eleanor Roosevelt and Kennedy. Stories from the last twenty years have also reflected the growing scholarly interest in first ladies, routinely quoting first ladies scholars or referencing recent books about presidents' wives.

Journalistic Practice and Press Framing

Gendered framing over the years has also impacted where a story is placed. The majority of first lady stories appeared in women's magazines and on women's pages in newspapers. Even in later periods, when the women's pages became "Style" or "Lifestyle" sections, this is where most first lady stories ran. Relegating first lady stories to women's publications implies they are newsworthy primarily for other women. Such placement reinforces the status of first ladies as role models for American women but also devalues their importance as public figures and political agents, thus containing their influence while further empowering men.[5] While first ladies were represented by the press as being central to the public and private life of the nation, the placement of stories about them asserts they are much less pivotal to U.S. political culture in general.

When first lady stories managed to make the front page or national sections, journalists often made a point of explicating the newsworthiness of their activities in order to justify the article's placement. Having to qualify the newsworthiness of a first lady, often by highlighting the unusualness of her actions, underscores the notion that she has limited significance within U.S. political culture. Since the late 1970s stories about first ladies have slowly shifted from the "Style" to the "National" section and to the editorial pages. Front-page coverage is still limited. Campaign coverage in particular justified story placement in higher-profile sections, particularly in years when the wives have been key players in the campaign. However, unusual behavior is still treated as more newsworthy.

Gendered elements such as story placement and personification framing contribute also to the characterization of first lady coverage as "soft news." News about national political figures has traditionally been treated as "hard news," appearing in the front sections of newspapers. Even articles that could be characterized as soft news, such as the president's weekending at Camp David, have appeared in the "National" section (sometimes even making the front page on a slow news day). First ladies have rarely been treated as hard news, and when they have, once again the unusualness of their actions is a feature. This framing places first ladies on the fringes of political culture, often characterizing them as interlopers when they move too far toward the center of political activity. Labeling first lady stories as soft news also contains women's political influence by reifying gendered boundaries that imply women's political activities are less newsworthy than those of men.

Journalists' Gender and Press Framing

The majority of stories about the first lady institution over the years have been written by women journalists, for most of the reporters routinely assigned to cover first ladies have been women. For women to cover women solved the problems of propriety, particularly during eras when women's addressing promiscuous audiences violated norms of gender etiquette. It was considered acceptable for the first lady to speak to women reporters, and such journalistic practices broke down barriers to the presence of women in the public sphere. Yet there was also the assumption that women understood each other and shared similar interests rooted primarily in home and family. As first ladies became more active both publicly and politically, the number of stories written by male journalists increased. The gender of the reporter has not prevented journalistic gendered framing from dominating the coverage of the first lady institution, however.

The relationship between first ladies and women journalists over the years warrants further study. Women journalists in some ways have benefited from assignments to cover first ladies. For example, Eleanor Roosevelt's practice of limiting her press conferences to women forced some news organizations to hire women and ensured that other female reporters would keep their jobs during the Depression. Roosevelt's constant activity and activism gave women reporters plenty to write about and sometimes even landed them on the front page, which meant their work was read by a larger audience. Similarly, Johnson's active schedule kept the women of the press corps busy, on occasion earning them a front-page byline. In turn women journalists often promoted the celebrity and political activism of the first lady. Women reporters, particularly those working for women's magazines, also wrote countless stories touting the first lady's domesticity, often promoting women's domestic empowerment. First ladies, through the visibility and duties associated with their position, were easy for women journalists to position as role models for their female readers. Thus, these women writers empowered the first ladies by contributing to their emergence as public women, political celebrities, and political activists.

Eventually, though, as coverage of the first lady institution became more critical, women journalists also participated actively in the critique of first ladies and thus played a major role in reifying the boundaries of first lady and gender performance. Women writers frequently pointed out the constraints of double binds, but they were also complicit in the creation of them, particularly when they characterized first ladies as political interlopers. Women journalists have acted as both supporters and critics of first ladies, creating an interesting dynamic between these public women.

Progress over the past century is visible as first ladies' participation in public life is normalized, and even anticipated. First ladies are expected now to use their influence to promote social causes, continuing women's legacy of volunteerism. Some have used the power of their position to push political initiatives, venturing into the male-dominated political sphere: Roosevelt promoted numerous reform efforts; Wilson and Johnson helped draft federal legislation; Ford and Carter lobbied for political and public support of the ERA; Carter, Clinton, and Laura Bush all testified before Congress. The public and political activities of these first ladies, even when arousing criticism, played a significant role in expanding the boundaries of their influence and legitimized women's entrance into the political sphere. The turn of the twenty-first century saw a first lady, Clinton, move from the White House to the floor of the U.S. Senate, which shows that some of the boundaries of containment can be eroded.

At the same time, however, some of the same obstacles to women's participation—in the political sphere, in particular—still persist. The question of women's "proper" place in political culture is as relevant today as it has been during any historical period. Press framing of the first lady institution still places the first lady at the heart of women's public culture, yet it continues to consign her to the periphery of U.S. political culture. By positioning her as a role model for American women, journalists imply, then, that women also function largely on the margins of U.S. political life, despite the increasing numbers of women (including a former first lady) who are pursuing political careers. Gender influenced the media coverage of some of the earliest, and most visible, public women. Just as first ladies are bound by a tradition dating back to Martha Washington, journalistic practices rooted to a great extent in nineteenth-century gender prescriptions continue to define media coverage of first ladies. Until such practices are more forcefully challenged, women will be relegated to their "more traditional" supporting role in U.S. political culture. As one journalist asserted, "The public will some day accept a fully independent first lady."[6] Some day.

Notes

Introduction—Press Images of First Ladies, 1900–2001

1. *Pennsylvania and Daily Advertiser,* 26 May 1789, 1.

2. While there are many definitions of gender, I agree with feminist media scholar Liesbet van Zoonen's description, "Gender can thus be thought of as a particular discourse, that is, a set of overlapping and often contradictory cultural descriptions and prescriptions referring to sexual difference, which arises from and regulates particular economic, social, political, technological and other non-discursive contexts" [Liesbet van Zoonen, *Feminist Media Studies* (London: Sage, 1994), 33]. As a social construction, gender has both prescriptive and performative aspects. Feminist media scholar Lana Rakow defines gender as "both something we do and something we think with, both a set of social practices and a system of cultural meanings. The social 'doing' of gender—and the cultural meanings—'thinking the world' using the categories and experiences of gender—constitute us as women or men, organized into a particular configuration of social relations" [Lana Rakow, "Rethinking Gender Research in Communication," *Journal of Communication* 36 (1986): 21].

3. Karlyn Kohrs Campbell, "The Discursive Performance of Femininity: Hating Hillary," *Rhetoric & Public Affairs* 1 (1998): 2–4. Rooted in the work of Judith Butler, Campbell argues that gender is a social construction that must be performed. She states, "gender is not a physical or biological given; it is enacted and performed bodily, and in order for a 'woman' or 'girl' to be an agent . . . she must 'cite' or 'enact' cultural norms of femininity" [p. 2].

4. Lewis L. Gould, "First Ladies," *American Scholar* 55 (1986): 529.

5. Robert P. Watson, *The Presidents' Wives: Reassessing the Office of First Lady* (Boulder, CO: Lynne Rienner, 2000), 110–11.

6. Maurine H. Beasley, *Eleanor Roosevelt and the Media: A Public Quest for Self-Fulfillment* (Urbana: University of Illinois Press, 1987), 38.

7. Lewis L. Gould, "First Ladies and the Press: Bess Truman to Lady Bird Johnson," *American Journalism* 1 (1986): 48–54.

8. Betty Houchin Winfield, "The Making of an Image: Hillary Rodham Clinton and American Journalists," *Political Communication* 14 (1997): 241.

9. Watson, *President's Wives*, 20–21; Karlyn Kohrs Campbell, "The Rhetorical Presidency: A Two-Person Career," in *Beyond the Rhetorical Presidency*, ed. Martin J. Medhurst (College Station: Texas A&M University Press, 1996), 181.

10. Samuel Kernell, *Going Public: New Strategies of Political Leadership*, 3rd ed. (Washington, DC: Congressional Quarterly Press, 1997).

11. Glenna Matthews, *The Rise of Public Woman: Woman's Power and Woman's Place in the United States, 1630–1970* (New York: Oxford University Press, 1992), 4; Maurine H. Beasley, *First Ladies and the Press: The Unfinished Partnership of the Media Age* (Evanston, IL: Northwestern University Press, 2005), 7 (quote).

12. Stephen D. Reese, Oscar H. Gandy, Jr., and August E. Grant, eds., *Framing Public Life: Perspectives on Media and Our Understanding of the Social World* (Mahwah, NJ: Lawrence Erlbaum Associates, 2001), 11 (quote). See also Shanto Iyengar and Donald R. Kinder, *News that Matters: Television and American Opinion* (Chicago: University of Chicago Press, 1993), 64.

13. Pippa Norris, ed., *Women, Media, and Politics* (New York: Oxford University Press, 1997), 6–7 (quote); Cynthia Carter, Gill Branston, and Stuart Allan, eds., *News, Gender, and Power* (London: Routledge, 1998), 7.

14. James W. Carey, "A Cultural Approach to Communication," *Communication* 2 (1975): 8.

15. Kathleen Hall Jamieson, *Beyond the Double Bind: Women and Leadership* (New York: Oxford University Press, 1995), 13, 16, 4; Rosalynn Carter, *First Lady from Plains* (New York: Ballantine Books, 1984), 175.

16. Barbie Zelizer, "Journalists as Interpretive Communities," *Critical Studies in Mass Communication* 10 (1993): 224 (quote); John Bodnar, "Public Memory in an American City: Commemoration in Cleveland," in *Commemorations: The Politics of National Identity*, ed. John R. Gillis (Princeton: Princeton University Press, 1992), 76 (quote); Bruce E. Gronbeck, "The Rhetorics of the Past: History, Argument, and Collective Memory," *Doing Rhetorical History: Concepts and Cases*, ed. Kathleen J. Turner (Tuscaloosa: University of Alabama Press, 1998), 57.

17. S. Paige Baty, *American Monroe: The Making of a Body Politic* (Berkeley and Los Angeles: University of California Press, 1995), 59–60.

18. Barbie Zelizer, "Reading the Past against the Grain: The Shape of Memory Studies," *Critical Studies in Mass Communication* 12 (1995): 224; Maurice Halbwachs, *On Collective Memory*, trans. and ed. Lewis A. Coser (Chicago: University of Chicago Press, 1992), 172.

19. Richard W. Waterman, Robert Wright, and Gilbert St. Clair, *The Image-Is-Everything Presidency: Dilemmas in American Leadership* (Boulder, CO: Westview Press, 1999), 128 (quote); Myra G. Gutin, *The President's Partner: The First Lady in the Twentieth Century* (New York: Greenwood Press, 1989), 176 (quote); Betty Houchin Winfield, "The First Lady's Relations with the Mass Media," *Laura Bush: The Report to the First Lady*, ed. Robert P. Watson (Huntington, NY: Nova History, 2001), 45–51.

20. Karrin Vasby Anderson, "The First Lady: A Site of 'American Womanhood,'" in Wertheimer, *Inventing a Voice*, 18.

21. Daniel J. Boorstin, *The Image: A Guide to Pseudo-Events in America*, 25th anniversary ed. (New York: Vintage Books, 1987), 57; Chris Rojek, *Celebrity* (London: Reaktion Books, 2001), 16.

22. P. David Marshall, *Celebrity and Power: Fame in Contemporary Culture* (Minneapolis: University of Minnesota Press, 1997), ix–x, 56–57.

23. Michael Schudson, *The Good Citizen: A History of American Civic Life* (New York: Free Press, 1998), 287.

24. Ibid., 178–80; Eleanor Flexner, *Century of Struggle: The Woman's Rights Movement in the United States* (New York: Atheneum, 1972), 179–80.

Chapter One—Representations of Womanhood in the American Press before 1900

1. Martha Washington to Fanny Bassett Washington, 8 June 1789, in *"Worthy Partner": The Papers of Martha Washington*, ed. Joseph E. Fields (Westport, CT: Green-

wood Press, 1994), 215; Republican papers quoted in Carl Sferrazza Anthony, *First Ladies: The Saga of Presidents' Wives and Their Power, 1789–1961* (New York: Quill, 1990), 48.

2. Catherine Allgor, *Parlor Politics: In Which the Ladies of Washington Helped Build a City and a Government* (Charlottesville: University Press of Virginia, 2000), 20.

3. Gaye Tuchman, "Introduction: The Symbolic Annihilation of Women by the Mass Media," in *Hearth and Home: Images of Women in the Mass Media,* ed. Gaye Tuchman, Arlene Kaplan Daniels, and James Benét (New York: Oxford University Press, 1978), 3; Liesbet van Zoonen, *Feminist Media Studies* (London: Sage, 1994), 30–31.

4. Anderson, "The First Lady," 18.

5. Matthews, *Rise of Public Woman;* Nan Johnson, *Gender and Rhetorical Space in American Life, 1866–1910* (Carbondale: Southern Illinois University Press, 2002), 2–18.

6. Linda K. Kerber, *Women of the Republic: Intellect and Ideology in Revolutionary America* (New York: W. W. Norton, 1986), 7 (quote); Linda K. Kerber, "Separate Spheres, Female Worlds, Woman's Place: The Rhetoric of Women's History," *Journal of American History* 75 (1988): 17–19.

7. Kerber, "Separate Spheres," 20 (quotes). See also Gail Collins, *America's Women: Four Hundred Years of Dolls, Drudges, Helpmates, and Heroines* (New York: HarperCollins, 2003), 86.

8. Catherine Allgor, "Political Parties: First Ladies and Social Events in the Formation of the Federal Government," in *The Presidential Companion: Readings on the First Ladies,* ed. Robert P. Watson and Anthony J. Eksterowicz (Columbia: University of South Carolina Press, 2003), 49, 41.

9. Watson, *Presidents' Wives,* 49.

10. Robert P. Watson, "Introduction," in Watson and Eksterowicz, *Presidential Companion,* 6. Although Rachel Jackson died on December 24, 1828, and thus never served as first lady, the campaign coverage of her warrants mention in this chapter. For more on Jackson, see Anthony, *First Ladies, 1789–1961,* 111–14; Allgor, *Parlor Politics,* 195–97.

11. Allgor, *Parlor Politics,* 1, 241.

12. Allgor, "Political Parties," 42; Patricia Brady, "Martha Washington and the Creation of the Role of the First Lady," in Watson and Eksterowicz, *Presidential Companion,* 26.

13. Campbell, "Rhetorical Presidency," 179–95; Betty Boyd Caroli, *First Ladies* (New York: Oxford University Press, 1995), xviii (quote).

14. Martha Washington to Fanny Bassett Washington, 8 June 1789, in Fields, *"Worthy Partner,"* 220; Abigail Adams quoted in Molly Meijer Wertheimer, "First Ladies' Fundamental Rhetorical Choices: When to Speak? What to Say? When to Remain Silent?" in Wertheimer, *Inventing a Voice,* 1.

15. Jeffrey L. Pasley, *"The Tyranny of Printers": Newspaper Politics in the Early American Republic* (Charlottesville: University Press of Virginia, 2001), 1–12; William David Sloan, "'Purse and Pen': Party-Press Relationships, 1789–1816," *American Journalism* 6 (1989): 103–27; David Sloan, "The Early Party Press," *Journalism History* 9 (1982): 19; Carol Sue Humphrey, *The Press of the Young Republic, 1783–1833* (Westport, CT: Greenwood Press, 1994), xiii–xiv.

16. Karen List, "The Media and the Depiction of Women," in *The Significance of the Media in American History,* ed. James D. Startt and William David Sloan (Northport, AL: Vision Press, 1994), 116.

17. Karen K. List, "Realities and Possibilities: The Lives of Women in Periodicals of the New Republic," *American Journalism* 11 (1994): 34; Matthews, *Rise of Public Woman,* 4.

18. List, "Women in Periodicals," 37.

19. Ibid., 35.

20. For "Lady Washington," see Anthony, *First Ladies, 1789–1961*, 48; Margaret Truman, *First Ladies* (New York: Random House, 1995), 18; for Adams, see Watson, *Presidents' Wives*, 10; Anthony, *First Ladies, 1789–1961*, 84 (Madison), 98 (Monroe).

21. Allgor, *Parlor Politics*, 148–52; Anthony, *First Ladies, 1789–1961*, 104–5, 110 (quote); Lewis L. Gould, *American First Ladies: Their Lives and Legacies* (New York: Garland, 1996), 76–77.

22. Allgor, *Parlor Politics*, 75–76; Anthony, *First Ladies, 1789–1961*, 83 (quote).

23. Allgor, *Parlor Politics*, 54.

24. Watson, *Presidents' Wives*, 75; Allgor, *Parlor Politics*, 98; Anthony, *First Ladies, 1789–1961*, 83, 94–95.

25. Anthony, *First Ladies, 1789–1961*, 103, 37–38.

26. Ibid., 54–55, 83, 94–95.

27. Allgor, *Parlor Politics*, 98.

28. Anthony, *First Ladies, 1789–1961*, 80; William David Sloan and James D. Startt, *The Media in America: A History*, 4th ed. (Northport, AL: Vision Press, 1999), 87.

29. See Allgor, *Parlor Politics*, 195; Mary French Caldwell, *General Jackson's Lady* (Nashville: Kingsport Press, 1936): 339–43.

30. Anthony, *First Ladies, 1789–1961*, 111; also Truman, *First Ladies*, 262–63.

31. Allgor, *Parlor Politics*, 196–97.

32. List, "The Media and the Depiction of Women," in Startt and Sloan, *The Significance of the Media in American History*, 110.

33. Gerda Lerner, *The Majority Finds Its Past: Placing Women in History* (New York: Oxford University Press, 1979), 18.

34. Quotes from Carl M. Degler, *At Odds: Women and the Family in America from the Revolution to the Present* (New York: Oxford University Press, 1980), 27; Karlyn Kohrs Campbell, *Man Cannot Speak for Her: A Critical Study of Early Feminist Rhetoric*, vol. 1 (New York: Praeger, 1989), 9–10. See also Barbara Welter, "The Cult of True Womanhood, 1820–1860," in The *American Family in Social-Historical Perspective*, ed. Michael Gordon (New York: St. Martin's, 1973), 225; Mary P. Ryan, "Gender and Public Access: Women's Politics in Nineteenth-Century America," in *Habermas and the Public Sphere*, ed. Craig Calhoun (Boston: MIT Press, 1992), 273.

35. Degler, *At Odds*, 26; Alexis de Tocqueville, "Chapter XII—How the Americans Understand the Equality of the Sexes," *Democracy in America* online text, <http://xroads.virginia.edu/~HYPER/DETOC/home.html>.

36. Glenna Matthews, *"Just a Housewife": The Rise and Fall of Domesticity in America* (New York: Oxford University Press, 1987), 34.

37. Collins, *America's Women*, 97–98; Matthews, *Rise of Public Woman*, 116.

38. A. Cheree Carlson, "Creative Casuistry and Feminist Consciousness: The Rhetoric of Moral Reform," *Quarterly Journal of Speech* 78 (1992): 17; Collins, *America's Women*, 188–92.

39. Flexner, *Century of Struggle*, 74–77; Janet Zollinger Giele, *Two Paths to Women's Equality: Temperance, Suffrage, and the Origins of Modern Feminism* (New York: Twayne, 1995), 56–62.

40. Watson, *Presidents' Wives*, 51; Elizabeth Lorelei Thacker-Estrada, "True Women: The Roles and Lives of Antebellum Presidential Wives Sarah Polk, Margaret Taylor, Abigail Fillmore, and Jane Pierce," in Watson and Eksterowicz, *Presidential Companion*, 77.

41. Gould, *American First Ladies*, 121–22, 140; Caroli, *First Ladies*, 73; Thacker-Estrada, "True Women," 80.

42. Gould, *American First Ladies*, 121, 140 (quote); Caroli, *First Ladies*, 73.

43. Thacker-Estrada, "True Women," 96.

44. Maurine H. Beasley and Sheila J. Gibbons, *Taking Their Place: A Documentary History of Women and Journalism*, 2nd ed. (State College, PA: Strata, 2003), 34–35; William E. Huntzicker, *The Popular Press, 1833–1865* (Westport, CT: Greenwood Press, 1999), 15.

45. Anthony, *First Ladies, 1789–1961*, 118 (Tyler), 171–76 (Lincoln); *Leslie's Weekly*, 22 February 1862, 1.

46. Katherine Fishburn, *Women in Popular Culture: A Reference Guide* (Westport, CT: Greenwood Press, 1982), 9; Caroli, *First Ladies*, 65; New York paper cited in Anthony, *First Ladies, 1789–1961*, 140.

47. Anthony, *First Ladies, 1789–1961*, 129–33; Caroli, *First Ladies*, 48; Gould, *American First Ladies*, 162.

48. Gould, *American First Ladies*, 187.

49. Anthony, *First Ladies, 1789–1961*, 181, 170.

50. Ibid., 129 (quote), 212–13, 132; Caroli, *First Ladies*, 46; Gould, *American First Ladies*, 190.

51. Caroli, *First Ladies*, 84–85.

52. Anne Firor Scott, *Making the Invisible Woman Visible* (Urbana: University of Illinois Press, 1984), 65–66.

53. Jennifer Scanlon, *Inarticulate Longings: The Ladies' Home Journal, Gender, and the Promises of Consumer Culture* (New York: Routledge, 1995), 2. The most popular and successful of these magazines became known as the "Big Six" and included *Ladies' Home Journal*, *McCall's*, and *Good Housekeeping*.

54. Matthews, *Rise of Public Woman*, 155; Flexner, *Century of Struggle*, 156–78; Giele, *Women's Equality*, 117; Campbell, *Man Cannot Speak for Her*, 11 (quote).

55. Caroli, *First Ladies*, 86 (quote); Flexner, *Century of Struggle*, 179; Matthews, *Rise of Public Woman*, 147–54.

56. Flexner, *Century of Struggle*, 182; Giele, *Women's Equality*, 109–11.

57. Matthews, *Rise of Public Woman*, 158–59; Estelle Freedman, "Separatism as Strategy: Female Institution Building and American Feminism, 1870–1930," *Feminist Studies* 5 (1979): 512–18.

58. Watson, *Presidents' Wives*, 52, 53 (quotes); Caroli, *First Ladies*, 84.

59. Anthony, *First Ladies, 1789–1961*, 221, 210.

60. Caroli, *First Ladies*, 91.

61. Collins, *America's Women*, 246; Caroli, *First Ladies*, 104–5.

62. Anthony, *First Ladies, 1789–1961*, 233, 241.

63. Ibid., 235; Watson, "Introduction," 6; Gould, *American First Ladies*, 287 (quote).

64. Beasley and Gibbons, *Taking Their Place*, 64–73; Ishbel Ross, *Ladies of the Press: The Story of Women in Journalism by an Insider* (New York: Harper and Brothers, 1936), 50–51; Agnes Hooper Gottlieb, "Women's Press Club of New York City, 1889–1980," in *Women's Press Organizations, 1881–1999*, ed. Elizabeth V. Burt (Westport: Greenwood Press, 2000), 251; Ross, *Ladies of the Press*, 44–45, 326.

65. Scanlon, *Inarticulate Longings*, 3; Susan Henry, "Changing Media History through Women's History," in *Women in Mass Communication*, ed. Pamela J. Creedon (Newbury Park: Sage, 1989), 51; Sloan and Startt, *Media in America*, 239, 244; Helen Damon-Moore, *Magazines for the Millions: Gender and Commerce in the Ladies' Home Journal and the Saturday Evening Post, 1880–1910* (Albany: State University of New York, 1994), 11.

66. Anthony, *First Ladies, 1789–1961*, 210.

67. See Emily Apt Greer, "Lucy Webb Hayes and Her Influence upon Her Era," *Hayes Historical Journal* 1 (1976): 27.

68. Mary Clemmer Ames, "Woman's Letter From Washington," *The Independent*, 15 March 1877, 2.

69. Caroli, *First Ladies*, 91; Anthony, *First Ladies, 1789–1961*, 263; Caroli, *First Ladies*, 104.

70. In Caroli, *First Ladies*, 90; Mary Clemmer Ames, "Woman's Letter From Washington," *The Independent*, 15 March 1877, 2; Caroli, *First Ladies*, 111.

71. "Mrs. McKinley, Mrs. Bryan: A Comparison," *Harper's Bazaar*, 11 August 1900.

72. Caroli, *First Ladies*, 98 (quote); Anthony, *First Ladies, 1789–1961*, 240 (Garfield's redecoration); Caroli, *First Ladies*, 106 (quote); Anthony, *First Ladies, 1789–1961*, 267–71 (Harrison's redecoration).

73. Anthony, *First Ladies, 1789–1961*, 253; Gould, *American First Ladies*, 259; Watson, *Presidents' Wives*, 89.

74. Greer, "Lucy Webb Hayes," 27.

75. Anthony, *First Ladies, 1789–1961*, 233, 237.

76. Truman, *First Ladies*, 51.

77. Anthony, *First Ladies, 1789–1961*, 267–71.

78. Ibid., 213; Caroli, *First Ladies*, 89.

79. Kerber, "Separate Spheres," 39.

80. Michael Calvin McGee, "The 'Ideograph': A Link between Rhetoric and Ideology," *Quarterly Journal of Speech* 66 (1980): 9; Scott, *Invisible Woman*, 65.

81. Wertheimer, "First Ladies' Fundamental Rhetorical Choices," 2.

Chapter Two — First Lady as Public Woman, 1900–1929

1. "Mrs. McKinley, Mrs. Bryan: A Comparison," *Harper's Bazaar*, 11 August 1900, 955.

2. Ibid., 955–56.

3. Watson, *Presidents' Wives*, 54.

4. Nancy F. Cott, *The Grounding of Modern Feminism* (New Haven: Yale University Press, 1987), 16, 22; J. Stanley Lemons, *The Woman Citizen: Social Feminism in the 1920s* (Urbana: University of Illinois Press, 1973), vii–xi; Carolyn Kitch, *The Girl on the Magazine Cover: The Origins of Visual Stereotypes in American Mass Media* (Chapel Hill: University of North Carolina Press, 2001), 8, 4.

5. Carrol Smith-Rosenberg, *Disorderly Conduct: Visions of Gender in Victorian America* (New York: Alfred A. Knopf, 1985), 224, 264.

6. Nancy S. Dye, "Introduction," in *Gender, Class, Race, and Reform in the Progressive Era*, ed. Noralee Frankel and Nancy S. Dye (Lexington: University Press of Kentucky, 1991), 3; Lemons, *Woman Citizen*, viii–ix.

7. Kitch, *Girl on the Magazine Cover*, 8; Mary P. Ryan, *Womanhood in America: From Colonial Times to Present* (New York: Viewpoints, 1975), 256–57; Cott, *Modern Feminism*, 39, 148; Mona Domosh and Joni Seager, *Putting Women in Place: Female Geographers Make Sense of the World* (New York: Guilford Press, 2001), 20; Robyn Muncy, *Creating a Female Dominion in American Reform, 1890–1935* (New York: Oxford University Press, 1991), 36–37.

8. Giele, *Women's Equality*, 159; Lemons, *Woman Citizen*, ix; Cott, *Modern Feminism*, 97–99; Lois Scharf and Joan M. Jensen, "Introduction," in *Decades of Discontent: The Women's Movement, 1920–1940*, ed. Lois Scharf and Joan M. Jensen (Boston: Northeastern University Press, 1987), 5.

9. Kitch, *Girl on the Magazine Cover*, 11–13, 184. Kitch is referring to Susan Faludi's *Backlash: The Undeclared War against American Women* (New York: Anchor Books, 1991).

10. "Mrs. Catt on Feminism," *Woman's Journal,* 9 January 1915, 12.

11. Giele, *Women's Equality,* 173.

12. Ida Clyde Clarke, "Feminism and the New Technique: Strike for High Places," *The Century* (April 1929): 753.

13. Kerber, *Women of the Republic,* 11–12; Giele, *Women's Equality,* 69 (citizen-mothers); Shawn J. Parry-Giles and Diane M. Blair, "The Rise of the Rhetorical First Lady: Politics, Gender Ideology, and Women's Voice, 1789–2002," *Rhetoric and Public Affairs* 5 (2002): 567.

14. Vanessa Beasley, "Engendering Democratic Change: How Three U.S. Presidents Discussed Female Suffrage," *Rhetoric and Public Affairs* 5 (2002): 87, 92, 93.

15. Freedman, "Separatism as Strategy"; Lemons, *Woman Citizen,* ix.

16. "Mrs. Hoover Seen as Cosmopolitan, Social Worker, Devoted Mother and Real Companion to Husband," *Washington Post,* 7 November 1928, 9; "The Lady of the White House," *New York Times Magazine,* 10 March 1929, 1; "The Wives behind Presidential Candidates," *New York Times,* 23 October 1904, 6.

17. "The Wives behind Presidential Candidates," *New York Times,* 23 October 1904, 6.

18. Ibid.

19. Maureen E. Montgomery, *Displaying Women: Spectacles of Leisure in Edith Wharton's New York* (New York: Routledge, 1998), 6; Cott, *Modern Feminism,* 165–66.

20. Theodore Roosevelt, *The Strenuous Life* (New York: Outlook, 1900), 5–6.

21. Mabel Porter Daggett, "Woodrow Wilson's Wife," *Good Housekeeping* (March 1913): 318, 323.

22. "Mrs. Hoover Seen as Cosmopolitan," 9; "The Lady of the White House," 1.

23. Dudley Harmon, "What Is Mrs. Wilson Doing? The Part the President's Wife and His Daughters Have in the War," *Ladies' Home Journal* (July 1918): 22, 44.

24. Beasley, "Engendering Democratic Change," 88.

25. Kerber, *Women of the Republic,* 12.

26. Warren G. Harding, "Inaugural Address," in *The Presidents Speak,* ed. Davis Newton Lott (New York: Henry Holt, 1994), 249. This portion of Harding's inaugural address was also quoted in Constance Drexel, "Mrs. Harding Shares Tasks of President," *Washington Post,* 5 March 1921, 2.

27. "Mrs. Harding on Tariff," *New York Times,* 19 January 1921, 2; Dye, "Introduction," 1. A "promiscuous audience" consists of both men and women. During this era the stigma surrounding women's speaking to a mixed audience was decreasing. For a more detailed discussion of female speakers and promiscuous audiences, see Susan Zaeske, "The 'Promiscuous Audience' Controversy and the Emergence of the Early Woman's Rights Movement," *Quarterly Journal of Speech* 81 (1995): 191–207.

28. Carl Sferrazza Anthony, *America's First Families* (New York: Simon and Schuster, 2000), 89; Jacob A. Riis, "Mrs. Roosevelt and Her Children," *Ladies' Home Journal* (August 1902): 6; "The Wives behind Presidential Candidates," 6.

29. Cott, *Modern Feminism,* 156; Riis, "Mrs. Roosevelt and Her Children," 6.

30. Princess Cantacuzene, "The First Lady of the Land at Home," *Ladies' Home Journal* (June 1924): 85; "When Mrs. Taft Replaces Mrs. Roosevelt," *New York Times,* 15 November 1908, 7.

31. Harmon, "What Is Mrs. Wilson Doing?" 22; "A Glimpse of Mrs. Harding," *New York Times,* 14 November 1920, 6.

32. Allgor, *Parlor Politics,* 23; Stephen Birmingham, *The Right People: A Portrait of the American Social Establishment* (Boston: Little, Brown, 1968), 227.

33. George Griswold Hill, "The Wife of the New President," *Ladies' Home Journal* (March 1909): 6; "Mrs. Hoover Seen as Cosmopolitan," 9.

34. Watson, *Presidents' Wives*, 76; Riis, "Mrs. Roosevelt and Her Children," 6.

35. "The New Regime within the White House," *New York Times*, 14 March 1909, 5:1; "The Lady of the White House," 1.

36. Notable examples include Myra Gutin, whose focus on first ladies as public communicators leads her to criticize the women she calls "social hostesses and ceremonial presences" (in *President's Partner*, 2), and Betty Houchin Winfield, who classifies hostessing as a more "traditional" and less political role (in "'Madam President': Understanding a New Kind of First Lady," *Media Studies Journal* 8 [1994]: 59).

37. Matthews, *Rise of Public Woman*, 172.

38. Mel Laracey, *Presidents and the People: The Partisan Story of Going Public* (College Station: Texas A&M Press, 2002), 8–9.

39. Caroli, *First Ladies*, 120–21.

40. "Glorious, Says Mrs. Taft: Loves Public Life," 3 (quotes); Lewis L. Gould, *The Modern American Presidency* (Lawrence: University Press of Kansas, 2003), 41; Flexner, *Century of Struggle*, 296.

41. "Glorious, Says Mrs. Taft: Loves Public Life," 3.

42. Daggett, "Woodrow Wilson's Wife," 323; Caroli, *First Ladies*, 140.

43. "Mrs. Harding Declaras [*sic*] Kansas: Delegates' Switch Made Her Sure Her Husband Would Be Nominee," *Washington Post*, 15 June 1920, 5.

44. Drexel, "Mrs. Harding Shares Tasks," 2.

45. "A Glimpse of Mrs. Harding," 6:8.

46. "Mrs. Coolidge at Rally," *New York Times*, 20 September 1924, 8; see also Beasley, "Engendering Democratic Change," 92–93.

47. "Mrs. Hoover Seen as Cosmopolitan," 9.

48. Beasley, "Engendering Democratic Change," 89; Kristi Anderson, *Beyond Suffrage* (Chicago: University of Chicago Press, 1996), 71–74.

49. Harmon, "What Is Mrs. Wilson Doing?" 22.

50. Frances Parkinson Keyes, "Letters from a Senator's Wife," *Good Housekeeping* (May 1922): 49; Dorothy Canfield, "A Good Girl Scout," *Good Housekeeping* (April 1930): 24.

51. "Mrs. Hoover Seen as Cosmopolitan," 9.

52. Matthews, *Rise of Public Woman*, 173.

53. Dye, "Introduction," 2.

54. "Mrs. Wilson Slumming," *New York Times*, 16 May 1913, 2.

55. "Cleansing Capital's Slums," *New York Times*, 23 May 1913, 1.

56. "Parks for Capital's Slums," *New York Times*, 24 May 1913, 4. For more, see Lisa M. Burns, "A Forgotten First Lady: A Rhetorical Reassessment of Ellen Axson Wilson," in Wertheimer, *Inventing a Voice*, 93.

57. Matthews, *Rise of Public Woman*, 178.

58. "The Lady of the White House," *New York Times Magazine*, 10 March 1929, 1.

59. Faludi, *Backlash*, xii–xiii.

Chapter Three—First Lady as Political Celebrity, 1932–1961

1. Alice Rogers Hagar, "Candidates for the Post of First Lady," *New York Times Magazine*, 2 October 1932, 5.

2. Ibid., 5, 16.

3. Gould, "First Ladies," 531.

4. Elaine Tyler May, *Homeward Bound: American Families in the Cold War Era* (New York: Basic Books, 1999), xxiv (quote); Matthews, *"Just a Housewife,"* 196. Ruth Schwartz

Cohen, "Two Washes in the Morning and a Bridge Party at Night: The American House-wife between the Wars," in Scharf and Jensen, *Decades of Discontent,* 177–78.

5. Janet M. Martin, *The Presidency and Women: Promise, Performance, and Illusion* (College Station: Texas A&M University Press, 2003), 23; Muncy, *Creating a Female Dominion,* 152–54; Lois Scharf, "'The Forgotten Woman': Working Women, the New Deal, and Women's Organizations," in Scharf and Jensen, *Decades of Discontent,* 243–45.

6. Susan M. Hartman, *The Home Front and Beyond: American Women in the 1940s* (Boston: Twayne, 1982), 1–5; Collins, *America's Women,* 394–95; Matthews, *Rise of Public Woman,* 222; Barbara Ryan, *Feminism and the Women's Movement: Dynamics of Change in Social Movement Ideology and Activism* (New York: Routledge, 1992), 36; Betty Friedan, *The Feminine Mystique* (New York: Dell, 1983), 15–32.

7. Lemons, *Woman Citizen,* 180; Nancy A. Walker, *Shaping Our Mothers' World: American Women's Magazines* (Jackson: University Press of Mississippi, 2000), ix.

8. William H. Chafe, *The Paradox of Change: American Women in the Twentieth Century* (New York: Oxford University Press, 1991), 47–49; Matthews, *"Just a House-wife,"* 160 (quote).

9. Kerber, *Women of the Republic,* 283 (quote); Maurine H. Beasley, "Eleanor Roosevelt's Press Conferences: Case Study in Class, Gender, and Race," *Social Science Journal* 37 (2000): 519.

10. Collins, *America's Women,* xv (quote), 385–88; Walker, *Shaping Our Mothers' World,* 80; Kerber, *Women of the Republic,* 11.

11. Susan J. Douglas, *Where the Girls Are: Growing Up Female with the Mass Media* (New York: Times Books, 1995), 47; Collins, *America's Women,* 394–95.

12. Karal Ann Marling, *As Seen on TV: The Visual Culture of Everyday Life in the 1950s* (Cambridge, MA: Harvard University Press, 1994), 5, 202–40; Matthews, *Rise of Public Woman,* 222; Walker, *Shaping Our Mothers' World,* 150; Collins, *America's Women,* 398 (quote).

13. Friedan, *Feminine Mystique,* 18; see also Lary May, *Recasting America: Culture and Politics in the Age of the Cold War* (Chicago: University of Chicago Press, 1989), 5; Walker, *Shaping Our Mothers' World,* 10.

14. Matthews, *Rise of Public Woman,* 188–89 (quote); Cohen, "American House-wife between the Wars," 177–78.

15. Ryan, *Feminism and the Women's Movement,* 41–42; Friedan, *Feminine Mystique,* 32; Martin, *The Presidency and Women,* 59–86.

16. Walker, *Shaping Our Mothers' World,* xi.

17. May, *Homeward Bound,* 63–64, 149–50; Walker, *Shaping Our Mothers' World,* 24.

18. Beasley, *Eleanor Roosevelt and the Media,* 42.

19. "Housewives Entitled to Fixed Salaries, like Any Worker, Mrs. Roosevelt Holds," *New York Times,* 13 May 1937, 1.

20. Parry-Giles and Blair, "Rhetorical First Lady," 576–77; "Crowd Mind Read by Mrs. Roosevelt," *Washington Post,* 5 March 1933, 7.

21. "First Lady Decries Home-Front Complaints and Urges Women to Do Utmost to Aid War," *New York Times,* 3 January 1945, 20 (all quotes); also Kerber, *Women of the Republic,* 35–67.

22. May, *Homeward Bound,* 13, 149.

23. Bess Furman, "Trumans Give Up Five-Room Residence," *New York Times,* 14 April 1945, 8; also Anne Norton, *Republic of Signs: Liberal Theory and American Popular Culture* (Chicago: University of Chicago Press, 1993), 91.

24. Martha Weinman, "First Ladies—In Fashion, Too?" *New York Times Magazine,* 11 September 1960, 130.

25. Marling, *As Seen on TV;* Waterman, Wright, and St. Clair, *Image-Is-Everything Presidency.*

26. Gould, "First Ladies," 533.

27. Weinman, "First Ladies—In Fashion, Too?" 32–33, 132.

28. Nan Robertson, "Mrs. Kennedy Defends Clothes: Is 'Sure' Mrs. Nixon Pays More," *New York Times,* 15 September 1960, 1.

29. Norton, *Republic of Signs,* 91.

30. Campbell, "Rhetorical Presidency," 180; *Ladies' Home Journal* quoted in Gil Troy, *Mr. and Mrs. President: From the Trumans to the Clintons* (Lawrence: University Press of Kansas, 2000), 3.

31. Furman, "Trumans Give Up Five-Room Residence," 8; "Capital Homemaker: Mamie Doud Eisenhower," *New York Times,* 14 November 1956, 24.

32. Lucy Freeman, "The General and His Wife," *New York Times,* 5 November 1952, 20; "It Was a Long, but Proud Day for Wife of the New President," *New York Times,* 21 January 1961, 11.

33. Rita S. Halle, "That First Lady of Ours," *Good Housekeeping* (December 1933): 195; Campbell, "Rhetorical Presidency," 181.

34. Furman, "Trumans Give Up Five-Room Residence," 8; "Capital Homemaker," 24.

35. "Mrs. Eisenhower a Mystery Fan," *New York Times,* 9 November 1952, 64; Laurie Johnston, "'Policeman for Ike' Is Wife's Idea of Her Principal Role in Public Life," *New York Times,* 3 September 1952, 23.

36. Nan Robertson, "Election 'Unreal' to Mrs. Kennedy," *New York Times,* 11 November 1960, 22.

37. "Capital Homemaker," 24; Kathleen McLaughlin, "Mrs. Roosevelt Goes Her Own Way," *New York Times Magazine,* 5 July 1936, 7.

38. Halle, "That First Lady of Ours," 195.

39. McLaughlin, "Mrs. Roosevelt Goes Her Own Way," 7.

40. Troy, *Mr. and Mrs. President,* 2; Anthony Leviero, "Campaigner Truman Makes Some Headway," *New York Times,* 13 June 1948, E7.

41. "Truman's Family Going Home," *New York Times,* 20 July 1948, 14; Anthony Leviero, "Truman in St. Louis Predicts Victory," *New York Times,* 31 October 1948, 1.

42. Watson, *Presidents' Wives,* 85; "Mrs. Eisenhower Will 'Miss Our Gang,' Calls People Nicest Part of Train Swing," *Washington Post,* 25 October 1952, 8.

43. Maurine Beasley and Paul Belgrade, "Media Coverage of a Silent Partner: Mamie Eisenhower as First Lady," *American Journalism* 3 (1986): 39; "Mrs. Eisenhower a Mystery Fan," 64.

44. "Women Extolled by Mrs. Roosevelt," *New York Times,* 1 November 1936, 1; Johnston, "Policeman for Ike," 23.

45. Gutin, *President's Partner,* 81–107; Diane M. Blair, "No Ordinary Time: Eleanor Roosevelt's Address to the 1940 Democratic National Convention," *Rhetoric and Public Affairs* 4 (2001): 203–22.

46. Kathleen McLaughlin, "No Campaigning, First Lady States," *New York Times,* 19 July 1940, 1.

47. Cott, *Modern Feminism,* 165.

48. "Mrs. Roosevelt for Home Science," *New York Times,* 27 March 1933, 17; "Crowd Mind Read by Mrs. Roosevelt," 7.

49. Furman, "Trumans Give Up Five-Room Residence," 8; "New First Lady Puts Housekeeping First," *Washington Post,* 14 June 1945, 16.

50. "Capital Homemaker," 24.

51. May, *Homeward Bound,* xxi–xxii.

52. Troy, *Mr. and Mrs. President,* ix.

53. Rojek, *Celebrity,* 13 (quote); Boorstin, *The Image,* 61; Robert S. Cathcart, "From Hero to Celebrity: The Media Connection," in *American Heroes in a Media Age,* ed. Susan J. Drucker and Robert S. Cathcart (Cresskill, NJ: Hampton Press, 1994), 36–46.

54. Halle, "That First Lady of Ours," 20; Elizabeth Gertrude Stein, "Exacting Role of the First Lady," *New York Times Magazine,* 14 March 1937, 144; McLaughlin, "Mrs. Roosevelt Goes Her Own Way," 7; Kathleen McLaughlin, "Mrs. Roosevelt Wants 'Just a Little Job,'" *New York Times,* 8 October 1944, 16.

55. "Debutantes Show 'Fair Wage' Gowns at $30, in Women Voters' Drive on the Sweatshop," *New York Times,* 21 April 1933, 19; "Fair Pay Plea Made by Mrs. Roosevelt," 20 June 1933, 21.

56. "Women Hear Plea for World Parley," *New York Times,* 18 February 1945: 24.

57. Beasley and Belgrade, "Silent Partner," 39, 43; Nona B. Brown, "Women's Vote: The Bigger Half?" *New York Times,* 21 October 1956, 28.

58. "Capital Homemaker," 24.

59. Marling, *As Seen on TV,* 26, 39, 38.

60. "White House Influence," *New York Times,* 8 February 1957, 20.

61. "Capital Homemaker," 24; May, *Homeward Bound,* xiii.

62. Marylin Bender, "The Woman Who Wins High Fashion's Vote Is Jacqueline Kennedy," *New York Times,* 15 July 1960, 17.

63. "Mild Fever Gets to City via Capital," *Washington Post,* 19 January 1961, 32.

64. Hamish Bowles, "Defining Style: Jacqueline Kennedy's White House Years," *Jacqueline Kennedy: The White House Years,* ed. Hamish Bowles (Boston: Little, Brown, 2001), 17.

65. Marshall, *Celebrity and Power,* xi.

66. Fannie Hurst, "Sees Mrs. Roosevelt as Tradition Breaker," *New York Times,* 26 June 1936, 12.

67. Troy, *Mr. and Mrs. President,* xiii.

Chapter Four—First Lady as Political Activist, 1964–1977

1. Katie Louchheim, "The Spotlight Shifts in Washington: A New First Lady Moves to Center Stage," *Ladies' Home Journal* (March 1964): 55.

2. Ibid., 55–56.

3. Gutin, *President's Partner,* 71.

4. Friedan, *Feminine Mystique,* 15–32.

5. Matthews, *Rise of Public Woman,* 223; Ryan, *Feminism and the Women's Movement,* 36; Estelle B. Freedman, *No Turning Back: The History of Feminism and the Future of Women* (New York: Ballantine Books, 2002), 5 (quote).

6. Martin, *The Presidency and Women,* 57–86; Ryan, *Feminism and the Women's Movement,* 43–44; Miriam Schneir, *Feminism in Our Time: The Essential Writings, World War II to the Present* (New York: Vintage Books, 1994), 71–75; Matthews, *Rise of Public Woman,* 229.

7. Chafe, *Paradox of Change,* 195; Friedan, *Feminine Mystique,* 15–32, 43 (quote); Chafe, *Paradox of Change,* 197.

8. Bonnie J. Dow, *Prime-Time Feminism: Television, Media Culture, and the Women's Movement since 1970* (Philadelphia: University of Pennsylvania Press, 1996), 29; Chafe, *Paradox of Change,* 201; Winifred D. Wandersee, *On the Move: American Women in the 1970s* (Boston: Twayne, 1988), 43; Bonnie J. Dow, "Fixing Feminism: Women's Liberation and the Rhetoric of Television Documentary," *Quarterly Journal of Speech* 90 (2004): 55–56.

9. Wandersee, *On the Move,* 182; Douglas, *Where the Girls Are,* 166; Ethel Klein, *Gender Politics* (Cambridge, MA: Harvard University Press, 1984), 24–25.

10. Douglas, *Where the Girls Are,* 233; Degler, *At Odds,* 447; Chafe, *Paradox of Change,* 203; Faludi, *Backlash,* xviii–xx.

11. Matthews, *Rise of Public Woman,* 223; Freedman, *No Turning Back,* 327.

12. "The Power of a Woman," *Ladies' Home Journal* (September 1969): 93.

13. "Women of the Year, 1976," *Ladies' Home Journal* (May 1976): 73.

14. Chafe, *Paradox of Change,* 223.

15. Margaret Mead, "Mrs. Lyndon B. Johnson: A New Kind of First Lady?" *Good Housekeeping* (July 1965): 12; Ruth Montgomery, "What Kind of Woman Is Our New First Lady?" *Good Housekeeping* (March 1964): 32; Christine Sadler, "Our Very Busy First Lady," *McCall's* (March 1964): 189; "Mrs. Johnson Cites Women's Challenges," *New York Times,* 4 June 1964, 27; Mead, "A New Kind of First Lady?" 20.

16. Montgomery, "What Kind of Woman Is Our New First Lady?" 32; William V. Shannon, "The Other Carter in the Running," *New York Times,* 15 September 1976, 45; Elizabeth Janeway, "The First Lady: A Professional at Getting Things Done," *Ladies' Home Journal* (April 1964): 64.

17. Wayne King, "Rosalynn Carter, a Tough, Tireless Campaigner, Displays Same Driving Quality as Her Husband," *New York Times,* 18 October 1976, 33; Judy Klemesrud, "For Mrs. Carter, a Rest at Last," *New York Times,* 11 June 1976, 1; Myra MacPherson, "First Families," *Washington Post,* 20 January 1977, 15.

18. Kandy Stroud, "Rosalynn's Agenda in the White House," *New York Times Magazine,* 20 March 1977, 20.

19. Myra MacPherson, "The Blooming of Betty Ford," *McCall's* (September 1975): 120; MacPherson, "First Families," 15; "Women of the Year, 1976," 74.

20. Jean Libman Block, "The Pat Nixon I Know," *Good Housekeeping* (July 1973): 126 (quote); Susanna McBee, "Pat Nixon and the First Lady Watchers," *McCall's* (September 1970): 140; May, *Homeward Bound,* 201; Lenore Hershey, "The 'New' Pat Nixon," *Ladies' Home Journal* (February 1972): 125; Flora Rheta Schreiber, "Pat Nixon Reveals for the First Time: 'I Didn't Want Dick to Run Again,'" *Good Housekeeping* (July 1968): 62.

21. Douglas, *Where the Girls Are,* 165.

22. Louchheim, "Spotlight Shifts in Washington," 56; Mead, "A New Kind of First Lady?" 12; John Herbers, "Mrs. Ford Tells News Parley She's Busy and Happy," *New York Times,* 5 September 1974, 25; "Mrs. Carter Planning Active Role in Capitol," *New York Times,* 18 November 1976, 26; Barbara Gamarekian, "A Spokesman Who's 'a Worrywort,'" *New York Times,* 3 February 1977, 50.

23. McBee, "First Lady Watchers," 140, 144.

24. "Our First Ninety Days in the White House," *Good Housekeeping* (May 1964): 150, 152; Sadler, "Our Very Busy First Lady," 79; "Mrs. Johnson Explains Her Role as a Leveler," *Washington Post,* 23 August 1964, 82; Nan Robertson, "Mrs. Johnson Holds the Bible for the Oath-Taking," *New York Times,* 21 January 1965, 16; Nan Robertson, "Public Writing Many Letters to Mrs. Johnson," *New York Times,* 1 March 1964, 54 (the article noted that Johnson received between fifteen hundred and two thousand letters a week).

25. King, "Rosalynn Carter," 33; Klemesrud, "For Mrs. Carter, a Rest at Last," 1. See also Trude B. Feldman, "Rosalynn Carter at Fifty," *McCall's* (August 1977): 126.

26. MacPherson, "Betty Ford," 124.

27. Trude B. Feldman, "Our Private Life in the White House," *Ladies' Home Journal* (October 1976): 84, 86.

28. See Nan Robertson, "Mrs. Johnson Sets a Campaign Tone," *New York Times,* 19 August 1964, 20; Nan Robertson, "Mrs. Johnson's Akron Visit Opens Campaign

Trip," *New York Times,* 18 September 1964, 20; Nan Robertson, "Mrs. Johnson, in Ohio Bastion of G.O.P., Praises Her Party," *New York Times,* 19 September 1964, 14; "Four Day Trip Planned by Mrs. Johnson," *Washington Post,* 23 October 1964, 28.

29. Nan Robertson, "First Lady Starts Solo Swing through the South Tomorrow," *New York Times,* 5 October 1964, 26; Liz Carpenter, *Ruffles and Flourishes* (Garden City, NJ: Doubleday, 1970), 144.

30. Nan Robertson, "Mrs. Johnson Ends Eight-State Rail Tour of the South," *New York Times,* 10 October 1964, 15.

31. Claude Sitton, "Mrs. Johnson's Southern Trip Spurs New Support," *New York Times,* 11 October 1964, 72; Robertston, "Mrs. Johnson Ends Eight-State Rail Tour of the South," 15.

32. King, "Rosalynn Carter," 33; Klemesrud, "For Mrs. Carter, a Rest at Last," 1 (quotes).

33. Feldman, "Rosalynn Carter at Fifty," 198; Megan Rosenfeld, "Candidates' Wives Carry Share of Load: Not Mere Symbols, They Have Their Own Charisma," *Washington Post,* 10 June 1977, C1.

34. "Mrs. Ford to Seek Votes in Minnesota for Husband," *Washington Post,* 22 June 1976, 26; "Transcripts of the Statements of the President and Mrs. Ford and Carter," *New York Times,* 4 November 1976, 23.

35. Charlotte Curtis, "Pat Nixon: Creature Comforts Don't Matter," *New York Times,* 3 July 1968, 30; "Mrs. Nixon Outlines Her Campaign Plans," *New York Times,* 16 August 1968, 37; Nan Robertson, "Mrs. Nixon Plans a Tour for the G.O.P.," *New York Times,* 8 October 1968, 32.

36. Sadler, "Our Very Busy First Lady," 188; Nan Robertson, "Mrs. Johnson Cheered in 'Poverty Pocket' Coal Towns," *New York Times,* 12 January 1964, 1.

37. "Mrs. Johnson to Give Poverty Project Tea," *Washington Post,* 14 February 1965, 56; "Mrs. Johnson Urges Help for Children," *New York Times,* 20 February 1965, 11.

38. The *New York Times* and *Washington Post* each carried fourteen articles about Carter's Latin American trip.

39. Laura Foreman, "Mrs. Carter Leaves on Latin Tour Today," *New York Times,* 30 May 1977, 4; Linda Charlton, "Mrs. Carter's Model Is Very Much Her Own: Mrs. F.D.R.," *New York Times,* 5 June 1977, 54; Susanna McBee, "Mrs. Carter's Trip Carefully Crafted to Make Policy Points," *Washington Post,* 29 May 1977, 6.

40. David Vidal, "Ambassador Rosalynn Carter: First Lady Confounds the Skeptics and Makes a Striking Success of Her Latin American Tour," *New York Times,* 14 June 1977, 18.

41. Carl Sferrazza Anthony, *First Ladies: The Saga of the Presidents' Wives and Their Power, 1961–1990* (New York: Quill, 1991), 114.

42. Nan Robertson, "Mrs. Johnson Leads Capital Tour," *New York Times,* 10 March 1965, 26. See also Lewis L. Gould, *Lady Bird Johnson: Our Environmental First Lady* (Lawrence: University Press of Kansas, 1999).

43. On September 28, 1974, the first stories ran regarding Ford's surgery, which received daily coverage for nearly two weeks, and the follow-up coverage continued throughout her time in the White House.

44. "Mrs. Ford's Ordeal," *New York Times,* 30 September 1974, 34; Betty Ford, "I Feel Like I've Been Reborn," *McCall's* (February 1975): 142.

45. "Mrs. Ford Cheered by Her Mail: Her Rapid Recovery Continues," *New York Times,* 4 October 1974, 16; also Lillian Barney, "Many More Women Seek Breast Cancer Exams, but Find Few Places to Go," *New York Times,* 20 October 1974, 118. Emanuel Perlmutter, "Mrs. Ford Asks Drive for Cancer Diagnosis," *New York Times,* 2 December 1976, 52.

46. James F. Clarity, "Mrs. Carter, at a Hearing, Opposes Sending Mentally Ill to Institutions," *New York Times*, 25 May 1977, 16; Marjorie Hunter, "Mrs. Carter's Mental Health Drive Has Tight Budget," *New York Times*, 22 April 1977, 17.

47. Nancy Hicks, "Mrs. Carter Plans White House Conference on Aging," *New York Times*, 16 (quote); also Donnie Radcliffe, "Mrs. Carter Begins Fulfilling Her Pledge: Launches Campaign to Aid Elderly, Mentally Disabled," *Washington Post*, 19 April 1977, 10; Donnie Radcliffe, "Rosalynn Carter Takes Up Cause of Nation's 22 Million Elderly," *Washington Post*, 11 May 1977, 5.

48. MacPherson, "Betty Ford," 122; "Women of the Year, 1976," 74; "Mrs. Ford Scored on Equality Plan: Letters Running 3 to 1 against Her Lobbying Efforts," *New York Times*, 21 February 1975, 32; MacPherson, "Betty Ford," 124.

49. Myra MacPherson, "Indiana Ratifies ERA—With Rosalynn Carter's Aid," *Washington Post*, 19 January 1977, 1. Senator Townsend later denied that Carter "swayed" his vote, though he admitted to speaking with her ("Mrs. Carter Intervenes in Indiana E.R.A. Vote," *New York Times*, 20 January 1977, 19).

50. Paul G. Edwards, "Rosalynn Carter Seeks Virginia Votes for ERA," *Washington Post*, 29 January 1977, B1.

51. "Miss Hayes Guest of Mrs. Johnson: First Lady Starts a Series of Informal Luncheons," *New York Times*, 17 January 1964, 22; Donnie Radcliffe, "A Different Kind of Tea," *Washington Post*, 5 April 1977, B2.

52. Block, "The Pat Nixon I Know," 126.

53. MacPherson, "Betty Ford," 93, 122.

54. Donnie Radcliffe, "A Low-Key Debut Appearance by the First Lady," *Washington Post*, 6 April 1977, D10.

55. MacPherson, "Betty Ford," 122. See also Jamieson, *Beyond the Double Bind*, 5.

56. McBee, "First Lady Watchers," 77; Zelizer, "Reading the Past against the Grain," 224.

57. Mead, "A New Kind of First Lady?" 12; Jessamyn West, "The Real Pat Nixon," *Good Housekeeping* (February 1971): 57; McBee, "First Lady Watchers," 77.

58. "Our First Ninety Days in the White House," 152; Robertson, "Many Letters to Mrs. Johnson," 54.

59. Charlton, "Mrs. Carter's Model," 54; Charlotte Curtis, "What Kind of First Lady Will She Be?" *McCall's* (January 1977): 22.

60. MacPherson, "Betty Ford," 93, 122 (quote).

61. West, "The Real Pat Nixon," 124; Hershey, "The 'New' Pat Nixon," 125.

62. Campbell, "Rhetorical Presidency," 181.

63. MacPherson, "Betty Ford," 124. See also Judy Klemesrud, "Mrs. Ford Helps 'Remember the Ladies' of Revolutionary Era," *New York Times*, 30 June 1976, 77.

64. MacPherson, "Betty Ford," 120, 124 (emphasis in original).

65. "Mrs. Ford Scored on Equality Plan," 32. However, a later article noted that "there was a dramatic turnaround" in the White House mail: "Of some 10,000 letters, the majority favored the ERA" (MacPherson, "Betty Ford," 124).

66. "Mrs. Ford Scored on Equality Plan," 32; MacPherson, "Betty Ford," 124; Candice Bergen, "An Intimate Look at the Fords," *Ladies' Home Journal* (May 1975): 75.

67. "Anti-ERA Protests Aimed at First Lady," *Washington Post*, 5 February 1977, B2; Stroud, "Rosalynn's Agenda," 20.

68. Douglas, *Where the Girls Are*, 221–44.

69. MacPherson, "First Families," 15 (quote); Jamieson, *Beyond the Double Bind*, 121.

70. "How Much Should a First Lady Say?" *McCall's* (February 1976): 49; Feldman, "Our Private Life in the White House," 84.

71. MacPherson, "First Families," 15; "Mrs. Ford and the Affair of the Daughter," *Ladies' Home Journal* (November 1975): 118.

72. "How Much Should a First Lady Say?" 49; MacPherson, "Betty Ford," 124.

73. Jamieson, *Beyond the Double Bind,* 80.

74. Stroud, "Rosalynn's Agenda," 58; Meg Greenfield, "Mrs. President," *Washington Post,* 15 June 1977, 17 (reprinted from *Newsweek*); Matthews, *Rise of Public Woman,* 4.

75. "Rosalynn Carter Elected," *New York Times,* 15 June 1977, 20; Greenfield, "Mrs. President," 17 (reprinted from *Newsweek*).

76. Jamieson, *Beyond the Double Bind,* 121.

77. McBee, "First Lady Watchers," 140.

78. Block, "The Pat Nixon I Know," 126. Stroud is quoted referring to Nixon as "Plastic Pat" in a *Women's Wear Daily* article.

79. Ibid.; McBee, "First Lady Watchers," 138, 77.

80. Nan Robertson, "Mrs. Nixon, on Seven-State Tour, Shuns Politics," *New York Times,* 23 September 1972, 14.

81. Jamieson, *Beyond the Double Bind,* 120; MacPherson, "First Families," 15.

82. Wandersee, *On the Move,* 162.

83. Halbwachs, *On Collective Memory,* 172.

84. David Weaver, "Women as Journalists," in Norris, *Women, Media, and Politics,* 38–39.

85. MacPherson, "First Families," 15.

Chapter Five—First Lady as Political Interloper, 1980–2001

1. Jan Jarboe Russell, "Not Queen, Not Prisoner—Just the President's Wife," *New York Times,* 30 August 2000, 23.

2. Troy, *Mr. and Mrs. President,* 392.

3. Ryan, *Feminism and the Women's Movement,* 54–55; Faludi, *Backlash,* xix (quote), 48–55.

4. May, *Homeward Bound,* 201.

5. Ryan, *Feminism and the Women's Movement,* 103; Mary Douglas Vavrus, *Postfeminist News: Political Women in Media Culture* (Albany: State University of New York Press, 2002), 16 (quote).

6. Faludi, *Backlash,* xviii; also Dow, *Prime-Time Feminism,* 87.

7. Judith Stacey, "Sexism by a Subtler Name? Postindustrial Conditions and Postfeminist Consciousness in the Silicon Valley," *Socialist Review* 17 (1987): 8.

8. Rayna Rapp, "Is the Legacy of Second-Wave Feminism Postfeminism?" *Socialist Review* 18 (1987): 32; Robert Goldman, Deborah Heath, and Sharon L. Smith, "Commodity Feminism," *Critical Studies in Mass Communication* 8 (1991): 333–51; Kitch, *Girl on the Magazine Cover,* 184; Douglas, *Where the Girls Are,* 270 (quote).

9. Faludi, *Backlash,* 77–78; Vavrus, *Postfeminist News,* 22, 17–19.

10. Faludi, *Backlash,* 56, 93.

11. Stacey, "Sexism by a Subtler Name," 11; Mary Douglas Vavrus, "Putting Ally on Trial: Contesting Postfeminism in Popular Culture," *Women's Studies in Communication* 23 (2000): 415.

12. Stacey, "Sexism by a Subtler Name," 24.

13. Lally Weymouth, "The Biggest Role of Nancy's Life," *New York Times Magazine,* 26 October 1980, 45; Enid Nemy, "Words from Friends: A New White House Style Is on the Way," *New York Times Magazine,* 9 November 1980, 80.

14. Alessandra Stanley, "Republicans Present Marilyn [Quayle] as a Self-Sacrificing 90s Supermom," *New York Times,* 18 August 1992, A7; Alessandra Stanley, "First Lady on Abortion: Not a Platform Issue," *New York Times,* 14 August 1992, A1.

15. Cindy Adams, "Talking with the Next First Lady," *Ladies' Home Journal* (October 1988): 154; Donnie Radcliffe, "Barbara Bush: Unassuming, Underestimated, Stumping for the Veep," *Washington Post,* 5 June 1988, F1.

16. Weymouth, "The Biggest Role of Nancy's Life," 45 (abortion on demand); "Nancy Reagan Face-Off," *Ladies' Home Journal* (October 1980): 111.

17. Sharon Olsen, "George and Barbara: A Sense of Sharing," *McCall's* (September 1988): 84; Bernard Weinraub, "Barbara Bush Links Her Weight to Thyroid Condition," *New York Times,* 30 March 1989, A17.

18. Frank Rich, "Whose Hillary?" *New York Times Magazine,* 13 June 1993, 70 (quote). See also Felicity Barringer, "From Lawyer to Mother: Now, Both of the Above," *New York Times,* 30 October 1992, A18; Felicity Barringer, "Hillary Clinton's New Role: The Description Is Wide Open," *New York Times,* 16 November 1992, A1.

19. Felicity Barringer, "The White House Office That Isn't There," *New York Times,* 6 December 1992, 4:1; Sally Quinn, "Is America Ready for Hillary Clinton? The Candidate's Wife Is the Very Model of the Modern Working Woman," *Washington Post,* 9 August 1992, C1; Catherine Breslin, "Hillary Clinton," *Ladies' Home Journal* (October 1992): 190.

20. Robin Toner, "Hillary Clinton Is Back! Details Inside," *New York Times,* 7 May 1993, A18; Steven R. Weisman, "St. Hillary's Homecoming," *New York Times,* 28 August 1996, A18.

21. Susan Faludi, "The Power Laugh," *New York Times,* 20 December 1992, 4:13.

22. Amy E. Schwartz, "'Good Girls, Bad Girls': Pitting Women against Each Other in a Family Values Farce," *Washington Post,* 5 September 1992, A29; Stanley, "Self-Sacrificing 90s Supermom," A7; Alessandra Stanley, "'Family Values' and Women: Is G.O.P. a House Divided?" *New York Times,* 21 August 1992, A1.

23. Lloyd Grove, "The Woman with a Ticket to Ride: Hillary Clinton's New Image, Fresh from the Oven," *Washington Post,* 16 July 1992, C1; Howard Kurtz, "Portraits of a First Lady: Media Strive to Define Hillary Clinton," *Washington Post,* 21 November 1992, A1.

24. Tamar Lewin, "Legal Scholars See Distortion in Attacks on Hillary Clinton," *New York Times,* 24 August 1992, A1.

25. Stanley, "Self-Sacrificing 90s Supermom," A7; Marjorie Williams, "Barbara Bush, Hillary Clinton, Marilyn Quayle, Tipper Gore," *Washington Post Magazine,* 1 November 1992, 11; "A Word from the Wives," *New York Times,* 21 August 1992, A24; Elizabeth Kolbert, "On TV, a Victory in Family Numbers," *New York Times,* 21 August 1992, A12.

26. Williams, "Barbara Bush, Hillary Clinton," 11; Frank Bruni, "Quiet Strength: For Laura Bush, a Direction She Never Wished to Go In," *New York Times,* 31 July 2000, A1; Lois Romano, "First Lady Puts Privacy First: Reluctant Star likely to Set Her Own Terms," *Washington Post,* 20 January 2001, A16.

27. Williams, "Barbara Bush, Hillary Clinton," 11.

28. Maureen Dowd, "First Lady Celebrated on 'a Great Day,'" *New York Times,* 23 August 1984, A24; John Corry, "Special Looks at Nancy Reagan and Her Power," *New York Times,* 24 June 1985, C14; Beth Weinhouse, "Nancy Reagan: Traditional First Lady," *Ladies' Home Journal* (May 1985): 138; Charlotte Curtis, "A Private Talk with Nancy Reagan," *Ladies' Home Journal* (June 1981): 132.

29. Bernard Weinraub, "A Down-to-Earth Tenant for an Exclusive Address," *New York Times,* 15 January 1989, 1; Donnie Radcliffe, "Vintage Barbara," *Washington Post,* 20 January 1989, 34.

30. Ann Gerhart, "Learning to Read Laura Bush: The First Lady's Quietude Masks a Passionate Interest in Ideas," *Washington Post,* 22 March 2001, C1; Alison

Mitchell, "The Governor's Wife: A Political Wallflower Has Full Dance Card," *New York Times,* 21 September 2000, A25; Bruni, "Quiet Strength," A1; Lois Romano, "Bushes Planning to Hit Campaign Trail Together," *Washington Post,* 4 August 2000, A16.

31. Steven R. Weisman, "Nancy Reagan's Role Grows," *New York Times,* 11 November 1984, 2; also Maureen Dowd, "A More Relaxed Nancy Reagan Tours the South," *New York Times,* 14 October 1984, 28; Donnie Radcliffe, "There Aren't Any Secrets between Us," *Washington Post,* 22 August 1984, B1; Bernard Weinraub, "The Washingtonization of Nancy Reagan," *New York Times,* 26 March 1985, A20.

32. Donnie Radcliffe, "Nancy Reagan: 'Vicious and Cruel' Carter Tactics Prompt Rare Outburst of Anger," *Washington Post,* 23 October 1980, D1; Bernard Weinraub, "Mrs. Reagan, in Campaign Ad, Assails Statements by Carter on Her Husband," *New York Times,* 26 October 1980, 41 (also Dudley Clendinen, "What a Woman Endures for Her Candidate," *New York Times,* 23 October 1980, B12); Weisman, "Nancy Reagan's Role Grows," 2.

33. Maureen Dowd, "Washington Talk: Politics," *New York Times,* 19 June 1989, B8; Alison Cook, "At Home with Barbara Bush," *Ladies' Home Journal* (March 1990): 230.

34. For more on Eisenhower as protector, see Johnston, "Policeman for Ike," 23; "Mrs. Eisenhower a Mystery Fan," 64.

35. Campbell, "Rhetorical Presidency," 181–88; Kati Marton, *Hidden Power: Presidential Marriages that Shaped Our Recent History* (New York: Pantheon Books, 2001), 3–11.

36. Radcliffe, "There Aren't Any Secrets between Us," B1; Donnie Radcliffe, "The Influential Nancy Reagan: Time Looks at Her Impact, Image, and the Great Birth-Date Issue," *Washington Post,* 7 January 1985, D1.

37. Weymouth, "The Biggest Role of Nancy's Life," 45; also Radcliffe, "There Aren't Any Secrets between Us," B1; Weinraub, "The Washingtonization of Nancy Reagan," A20.

38. Francis X. Clines, "Avoiding Discouraging Words at the Ranch," *New York Times,* 5 August 1984, E3; "Nancy Reagan Denies Giving President Cue," *New York Times,* 19 August 1984, 29; Weymouth, "The Biggest Role of Nancy's Life," 45 (quote). See also "Nancy Reagan Criticizes Aides to President," *New York Times,* 13 November 1988, 1; Michael Wines, "First Lady Hopes for Unglamorous Legacy," *New York Times,* 15 January 1989, 20.

39. Radcliffe, "There Aren't Any Secrets between Us," B1; Radcliffe, "The Influential Nancy Reagan," D1.

40. "Nancy Reagan Criticizes Aides to President," 30.

41. Gwen Ifill, "Clinton Wants Wife at Cabinet Table," *New York Times,* 19 December 1992, 8; Gail Collins, "The Age of the Smart Woman," *Ladies' Home Journal* (April 1993): 146; Mary McGrory, "A Worthy Mission for Hillary," *Washington Post,* 26 November 1992, A2.

42. Ifill, "Clinton Wants Wife at Cabinet Table," 8; Alessandra Stanley, "A Softer Image for Hillary Clinton," *New York Times,* 13 July 1992, B1; Breslin, "Hillary Clinton," 190.

43. Williams, "Barbara Bush, Hillary Clinton," 11; Quinn, "Is America Ready for Hillary Clinton?" C1.

44. Williams, "Barbara Bush, Hillary Clinton," 11; Barringer, "Hillary Clinton's New Role," A1.

45. Linda Witt, Karen M. Paget, and Glenna Matthews, *Running as a Woman: Gender and Power in American Politics* (New York: Free Press, 1995), 194; Grove, "Hillary Clinton's New Image," C1.

46. Thomas L. Friedman, "Hillary Clinton to Head Panel on Health Care," *New York Times,* 26 January 1993, A1; Robert Pear, "Settling In: First Lady Hillary Clinton

Gets Policy Job and New Office," *New York Times,* 22 January 1993, A1; Michael Kelly, "Hillary Clinton Visits Capitol in Vivid Display of Her Clout," *New York Times,* 5 February 1993, A1.

47. Blaine Harden, "Finely Tailored Roles: Candidates' Wives Display Distinct Campaign Styles," *Washington Post,* 1 October 1996, A1; David Maraniss, "First Lady in Prime Time: Target for Criticism Recaptures Spotlight," *Washington Post,* 27 August 1996, A1.

48. James Bennet, "The First Lady: Hillary Clinton, an Evolutionary Tale," *New York Times,* 20 January 1997, A14; Peter Baker, "First Lady Remains Vital Force in White House," *Washington Post,* 20 January 1997, A20.

49. Robin Toner, "Backlash for Hillary Clinton," *New York Times,* 24 September 1992, A1.

50. Matthews, *Rise of Public Woman,* 4.

51. Diana McLellan, "Barbara Bush," *Ladies' Home Journal* (October 1992): 192; Radcliffe, "Barbara Bush: Unassuming," F1.

52. Romano, "First Lady Puts Privacy First," A16; Bruni, "Quiet Strength," A1; Marian Burros, "Making the White House a Home," *New York Times,* 23 February 2001, A11.

53. McLellan, "Barbara Bush," 192; Donnie Radcliffe, "Granny Get Your Gun: The Other Mrs. Bush," *Washington Post,* 19 August 1992, B1.

54. Donnie Radcliffe, "Barbara Bush's Vow of Silence: Decision to Be Mum on Controversial Issues Announced in Tokyo," *Washington Post,* 24 February 1989, C1; Stanley, "First Lady on Abortion," A1; Alessandra Stanley, "Barbara Bush: The Un-Secret Weapon," *New York Times,* 19 August 1992, A15.

55. Campbell, "Rhetorical Presidency," 181 (emphasis in original); Williams, "Barbara Bush, Hillary Clinton," 11.

56. David S. Broder, "The Special Strengths of Barbara Bush," *Washington Post,* 22 January 1989, D7.

57. Sarah Booth Conroy, "For Iona House, Mrs. Bush's Name Means Magic," *Washington Post,* 7 May 1989, F1; Sarah Booth Conroy, "The Benefit of Borrowing a Name," *Washington Post,* 13 December 1992, F1.

58. Lois Romano, "The Hug that Says It All: Barbara Bush Visits AIDS Infants," *Washington Post,* 23 March 1989, D2.

59. Barbara Gamarekian, "Barbara Bush Announces Formation of Literacy Foundation," *New York Times,* 7 March 1989, A16; William Raspberry, "Barbara Bush's Pet Project," *Washington Post,* 11 March 1989, A23; Ann Gerhart, "The First Lady's School Cheer: Mrs. Bush Stresses Need for Teachers," *Washington Post,* 27 February 2001, C1.

60. Chuck Conconi, "Personalities," *Washington Post,* 18 March 1985, D3.

61. Sally Koslow, "Hillary Rodham Clinton," *McCall's* (November 1996): 199; Victoria Falls, "The Woman behind the Mask: Away from Washington, Hillary Clinton Shows a Different Face," *Washington Post,* 27 March 1997, B1. *See also* Koslow, "Hillary Rodham Clinton," 148.

62. James Bennet, "Abortion-Rights Backers Win High-Level Support," *New York Times,* 23 January 1997, A14; Peter Baker, "Addressing a Conflict Raised by Families, Women's Careers: Hillary Clinton Hosts Conference on Early Childhood Education," *Washington Post,* 17 April 1997, A3; Peter Baker, "Saying Her Views Haven't Changed, First Lady Takes on 'Micro' Agenda," *Washington Post,* 31 January 1997, A6; James Bennet, "First Lady Re-Emerges with an Aid Plan for Tiny Businesses," *New York Times,* 31 January 1997, A19.

63. Bennet, "First Lady: Hillary Clinton," A14; Parry-Giles and Blair, "Rhetorical First Lady," 582.

64. Witt, Paget, and Matthews, *Running as a Woman,* 182.

65. Ifill, "Clinton Wants Wife at Cabinet Table," 8; Weymouth, "The Biggest Role of Nancy's Life," 45; Dowd, "A More Relaxed Nancy Reagan Tours the South," 28.

66. Stanley, "A Softer Image for Hillary," B1; Grove, "Hillary Clinton's New Image," C1. Other stories that referenced Reagan and Carter together include Quinn, "Is America Ready for Hillary Clinton?" C1; Stanley, "A Softer Image for Hillary Clinton," B1.

67. Koslow, "Hillary Rodham Clinton," 43; Kurtz, "Portraits of a First Lady," A1.

68. Richard Berke, "The Transition: The Other Clinton Helps Shape the Administration," *New York Times,* 14 December 1992, B6; Quinn, "Is America Ready for Hillary Clinton?" C1; Kevin Sack, "Mrs. Clinton Invokes Memories of Famed and Faulted," *New York Times,* 27 August 1996, A11; Francis X. Clines, "Mrs. Clinton Calls Sessions Intellectual, Not Spiritual," *New York Times,* 25 June 1996, A13; Mary McGrory, "Not Messianic, Maybe, but Messy," *Washington Post,* 25 June 1996, A2.

69. Broder, "Special Strengths of Barbara Bush," D7; Patricia Leigh Brown, "The First Lady-Elect: What She Is and Isn't," *New York Times,* 11 December 1988, 42; Elaine Sciolino, "Laura Bush Sees Everything in Its Place, Including Herself," *New York Times,* 15 January 2001, A1.

70. Cook, "At Home with Barbara Bush," 159; Brown, "The First Lady-Elect," 42 (quote).

71. Stanley, "Barbara Bush," A15; Weinraub, "A Down-to-Earth Tenant for an Exclusive Address," 1.

72. Sciolino, "Laura Bush," A1 (quote).

73. Anne-Marie Schiro, "It Began with Dolley Madison," *New York Times,* 18 October 1988, A26; Donnie Radcliffe, "The First Lady Reshapes Her Royal Image," *Washington Post,* 21 January 1985, G7; Curtis, "A Private Talk with Nancy Reagan," 134.

74. Collins, "The Age of the Smart Woman," 146; Radcliffe, "The First Lady Reshapes Her Royal Image," G7; Leslie Bennetts, "With a New First Lady, a New Style," *New York Times,* 21 January 1981, B6.

75. Bennetts, "With a New First Lady, a New Style," B6; Schiro, "It Began with Dolley Madison," A26.

76. Judy Mann, "Homemakers on Parade," *Washington Post,* 12 August 1992, E15; Williams, "Barbara Bush, Hillary Clinton," 11; Lewin, "Distortion in Attacks on Hillary Clinton," A1; Mann, "Homemakers on Parade," E15.

77. "Barbara Bush: Her Lifestyle," *Ladies' Home Journal* (June 1989): 11; Charles Strum, "Barbara Bush: Bush's 'Secret Weapon' Enters New Jersey Battle," *New York Times,* 22 October 1992, A21; Stanley, "Barbara Bush," A15 (quote).

78. Stanley, "Barbara Bush," A15; Radcliffe, "Granny Get Your Gun," B1.

79. Toner, "Backlash for Hillary Clinton," A1; Anna Quindlen, "Public and Private: Wives for Wives' Sake," *New York Times,* 9 August 1992, 4:17; Catherine Manegold, "Women Get into Political Football—as the Ball," *New York Times,* 23 August 1992, 4:1; Mann, "Homemakers on Parade," E15.

80. Manegold, "Women Get into Political Football—as the Ball," 4:1; Karen Lehrman, "Beware the Cookie Monster," *New York Times,* 18 July 1992, 23.

81. Manegold, "Women Get into Political Football—as the Ball," 4:1.

82. Schwartz, "Good Girls, Bad Girls," A29; Douglas, *Where the Girls Are,* 243.

83. Schwartz, "Good Girls, Bad Girls," A29; Williams, "Barbara Bush, Hillary Clinton," 11.

84. Gerhart, "Learning to Read Laura Bush," C1.

85. Radcliffe, "Granny Get Your Gun," B1; Quinn, "Is America Ready for Hillary Clinton?" C1.

86. Quinn, "Is America Ready for Hillary Clinton?" C1; Joyce Purnick, "Let Hillary Be Hillary," *New York Times*, 15 July 1992, A20; Anna Quindlen, "Public and Private: The Two Faces of Eve," *New York Times*, 15 July 1992, A21; Williams, "Barbara Bush, Hillary Clinton," 11.

87. Russell, "Not Queen, Not Prisoner," A23.

88. Christine Reinhardt, "Personal Pleasures," *McCall's* (October 1992): 40; Quinn, "Is America Ready for Hillary Clinton?" C1.

Conclusion—A Century of Press Framing

1. Mark Leibovich, "On the Campaign Trail, Laura Bush Is 180 Degrees from Teresa Kerry," *Washington Post*, 11 August 2004, C1.

2. "Mrs. McKinley, Mrs. Bryan: A Comparison," *Harper's Bazaar*, 11 August 1900, 955–56.

3. Stephen D. Reese, "Prologue—Framing Public Life: A Bridging Model for Media Research," in Reese, Gandy, and Grant, *Framing Public Life*, 19.

4. Zelizer, "Journalists as Interpretive Communities," 224.

5. Witt, Paget, and Matthews, *Running as a Woman*, 181–208.

6. Joyce Purnick, "To Become First Lady, Just Stand By," *New York Times*, 29 July 2004, B1.

References

Abbott, James, and Elaine Rice. *Designing Camelot: The Kennedy White House Restoration.* New York: Van Nostrand, 1998.

Abzug, Bella, and Mim Kelber. *The Gender Gap: Bella Abzug's Guide to Political Power for American Women.* Boston: Houghton Mifflin, 1984.

Adams, Cindy. "Talking with the Next First Lady." *Ladies' Home Journal* (October 1988): 151, 154.

Allgor, Catherine. *Parlor Politics: In Which the Ladies of Washington Helped Build a City and a Government.* Charlottesville: University Press of Virginia, 2000.

———. "Political Parties: First Ladies and Social Events in the Formation of the Federal Government." In Watson and Eksterowicz, *Presidential Companion,* 35–53.

Ames, William E. *A History of the National Intelligencer.* Chapel Hill: University of North Carolina Press, 1972.

Anderson, Christopher. *George and Laura: Portrait of an American Marriage.* New York: William Morrow, 2002.

Anderson, Karrin Vasby. "The First Lady: A Site of 'American Womanhood.'" In Wertheimer, *Inventing a Voice,* 17–30.

Anderson, Kristi. *Beyond Suffrage.* Chicago: University of Chicago Press, 1996.

Anthony, Carl Sferrazza. *America's First Families.* New York: Simon and Schuster, 2000.

———. *First Ladies: The Saga of Presidents' Wives and Their Power, 1789–1961.* New York: Quill, 1990.

———. *First Ladies: The Saga of Presidents' Wives and Their Power, 1961–1990.* New York: Quill, 1991.

———. *Florence Harding: The First Lady, the Jazz Age, and the Death of America's Most Scandalous President.* New York: Quill, 1998.

Arnett, Ethel Stephens. *Mrs. James Madison: The Incomparable Dolley.* Greenville, SC: Piedmont Press, 1972.

Baron, Ava. *Work Engendered: Toward a New History of American Labor.* Ithaca: Cornell University Press, 1991.

Barringer, Felicity. "Hillary Clinton's New Role: The Description Is Wide Open." *New York Times,* 16 November 1992, A1.

Baty, S. Paige. *American Monroe: The Making of a Body Politic.* Berkeley and Los Angeles: University of California Press, 1995.

Baumgardner, Jennifer, and Amy Richards. *Manifesta: Young Women, Feminism, and the Future.* New York: Farrar, Straus and Giroux, 2000.

Beasley, Maurine H. "The Curious Career of Anne Royall." *Journalism History* 3 (1976–1977): 98–102.

———. *Eleanor Roosevelt and the Media: A Public Quest for Self-Fulfillment.* Urbana: University of Illinois Press, 1987.

———. "Eleanor Roosevelt's Press Conferences: Case Study in Class, Gender, and Race." *Social Science Journal* 37 (2000): 517–28.

———. *First Ladies and the Press: The Unfinished Partnership of the Media Age.* Evanston, IL: Northwestern University Press, 2005.

Beasley, Maurine, and Paul Belgrade. "Media Coverage of a Silent Partner: Mamie Eisenhower as First Lady." *American Journalism* 3 (1986): 39–49.

Beasley, Maurine H., and Sheila J. Gibbons. *Taking Their Place: A Documentary History of Women and Journalism,* 2nd ed. State College, PA: Strata, 2003.

Beasley, Vanessa. "Engendering Democratic Change: How Three U.S. Presidents Discussed Female Suffrage." *Rhetoric and Public Affairs* 5 (2002): 79–103.

Bennet, James. "The First Lady: Hillary Clinton, an Evolutionary Tale." *New York Times,* 20 January 1997, A14.

Benze, James G. Jr. "Nancy Reagan: China Doll or Dragon Lady." *Presidential Studies Quarterly* 20 (1990): 777–90.

Berkin, Carol Ruth, and Mary Beth Norton. *Women of America: A History.* Boston: Houghton Mifflin, 1979.

Birmingham, Stephen. *Jacqueline Bouvier Kennedy Onassis.* New York: Grosset, 1978.

———. *The Right People: A Portrait of the American Social Establishment.* Boston: Little, Brown, 1968.

Black, Allida M. *Casting Her Own Shadow: Eleanor Roosevelt and the Shaping of Postwar Liberalism.* New York: Columbia University Press, 1996.

———, ed. *What I Want to Leave Behind: The Essential Essays of Eleanor Roosevelt.* New York: Columbia University Press, 1995.

Blair, Diane M. "No Ordinary Time: Eleanor Roosevelt's Address to the 1940 Democratic National Convention." *Rhetoric and Public Affairs* 4 (2001): 203–22.

Block, Jean Libman. "The Pat Nixon I Know." *Good Housekeeping* (July 1973): 72, 124–28.

Bodnar, John. "Public Memory in an American City: Commemoration in Cleveland." In *Commemorations: The Politics of National Identity,* ed. John R. Gillis. Princeton: Princeton University Press, 1992.

Boorstin, Daniel J. *The Image: A Guide to Pseudo-Events in America.* 25th anniversary ed. New York: Antheneum, 1987.

Bowles, Hamish. *Jacqueline Kennedy: The White House Years.* Boston: Little, Brown and Company, 2001.

Brady, Patricia. "Martha Washington and the Creation of the Role of the First Lady." In Watson and Eksterowicz, *Presidential Companion,* 21–34.

Breslin, Catherine. "Hillary Clinton." *Ladies' Home Journal* (October 1992): 126, 189–91.

Broder, David S. "The Special Strengths of Barbara Bush." *Washington Post,* 22 January 1989, D7.

Bruni, Frank. "Quiet Strength: For Laura Bush, a Direction She Never Wished to Go In." *New York Times,* 31 July 2000, A1.

Burnham, John C. "Medical Specialists and Movements Toward Social Control in the Progressive Era." In *Building the Organizational Society: Essays on Associational Activities in Modern America,* ed. Jerry Israel, 19–30. New York: Free Press, 1972.

Burns, Lisa M. "A Forgotten First Lady: A Rhetorical Reassessment of Ellen Axson Wilson." In Wertheimer, *Inventing a Voice,* 79–102.

Bush, Barbara. *Barbara Bush: A Memoir.* New York: St. Martin's Paperbacks, 1994.

Caldwell, Mary French. *General Jackson's Lady.* Nashville: Kingsport Press, 1936.

Campbell, Karlyn Kohrs. "The Discursive Performance of Femininity: Hating Hillary." *Rhetoric & Public Affairs* 1 (1998): 1–19.

——. *Man Cannot Speak for Her: A Critical Study of Early Feminist Rhetoric*. Vol. 1. New York: Praeger, 1989.

——. "The Rhetorical Presidency: A Two-Person Career." In *Beyond the Rhetorical Presidency,* ed. Martin J. Medhurst, 179–95. College Station: Texas A&M University Press, 1996.

"Capital Homemaker: Mamie Doud Eisenhower." *New York Times,* 14 November 1956, 24.

Carey, James W. "A Cultural Approach to Communication." *Communication* 2 (1975): 1–22.

——, ed. *Media, Myths, and Narratives: Television and the Press*. Newbury Park: Sage, 1988.

Carlson, A. Cheree. "Creative Casuistry and Feminist Consciousness: The Rhetoric of Moral Reform." *Quarterly Journal of Speech* 78 (1992): 16–32.

Caroli, Betty Boyd. *First Ladies*. New York: Oxford University Press, 1995.

Carpenter, Liz. *Ruffles and Flourishes*. Garden City, NJ: Doubleday, 1970.

Carter, Cynthia, Gill Branston, and Stuart Allan, eds. *News, Gender, and Power*. London: Routledge, 1998.

Carter, Rosalynn. *First Lady from Plains*. New York: Ballantine Books, 1984.

Cathcart, Robert S. "From Hero to Celebrity: The Media Connection." In *American Heroes in a Media Age,* ed. Susan J. Drucker and Robert S. Cathcart, 36–46. Cresskill, NJ: Hampton Press, 1994.

Chafe, William H. *The Paradox of Change: American Women in the Twentieth Century*. New York: Oxford University Press, 1991.

Charlton, Linda. "Mrs. Carter's Model Is Very Much Her Own: Mrs. F.D.R." *New York Times,* 5 June 1977, 54.

Claxton, Jimmie Lou Sparkman. *88 Years With Sarah Polk*. New York: Vantage Press, 1972.

Cohen, Jeffrey E. "The Polls: Public Favorability Toward the First Lady, 1993–1999." *Presidential Studies Quarterly* 30 (2000): 575–85.

Cohen, Ruth Schwartz. "Two Washes in the Morning and a Bridge Party at Night: The American Housewife between the Wars." In Scharf and Jensen, *Decades of Discontent,* 177–98.

Collins, Gail. "The Age of the Smart Woman." *Ladies' Home Journal* (April 1993): 146–48.

——. *America's Women: Four Hundred Years of Dolls, Drudges, Helpmates, and Heroines*. New York: HarperCollins, 2003.

Cook, Alison. "At Home with Barbara Bush." *Ladies' Home Journal* (March 1990): 157–59, 229–32.

Cook, Blanche Wiesen. *Eleanor Roosevelt, Volume I, 1884–1933*. New York: Viking, 1992.

——. *Eleanor Roosevelt, Volume II, 1933–1938*. New York: Viking, 1999.

Cott, Nancy F. *The Bonds of Womanhood: "Woman's Sphere" in New England, 1780–1835*. New Haven: Yale University Press, 1977.

——. *The Grounding of Modern Feminism*. New Haven: Yale University Press, 1987.

——, ed. *Root of Bitterness: Documents of the Social History of Women*. New York: E.P. Dutton, 1972.

Creedon, Pamela J., ed. *Women in Mass Communication*. Newbury Park: Sage, 1989.

"Crowd Mind Read by Mrs. Roosevelt." *Washington Post,* 5 March 1933, 7.

Curren, James, and Michael Gurevitch, eds. *Mass Media and Society*. New York: Arnold, 1996.

Curtis, Charlotte. "A Private Talk with Nancy Reagan." *Ladies' Home Journal* (June 1981): 71, 131–34.

Daggett, Mabel Porter. "Woodrow Wilson's Wife." *Good Housekeeping* (March 1913): 316–23.

Damon-Moore, Helen. *Magazines for the Millions: Gender and Commerce in the Ladies' Home Journal and the Saturday Evening Post, 1880–1910.* Albany: State University of New York, 1994.

D'Angelo, Paul. "News Framing as a Multiparadigmatic Research Program: A Response to Entman." *Journal of Communication* 52 (2002): 870–88.

Danner, Laura, and Susan Walsh. "'Radical' Feminists and 'Bickering' Women: Backlash in U.S. Media Coverage of the United Nations Fourth World Conference on Women." *Critical Studies in Mass Communication* 16 (1999): 63–84.

David, Lester. *The Lonely Lady of San Clemente: The Story of Pat Nixon.* New York: Thomas Y. Crowell, 1978.

David, Lester, and Irene David. *Ike and Mamie: The Story of a General and His Lady.* New York: World Publishing, 1981.

Degler, Carl M. *At Odds: Women and the Family in America from the Revolution to the Present.* New York: Oxford University Press, 1980.

Domosh, Mona, and Joni Seager. *Putting Women in Place: Female Geographers Make Sense of the World.* New York: Guilford Press, 2001.

Douglas, Susan J. *Where the Girls Are: Growing Up Female with the Mass Media.* New York: Times Books, 1995.

Douglass, George H. *The Golden Age of the Newspaper.* Westport, CT: Greenwood Press, 1999.

Dow, Bonnie J. "Fixing Feminism: Women's Liberation and the Rhetoric of Television Documentary." *Quarterly Journal of Speech* 90 (2004): 53–81.

———. *Prime-Time Feminism: Television, Media Culture, and the Women's Movement since 1970.* Philadelphia: University of Pennsylvania Press, 1996.

Dowd, Maureen. "A More Relaxed Nancy Reagan Tours the South." *New York Times,* 14 October 1984, 28.

Drexel, Constance. "Mrs. Harding Shares Tasks of President." *Washington Post,* 5 March 1921, 2.

Dye, Nancy S. "Introduction." In *Gender, Class, Race, and Reform in the Progressive Era,* ed. Noralee Frankel and Nancy S. Dye, 1–9. Lexington: University Press of Kentucky, 1991.

Edwards, Janis L., and Huey-Rong Chen. "The First Lady/First Wife in Editorial Cartoons: Rhetorical Visions Through Gendered Lenses." *Women's Studies in Communication* 23 (2000): 367–91.

Eisenhower, Julie Nixon. *Pat Nixon: The Untold Story.* New York: Simon and Schuster, 1986.

———. *Special People.* New York: Simon, 1977.

Eisenhower, Susan. *Mrs. Ike: Memories and Reflections on the Life of Mamie Eisenhower.* New York: Farrar, Straus, and Giroux, 1996.

Emblidge, David, ed. *My Day: The Best of Eleanor Roosevelt's Acclaimed Newspaper Columns, 1936–1962.* New York: Da Capo Press, 2001.

Emery, Michael, Edwin Emery, and Nancy L. Roberts. *The Press and America: An Interpretive History of the Mass Media.* Needham Heights, MA: Allyn and Bacon, 2000.

Endres, Kathleen. "Jane Grey Swisshelm: 19th Century Journalist and Feminist." *Journalism History* 2 (1975/76): 128–32.

Entman, Robert M. "Framing: Toward a Clarification of a Fractured Paradigm." *Journal of Communication* 43 (1993): 51–58.

Faludi, Susan. *Backlash: The Undeclared War against American Women.* New York: Anchor Books, 1991.

Feldman, Trude B. "Our Private Life in the White House." *Ladies' Home Journal* (October 1976): 84–86, 185.

———. "Rosalynn Carter at Fifty." *McCall's* (August 1977): 126, 198.

Felix, Antonia. *America's First Lady, First Mother.* New York: Adams Media Corporation, 2002.

Ferrell, Robert H. *Dear Bess: The Letters From Harry to Bess Truman, 1910–1959.* New York: W.W. Norton and Company, 1983.

Fields, Joseph E, ed. *"Worthy Partner": The Papers of Martha Washington.* Westport, CT: Greenwood Press, 1994.

Fishburn, Katherine. *Women in Popular Culture: A Reference Guide.* Westport, CT: Greenwood Press, 1982.

Fisher, Walter R. *Human Communication as Narration: Toward a Philosophy of Reason, Value, and Action.* Columbia: University of South Carolina Press, 1984.

Flexner, Eleanor. *Century of Struggle: The Woman's Rights Movement in the United States.* New York: Atheneum, 1972.

Ford, Betty, with Chris Chase. *The Times of My Life.* New York: Ballantine Books, 1979.

Frankel, Noralee, and Nancy S. Dye, eds. *Gender, Class, Race, and Reform in the Progressive Era.* Lexington: University Press of Kentucky, 1991.

Freedman, Estelle B. *No Turning Back: The History of Feminism and the Future of Women.* New York: Ballantine Books, 2002.

———. "Separatism as Strategy: Female Institution Building and American Feminism, 1870–1930." *Feminist Studies* 5 (1979): 512–29.

Freeman, Jo. *The Politics of Women's Liberation.* New York: David McKay Company, Inc., 1975.

Friedan, Betty. *The Feminine Mystique.* New York: Dell, 1983.

Furman, Bess. "Trumans Give Up Five-Room Residence." *New York Times,* 14 April 1945, 8.

Gamson, Joshua. *Claims to Fame: Celebrity in Contemporary America.* Berkeley and Los Angeles: University of California Press, 1994.

Gerhart, Ann. "Learning to Read Laura Bush: The First Lady's Quietude Masks a Passionate Interest in Ideas." *Washington Post,* 22 March 2001, C1.

———. *The Perfect Wife: The Life and Choices of Laura Bush.* New York: Simon and Schuster, 2004.

Giele, Janet Zollinger. *Two Paths to Women's Equality: Temperance, Suffrage, and the Origins of Modern Feminism.* New York: Twayne, 1995.

Gitlin, Todd. *The Whole World Is Watching: Mass Media In the Making and the Unmaking of the New Left.* Berkeley: University of California Press, 1980.

"A Glimpse of Mrs. Harding." *New York Times,* 14 November 1920, 6:8.

Golding, Peter, and Phillip Elliot. "News Departments and Broadcasting Organizations the Institutionalization of Objectivity." In *Approaches to Media: A Reader,* ed. Oliver Boyd-Barrett and Chris Newbold, 300–305. London: Arnold, 1995.

Goldman, Robert, Deborah Heath, and Sharon L. Smith. "Commodity Feminism." *Critical Studies in Mass Communication* 8 (1991): 333–51.

Goodall, Sandra. "De/Reconstructing Hillary: From the Retro Ashes of the Donna Reed Fantasy to a '90s View of Women and Politics." In *Bill Clinton on Stump, State, and Stage,* ed. Stephen A. Smith, 163–85. Fayetteville: The University of Arkansas Press, 1994.

Goodwin, Doris Kearns. *No Ordinary Times: Franklin and Eleanor Roosevelt, The Home Front in World War II.* New York: Simon and Schuster, 1994.

Gottlieb, Agnes Hooper. "Women's Press Club of New York City, 1889–1980." In *Women's Press Organizations, 1881–1999,* ed. Elizabeth V. Burt. Westport: Greenwood Press, 2000.

Gould, Lewis L. *American First Ladies: Their Lives and Legacies.* New York: Garland, 1996.

———. "First Ladies." *American Scholar* 55 (1986): 528–35.

———. "First Ladies and the Press: Bess Truman to Lady Bird Johnson." *American Journalism* 1 (1986): 47–62.

———. *Lady Bird Johnson: Our Environmental First Lady.* Lawrence: University Press of Kansas, 1999.

———. *The Modern American Presidency.* Lawrence: University Press of Kansas, 2003.

———. "Modern First Ladies: An Institutional Perspective." *Prologue: Journal of the National Archives* 19 (1987): 71–83.

Graff, Henry F., ed. *The Presidents: A Reference History,* 2nd ed. New York: Simon & Schuster Macmillan, 1997.

Grayson, Benson Lee. *The Unknown President: The Administration of Millard Fillmore.* Washington, DC: University Press of America, 1981.

Greenfield, Meg. "Mrs. President." *Washington Post,* 15 June 1977, 17. Reprinted from *Newsweek.*

Greer, Emily Apt. *First Lady: The Life of Lucy Webb Hayes.* Kent State: Kent State University Press, 1984.

———. "Lucy Webb Hayes and Her Influence upon Her Era." *Hayes Historical Journal* 1 (1976): 25–32.

Gronbeck, Bruce E. "The Presidency in the Age of Second Orality." In *Beyond the Rhetorical Presidency,* ed. Martin J. Medhurst, 30–49. College Station: Texas A&M University Press, 1996.

———. "The Rhetorics of the Past: History, Argument, and Collective Memory." In *Doing Rhetorical History: Concepts and Cases,* ed. Kathleen J. Turner, 47–60. Tuscaloosa: University of Alabama Press, 1998.

Grove, Lloyd. "The Woman with a Ticket to Ride: Hillary Clinton's New Image, Fresh from the Oven." *Washington Post,* 16 July 1992, C1.

Gutin, Myra G. *The President's Partner: The First Lady in the Twentieth Century.* New York: Greenwood Press, 1989.

Habermas, Juergen. "The Public Sphere: An Encyclopedia Article." *New German Critique* 3 (1974): 49–55.

Halbwachs, Maurice. *On Collective Memory.* Translated and edited by Lewis A. Coser. Chicago: University of Chicago Press, 1992.

Halle, Rita S. "That First Lady of Ours." *Good Housekeeping* (December 1933): 29–31, 195–96.

Harmon, Dudley. "What Is Mrs. Wilson Doing? The Part the President's Wife and His Daughters Have in the War." *Ladies' Home Journal* (July 1918): 22, 44.

Hart, Roderick P. *Campaign Talk: Why Elections Are Good For Us.* Princeton: Princeton University Press, 2000.

Hartman, Susan M. *The Home Front and Beyond: American Women in the 1940s.* Boston: Twayne, 1982.

Henry, Susan. "Changing Media History through Women's History." In *Women in Mass Communication,* ed. Pamela J. Creedon. Newbury Park: Sage, 1989.

Hershey, Lenore. "The 'New' Pat Nixon." *Ladies' Home Journal* (February 1972): 89–90, 124–26.

Holbrook, Thomas M. *Do Campaigns Matter?* Thousand Oaks, CA: Sage Publications, 1996.

"How Much Should a First Lady Say?" *McCall's* (February 1976): 49–50.

Humphrey, Carol Sue. *The Press of the Young Republic, 1783–1833.* Westport, CT: Greenwood Press, 1994.

Huntzicker, William E. *The Popular Press, 1833–1865.* Westport, CT: Greenwood Press, 1999.

Ifill, Gwen. "Clinton Wants Wife at Cabinet Table." *New York Times*, 19 December 1992, 8.

Iyengar, Shanto, and Donald R. Kinder. *News that Matters: Television and American Opinion*. Chicago: University of Chicago Press, 1993.

James, Bessie Rowland. *Ann Royall's U.S.A.* New Brunswick, NJ: Rutgers University Press, 1972.

Jamieson, Kathleen Hall. *Beyond the Double Bind: Women and Leadership*. New York: Oxford University Press, 1995.

———. *Packaging the Presidency: A History and Criticism of Presidential Campaign Advertising*. New York: Oxford, 1996.

Jamieson, Kathleen Hall, and Paul Waldman. *The Press Effect: Politicians, Journalists, and the Stories That Shape the Political World*. New York: Oxford University Press, 2003.

Jensen, Faye Lind. "An Awesome Responsibility: Rosalynn Carter as First Lady." *Presidential Studies Quarterly* 20 (1990): 769–76.

Johnson, Lady Bird. *A White House Diary*. New York: Holt, Rinehart and Winston, 1970.

Johnson, Nan. *Gender and Rhetorical Space in American Life, 1866–1910*. Carbondale: Southern Illinois University Press, 2002.

Johnston, Laurie. "'Policeman for Ike' Is Wife's Idea of Her Principal Role in Public Life." *New York Times*, 3 September 1952, 23.

Juergens, George. *Joseph Pulitzer and the New York World*. Princeton: Princeton University Press, 1966.

Kalendin, Eugenia. *Daily Life in the United States, 1940–1959: Shifting Worlds*. Westport, CT: Greenwood Press, 2000.

Kaplan, Richard L. *Politics and the American Press: The Rise of Objectivity, 1865–1920*. Cambridge, MA: Cambridge University Press, 2002.

Kendall, Kathleen E. *Communication in the Presidential Primaries: Candidates and the Media, 1912–2000*. Westport, CT: Praeger, 2000.

Kerber, Linda K. "Daughters of Columbia: Educating Women for the Republic, 1787–1805." In *The Hofstadter Aegis: A Memorial*, ed. Stanley Elkins and Eric McKitrick, 35–59. New York: Knopf, 1974.

———. "Separate Spheres, Female Worlds, Woman's Place: The Rhetoric of Women's History." *Journal of American History* 75 (1988): 9–39.

———. *Women of the Republic: Intellect and Ideology in Revolutionary America*. New York: W. W. Norton, 1986.

Kernell, Samuel. *Going Public: New Strategies of Political Leadership*, 3rd ed. Washington, D.C.: Congressional Quarterly Press, 1997.

King, Wayne. "Rosalynn Carter, a Tough, Tireless Campaigner, Displays Same Driving Quality as Her Husband." *New York Times*, 18 October 1976, 33.

Kitch, Carolyn. *The Girl on the Magazine Cover: The Origins of Visual Stereotypes in American Mass Media*. Chapel Hill: University of North Carolina Press, 2001.

Klapthor, Margaret Brown. *The First Ladies*. Washington, D.C.: White House Historical Association, 1994.

Klein, Ethel. *Gender Politics*. Cambridge, MA: Harvard University Press, 1984.

Klemesrud, Judy. "For Mrs. Carter, a Rest at Last." *New York Times*, 11 June 1976, 1.

Knight, Myra Gregory. "Issues of Openness and Privacy: Press and Public Response to Betty Ford's Breast Cancer." *American Journalism* (2000): 53–71.

Koslow, Sally. "Hillary Rodham Clinton." *McCall's* (November 1996): 199.

Kurtz, Howard. "Portraits of a First Lady: Media Strive to Define Hillary Clinton." *Washington Post*, 21 November 1992, A1.

Kyvig, David E. *Daily Life in the United States, 1920–1939*. Westport, CT: Greenwood Press, 2002.

"The Lady of the White House." *New York Times Magazine,* 10 March 1929, 1–2, 15.

Laracey, Mel. *Presidents and the People: The Partisan Story of Going Public.* College Station: Texas A&M Press, 2002.

Lash, Joseph P. *Eleanor and Franklin.* New York: Norton, 1971.

Leaming, Barbara. *Mrs. Kennedy: The Missing History of the Kennedy Years.* New York: The Free Press, 2001.

Lemons, J. Stanley. *The Woman Citizen: Social Feminism in the 1920s.* Urbana: University of Illinois Press, 1973.

Lerner, Gerda. *The Majority Finds Its Past: Placing Women in History.* New York: Oxford University Press, 1979.

Lewin, Tamar. "Legal Scholars See Distortion in Attacks on Hillary Clinton." *New York Times,* 24 August 1992, A1.

List, Karen K. "The Media and the Depiction of Women." In *The Significance of the Media in American History,* ed. James D. Startt and William David Sloan, 106–28. Northport, AL: Vision Press, 1994.

———. "Realities and Possibilities: The Lives of Women in Periodicals of the New Republic." *American Journalism* 11 (1994): 20–39.

Lont, Cynthia M. *Women and Media: Content, Careers, and Criticism.* Belmont, CA: Wadsworth Publishing Company, 1995.

Lott, Davis Newton, ed. *The Presidents Speak.* New York: Henry Holt, 1994.

Louchheim, Katie. "The Spotlight Shifts in Washington: A New First Lady Takes Center Stage." *Ladies' Home Journal* (March 1964): 55–56, 126.

MacPherson, Myra. "The Blooming of Betty Ford." *McCall's* (September 1975): 93, 120–26.

———. "First Families." *Washington Post,* 20 January 1977, 15.

Mann, Judy. "Homemakers on Parade." *Washington Post,* 12 August 1992, E15.

Marling, Karal Ann. *As Seen on TV: The Visual Culture of Everyday Life in the 1950s.* Cambridge, MA: Harvard University Press, 1994.

Marshall, P. David. *Celebrity and Power: Fame in Contemporary Culture.* Minneapolis: University of Minnesota Press, 1997.

Martin, Janet M. *The Presidency and Women: Promise, Performance, and Illusion.* College Station: Texas A&M University Press, 2003.

Marton, Kati. *Hidden Power: Presidential Marriages that Shaped Our Recent History.* New York: Pantheon Books, 2001.

Matthews, Glenna. *"Just a Housewife": The Rise and Fall of Domesticity in America.* New York: Oxford University Press, 1987.

———. *The Rise of Public Woman: Woman's Power and Woman's Place in the United States, 1630–1970.* New York: Oxford University Press, 1992.

Maxwell, Alice S., and Marion B. Dunlevy. *Virago! The Story of Ann Newport Royall (1769–1854).* Jefferson: McFarland, 1985.

May, Elaine Tyler. *Homeward Bound: American Families in the Cold War Era.* New York: Basic Books, 1999.

May, Lary. *Recasting America: Culture and Politics in the Age of the Cold War.* Chicago: University of Chicago Press, 1989.

Mayo, Edith P., and Denise D. Meringolo. *First Ladies: Political Role and Public Image.* Washington, D.C.: Smithsonian Institution, 1994.

McBee, Susanna. "Pat Nixon and the First Lady Watchers." *McCall's* (September 1970): 76–77, 137–44.

McGee, Michael Calvin. "The 'Ideograph': A Link between Rhetoric and Ideology." *Quarterly Journal of Speech* 66 (1980): 1–16.

McLaughlin, Kathleen. "Mrs. Roosevelt Goes Her Own Way." *New York Times Magazine,* 5 July 1936, 7, 15.

McLellan, Diana. "Barbara Bush." *Ladies' Home Journal* (October 1992): 192.

Mead, Margaret. "Mrs. Lyndon B. Johnson: A New Kind of First Lady?" *Good Housekeeping* (July 1965): 12–14, 20.

Medhurst, Martin J., ed. *Beyond the Rhetorical Presidency*. College Station: Texas A&M University Press, 1996.

Meyerowitz, Joanne. *Not June Cleaver: Women and Gender in Postwar America, 1945–1960*. Philadelphia: Temple University Press, 1994.

Mezzack, Janet L. "'Without Manners You Are Nothing': Lady Bird Johnson, Eartha Kitt, and the Women's Doers Luncheon of January 18, 1968." *Presidential Studies Quarterly* 20 (1990): 745–60.

Mills, Kay. *From Pocahontas to Power Suits: Everything You Need to Know About Women's History in America*. New York: Plume, 1995.

Mitchell, Juliet. *Woman's Estate*. New York: Penguin, 1971.

Montgomery, Maureen E. *Displaying Women: Spectacles of Leisure in Edith Wharton's New York*. New York: Routledge, 1998.

Montgomery, Ruth. "What Kind of Woman Is Our New First Lady?" *Good Housekeeping* (March 1964): 32–40.

Morgan, Robin, ed. *Sisterhood Is Global: The International Women's Movement Anthology*. Garden City, NY: Anchor Books, 1984.

———. *Sisterhood Is Powerful: An Anthology of Writings From the Women's Liberation Movement*. New York: Vintage Books, 1970.

"Mrs. Eisenhower a Mystery Fan." *New York Times,* 9 November 1952, 64.

"Mrs. Ford Scored on Equality Plan: Letters Running 3 to 1 against Her Lobbying Efforts." *New York Times,* 21 February 1975, 32.

"Mrs. Hoover Seen as Cosmopolitan, Social Worker, Devoted Mother and Real Companion to Husband." *Washington Post,* 7 November 1928, 9.

Muir, Janette Kenner, and Lisa M. Benitez. "Redefining the Role of the First Lady: The Rhetorical Style of Hillary Rodham Clinton." In *The Clinton Presidency: Images, Issues, and Communication Strategies,* ed. Robert E. Denton Jr. and Rachel L. Holloway, 187–200. Westport: Praeger, 1996.

Muncy, Robyn. *Creating a Female Dominion in American Reform, 1890–1935*. New York: Oxford University Press, 1991.

"Nancy Reagan Criticizes Aides to President." *New York Times,* 13 November 1988, 1.

Nerone, John, and Ellen Wartella. "Social Memory." *Communication* 11 (1989): 85–88.

Norris, Pippa, ed. *Women, Media, and Politics*. New York: Oxford University Press, 1997.

Norton, Anne. *Republic of Signs: Liberal Theory and American Popular Culture*. Chicago: University of Chicago Press, 1993.

Norton, Mary Beth. *Founding Mothers and Fathers: Gendered Power and the Forming of American Society*. New York: Knopf, 1996.

———. *Liberty's Daughters: The Revolutionary Experience of American Women, 1750–1800*. Ithaca, NY: Cornell University Press, 1980.

O'Connor, Karen, Bernadette Nye, and Laura Van Assendelft. "Wives in the White House: The Political Influence of First Ladies." *Presidential Studies Quarterly* 26 (1996): 835–51.

"Our First Ninety Days in the White House." *Good Housekeeping* (May 1964): 87–88, 146–54.

Parry-Giles, Shawn J. "Mediating Hillary Rodham Clinton: Television News Practices and Image-Making in the Postmodern Age." *Critical Studies in Media Communication* 17 (2000): 205–26.

Parry-Giles, Shawn J., and Diane M. Blair. "The Rise of the Rhetorical First Lady: Politics, Gender Ideology, and Women's Voice, 1789–2002." *Rhetoric and Public Affairs* 5 (2002): 565–99.

Pasley, Jeffrey L. *"The Tyranny of Printers": Newspaper Politics in the Early American Republic*. Charlottesville: University Press of Virginia, 2001.

Prindiville, Kathleen. *First Ladies*, 2nd ed. New York: MacMillan, 1964.

Quinn, Sally. "Is America Ready for Hillary Clinton? The Candidate's Wife Is the Very Model of the Modern Working Woman." *Washington Post*, 9 August 1992, C1.

Radcliffe, Donnie. "Barbara Bush: Unassuming, Underestimated, Stumping for the Veep." *Washington Post*, 5 June 1988, F1.

———. "The First Lady Reshapes Her Royal Image." *Washington Post*, 21 January 1985, G7.

———. "Granny Get Your Gun: The Other Mrs. Bush." *Washington Post*, 19 August 1992, B1.

———. "The Influential Nancy Reagan: Time Looks at Her Impact, Image, and the Great Birth-Date Issue." *Washington Post*, 7 January 1985, D1.

———. "There Aren't Any Secrets between Us." *Washington Post*, 22 August 1984, B1.

Rakow, Lana. "Rethinking Gender Research in Communication." *Journal of Communication* 36 (1986), 11–26.

Reagan, Nancy, with William Novak. *My Turn: The Memoirs of Nancy Reagan*. New York: Random House, 1989.

Reese, Stephen D., Oscar H. Gandy, Jr., and August E. Grant, eds. *Framing Public Life: Perspectives on Media and Our Understanding of the Social World*. Mahwah, NJ: Lawrence Erlbaum Associates, 2001.

Riis, Jacob A. "Mrs. Roosevelt and Her Children." *Ladies' Home Journal* (August 1902): 5–6.

Riley, Denise. *"Am I That Name?": Feminism and the Category of "Women" in History*. Minneapolis: University of Minnesota Press, 1988.

Riley, Glenda. *Inventing the American Woman: A Perspective on Women's History, 1865 to the Present*, vol. 2. Arlington Heights: Harlan Davidson, 1986.

Ritchie, Donald A. *Press Gallery: Congress and the Washington Correspondents*. Cambridge, MA: Harvard University Press, 1991.

Robertson, Nan. "Mrs. Johnson Ends Eight-State Rail Tour of the South." *New York Times*, 10 October 1964, 15.

———. "Public Writing Many Letters to Mrs. Johnson." *New York Times*, 1 March 1964, 54.

Rojek, Chris. *Celebrity*. London: Reaktion Books, 2001.

Romano, Lois. "First Lady Puts Privacy First: Reluctant Star likely to Set Her Own Terms." *Washington Post*, 20 January 2001, A16.

Roosevelt, Eleanor. *The Autobiography of Eleanor Roosevelt*. New York: Harper, 1961.

———. *This I Remember*. New York: Harper, 1949.

———. *This Is My Story*. New York: Garden, 1937.

Roosevelt, Theodore. *The Strenuous Life*. New York: Outlook, 1900.

Rosenfeld, Richard N. *American Aurora: A Democratic-Republican Returns*. New York: St. Martin's Press, 1997.

Ross, Ishbel. *Grace Coolidge and Her Era: The Story of a President's Wife*. New York: Dodd, Mead, and Company, 1962.

———. *Ladies of the Press: The Story of Women in Journalism by an Insider*. New York: Harper and Brothers, 1936.

Russell, Jan Jarboe. *Lady Bird: A Biography of Mrs. Johnson*. New York: Scribner, 1999.

———. "Not Queen, Not Prisoner—Just the President's Wife." *New York Times*, 30 August 2000, 23.

Ryan, Barbara. *Feminism and the Women's Movement: Dynamics of Change in Social Movement Ideology and Activism*. New York: Routledge, 1992.

Ryan, Mary P. "Gender and Public Access: Women's Politics in Nineteenth-Century America." In *Habermas and the Public Sphere,* ed. Craig Calhoun, 259–87. Boston: MIT Press, 1992.

———. *Womanhood in America: From Colonial Times to Present.* New York: Viewpoints, 1975.

Sadler, Christine. "Our Very Busy First Lady." *McCall's* (March 1964): 79–81, 187–89.

Scanlon, Jennifer. *Inarticulate Longings: The Ladies' Home Journal, Gender, and the Promises of Consumer Culture.* New York: Routledge, 1995.

———. "Old Housekeeping, New Housekeeping, or No Housekeeping? The Kitchenless Home Movement and Women's Service Magazines." *Journalism History* 30 (2004): 2–10.

Scharf, Lois, and Joan M. Jensen, eds. *Decades of Discontent: The Women's Movement, 1920–1940.* Boston: Northeastern University Press, 1987.

Scharrer, Erica, and Kim Bissell. "Overcoming Traditional Boundaries: The Role of Political Activity in Media Coverage of First Ladies." *Women and Politics* 21 (2000): 55–83.

Schickel, Richard. *Intimate Strangers: The Culture of Celebrity.* New York: Fromm International Publishing, 1986.

Schiro, Anne-Marie. "It Began with Dolley Madison." *New York Times,* 18 October 1988, A26.

Schneider, Beth E. "Political Generations and the Contemporary Women's Movement." *Sociological Inquiry* 58 (1988): 4–21.

Schneir, Miriam. *Feminism in Our Time: The Essential Writings, World War II to the Present.* New York: Vintage Books, 1994.

Schudson, Michael. *Discovering the News: A Social History of American Newspapers.* New York: Basic Books, 1978.

———. *The Good Citizen: A History of American Civic Life.* New York: Free Press, 1998.

Schwartz, Amy E. "'Good Girls, Bad Girls': Pitting Women against Each Other in a Family Values Farce." *Washington Post,* 5 September 1992, A29.

Sciolino, Elaine. "Laura Bush Sees Everything in Its Place, Including Herself." *New York Times,* 15 January 2001, A1.

Scott, Anne Firor. *Making the Invisible Woman Visible.* Urbana: University of Illinois Press, 1984.

Scott, Joan W. "Gender: A Useful Category of Historical Analysis." *American Historical Association* 5 (December 1986), 1053–75.

Seager, Robert. *And Tyler Too.* New York: McGraw Hill, 1962.

Sellars, Charles. *James K. Polk.* Princeton: Princeton University Press, 1966.

Shreve, Anita. *Women Together, Women Alone: The Legacy of the Consciousness Raising Movement.* New York: Viking, 1989.

Simonton, Dean Keith. "Presidents' Wives and First Ladies: On Achieving Eminence Within a Traditional Gender Role." *Sex Roles* 35 (1996): 309–36.

Sloan, William David. "The Early Party Press." *Journalism History* 9 (1982): 19.

———. "'Purse and Pen': Party-Press Relationships, 1789–1816." *American Journalism* 6 (1989): 103–27.

Sloan, William David, and James D. Startt, eds. *The Media in America: A History,* 4th ed. Northport, AL: Vision Press, 1999.

Smith, Nancy Keegan. "Private Reflections on a Public Life: The Papers of Lady Bird Johnson at the LBJ Library." *Presidential Studies Quarterly* 20 (1990): 737–44.

Smith-Rosenberg, Carrol. *Disorderly Conduct: Visions of Gender in Victorian America.* New York: Alfred A. Knopf, 1985.

Soloman, Martha M. "The Positive Woman's Journey: A Mythical Analysis of the Rhetoric of STOP ERA." *Quarterly Journal of Speech* 65 (1979): 345–57.

———. *A Voice of Their Own: The Woman Suffrage Press, 1840–1910.* Tuscaloosa: The University of Alabama Press, 1991.

Stacey, Judith. "Sexism by a Subtler Name? Postindustrial Conditions and Postfeminist Consciousness in the Silicon Valley." *Socialist Review* 17 (1987): 7–28.

Stanley, Alessandra. "Barbara Bush: The Un-Secret Weapon." *New York Times,* 19 August 1992, A15.

———. "First Lady on Abortion: Not a Platform Issue." *New York Times,* 14 August 1992, A1.

———. "Republicans Present Marilyn as a Self-Sacrificing 90s Supermom." *New York Times,* 18 August 1992, A7.

———. "A Softer Image for Hillary Clinton." *New York Times,* 13 July 1992, B1.

Startt, James D., and William David Sloan, eds. *The Significance of the Media in American History.* Northport, AL: Vision Press, 1994.

Stephens, Mitchell. *A History of News.* Fort Worth, TX: Harcourt Brace, 1997.

Stroud, Kandy. "Rosalynn's Agenda in the White House." *New York Times Magazine,* 20 March 1977, 19–20, 58–60.

Swanberg, W.A. *Pulitzer.* New York: Scribner's, 1967.

Tag, James. *Benjamin Franklin Bache and the Philadelphia Aurora.* Philadelphia: University of Pennsylvania Press, 1991.

Templin, Charlotte. "Hillary Clinton as Threat to Gender Norms: Cartoon Images of the First Lady." *Journal of Communication Inquiry* 23 (1999): 20–36.

Thacker-Estrada, Elizabeth Lorelei. "True Women: The Roles and Lives of Antebellum Presidential Wives Sarah Polk, Margaret Taylor, Abigail Fillmore, and Jane Pierce." In Watson and Eksterowicz, *Presidential Companion,* 77–101.

Tobin, Leesa. "Betty Ford as First Lady: A Woman for Women." *Presidential Studies Quarterly* 20 (1990): 761–68.

Tonkovich, Nicole. *Domesticity With a Difference: The Nonfiction of Catherine Beecher, Sarah J. Hale, Fanny Fern, and Margaret Fuller.* Jackson: University Press of Mississippi, 1997.

Troy, Gil. *Mr. and Mrs. President: From the Trumans to the Clintons.* Lawrence: University Press of Kansas, 2000.

Truman, Margaret. *Bess W. Truman.* New York: Jove Books, 1987.

———. *First Ladies.* New York: Random House, 1995.

Tuchman, Gaye. *Making News.* New York: The Free Press, 1978.

Tuchman, Gaye, Arlene Kaplan Daniels, and James Benét, eds. *Hearth and Home: Images of Women in the Mass Media.* New York: Oxford University Press, 1978.

Tugwell, Rexford. *Grover Cleveland.* New York: Macmillan, 1968.

Tulis, Jeffrey K. *The Rhetorical Presidency.* Princeton, NJ: Princeton University Press, 1987.

Turner, Kathleen J., ed. *Doing Rhetorical History: Concepts and Cases.* Tuscaloosa: The University of Alabama Press, 1998.

Van Rensselaer, Mary. *Jacqueline Kennedy: The White House Years.* Boston: Little, Brown, 1967.

Van Zoonen, Liesbet. *Feminist Media Studies.* London: Sage, 1994.

Vavrus, Mary Douglas. *Postfeminist News: Political Women in Media Culture.* Albany: State University of New York Press, 2002.

———. "Putting Ally on Trial: Contesting Postfeminism in Popular Culture." *Women's Studies in Communication* 23 (2000): 413–28.

Walker, Nancy A. *Shaping Our Mothers' World: American Women's Magazines.* Jackson: University Press of Mississippi, 2000.

Wandersee, Winifred D. *On the Move: American Women in the 1970s.* Boston: Twayne, 1988.

Waterman, Richard W., Robert Wright, and Gilbert St. Clair. *The Image-Is-Everything Presidency: Dilemmas in American Leadership.* Boulder, CO: Westview Press, 1999.

Watson, Robert P. "Introduction." In Watson and Eksterowicz, *Presidential Companion,* 3–16.

———. *The Presidents' Wives: Reassessing the Office of First Lady.* Boulder, CO: Lynne Rienner, 2000.

Watson, Robert P., and Anthony J. Eksterowicz, eds. *The Presidential Companion: Readings on the First Ladies.* Columbia: University of South Carolina Press, 2003.

Watts, Liz. "Magazine Coverage of First Ladies From Hoover to Clinton: From Election Through the First One Hundred Days of Office." *American Journalism* 14 (1997): 495–519.

Weaver, David. "Women as Journalists." In Norris, *Women, Media, and Politics,* 21–40.

Weinman, Martha. "First Ladies—In Fashion, Too?" *New York Times Magazine,* 11 September 1960, 32–33, 130–32.

Weinraub, Bernard. "A Down-to-Earth Tenant for an Exclusive Address." *New York Times,* 15 January 1989, 1.

———. "The Washingtonization of Nancy Reagan." *New York Times,* 26 March 1985, A20.

Weisman, Steven R. "Nancy Reagan's Role Grows." *New York Times,* 11 November 1984, 2.

Welter, Barbara. "The Cult of True Womanhood, 1820–1860." In *The American Family in Social-Historical Perspective,* ed. Michael Gordon, 224–50. New York: St. Martin's, 1973.

Wertheimer, Molly Meijer. "First Ladies' Fundamental Rhetorical Choices: When to Speak? What to Say? When to Remain Silent?" In Wertheimer, *Inventing a Voice,* 1–15.

———, ed. *Inventing a Voice: The Rhetoric of American First Ladies of the Twentieth Century.* Lanham, MD: Rowman and Littlefield, 2004.

West, Jessamyn. "The Real Pat Nixon." *Good Housekeeping* (February 1971): 57–59, 124–28.

Weymouth, Lally. "The Biggest Role of Nancy's Life." *New York Times Magazine,* 26 October 1980, 45–48.

Williams, Marjorie. "Barbara Bush, Hillary Clinton, Marilyn Quayle, Tipper Gore." *Washington Post Magazine,* 1 November 1992, 11–14.

Winfield, Betty Houchin. "The First Lady, Political Power, and the Media: Who Elected Her Anyway?" In Norris, *Women, Media, and Politics,* 166–80.

———. "The First Lady's Relations with the Mass Media." In *Laura Bush: The Report to the First Lady,* ed. Robert P. Watson, 45–51. Huntington, NY: Nova History, 2001.

———. "'Madam President': Understanding a New Kind of First Lady." *Media Studies Journal* 8 (1994): 59–71.

———. "The Making of an Image: Hillary Rodham Clinton and American Journalists." *Political Communication* 14 (1997): 241–53.

Witt, Linda, Karen M. Paget, and Glenna Matthews. *Running as a Woman: Gender and Power in American Politics.* New York: Free Press, 1995.

"Women of the Year, 1976." *Ladies' Home Journal* (May 1976): 73–74.

Zaeske, Susan. "The 'Promiscuous Audience' Controversy and the Emergence of the Early Women's Rights Movement." *Quarterly Journal of Speech* 81 (1995): 191–207.

Zelizer, Barbie. *Covering the Body: The Kennedy Assassination, the Media, and the Shaping of Collective Memory.* Chicago: The University of Chicago Press, 1992.

———. "Journalists as Interpretive Communities." *Critical Studies in Mass Communication* 10 (1993): 219–37.

———. "Reading the Past against the Grain: The Shape of Memory Studies." *Critical Studies in Mass Communication* 12 (1995): 214–39.

Index